This edition published in 2019

Copyright © Carlton Books Limited 2019

Carlton Books Limited
20 Mortimer Street
London W1T 3JW

A CIP catalogue record for this book is available from
the British Library

10 9 8 7 6 5 4 3 2 1

ISBN: 978-1-78739-325-7

Editorial Director: Martin Corteel
Project Editor: Ross Hamilton
Editorial Contributor: Mark White
Design: Amazing 15 and Stephen Cary
Picture research: Paul Langan
Production: Rachel Burgess

Printed in Slovenia

WORLD FOOTBALL RECORDS

ELEVENTH EDITION

KEIR RADNEDGE

CARLTON
BOOKS

CONTENTS

INTRODUCTION

Football is a phenomenon: not only a sport for the masses and a high-quality, highly paid elite but a source of passion, delight and despair which unites billions around the planet.

Evidence over the past year has been demonstrated by the speed with which the game has moved on from the dramas of the 2018 FIFA World Cup finals in Russia. Tradition was rewarded with Copa America success for Brazil and UEFA Champions League resurgence for Liverpool. Yet Qatar, the 2022 World Cup hosts, raised a warning for the old guard by winning the Asian Cup for the first time.

The internationalisation of the game proceeds apace with the free-flowing transfer of players between not only countries but continents, accompanied by cross-border financial investment from China, the Middle East and the United States. Simultaneously the FIFA Women's World Cup in France attracted a new audience for female football.

Football boasts a unique, mesmeric power in its matrix of team tradition and individual brilliance. Personification is evident in the goal-scoring achievements for both countries and clubs of Portugal's Cristiano Ronaldo and Argentina's Lionel Messi.

Ronaldo marked 2019 by winning the inaugural UEFA Nations League with European champions Portugal and Italy's Serie A with his latest club, Juventus; Messi was a Spanish champion yet again with Barcelona and won the European Golden Boot as the continent's leading league marksman for a record-extending sixth season.

All the many aspects of this grand football landscape feature in this latest, 11th edition of *World Football Records*. Here are the achievements and stars, old and new, from all of football's major international tournaments for men and women at senior and junior levels... and maybe tomorrow's superstars as well.

Keir Radnedge
London, July 2019

In one of the most-watched moment in football in 2019, the USA retained their FIFA Women's World Cup title.

THE COUNTRIES

The history of football is a long and illustrious journey, with every corner of the planet having played its part in a chapter or two.

F ootball is known as the global game. It knows no boundaries of politics or religion or race, and at its heart is a simple structure that has worked effectively for well over a century.

At the head of the global football pyramid is FIFA, the world federation. Supporting FIFA's work are national associations of 211 countries, across the six regional geographical federations: Africa, Asia, Europe, Oceania, South America, plus the Caribbean, Central and North America. These associations not only field the national teams who have built sporting history, but they also oversee the growth of football in their countries, from professional leagues to grassroots.

It was England and Scotland that played the first international football football in the late 19th century; the British home championship followed, laying the foundations for international tournaments to come, with the Copa America of South America and FIFA World Cup following in 1916 and 1930 respectively.

Regional continental championships, and such traditional events may yet be supplemented by the exciting prospect of a global nations league. The competitive structure of the world game is always evolving. Football is indeed a game of perpetual motion.

CONCACAF

Founded: 1961

Number of Federations: 41

Headquarters: Miami, United States

CONMEBOL

Founded: 1916

Number of Federations: 10

Headquarters: Luque, Paraguay

UEFA

Founded: 1954

Number of Federations: 55

Headquarters: Nyon, Switzerland

OFC

Founded: 1966

Number of Federations: 11 (+3 non-FIFA members)

Headquarters: Auckland, New Zealand

AFC

Founded: 1954

Number of Federations: 47

Headquarters: Bukit Jalil, Kuala Lumpur, Malaysia

CAF

Founded: 1956

Number of Federations: 56

Headquarters: Cairo, Egypt

EUROPE

At both club and international level, European football sides have dominated the beautiful game.

Confederation Founded: 1954

Number of Federations: 55

Headquarters: Nyon, Switzerland

Most Continental Championship Wins: Germany, Spain (three each)

55

There are **55 full member nations** of UEFA, the governing body of European football

88

The semi-final between Italy and USSR of the 1968 UEFA European Championship was decided by a **coin toss**. Italy guessed correctly to progress to the final.

Cristiano Ronaldo has scored more international goals than any other European player.

CRISTIANO
RONALDO

In 2020, the European Championships will be held in 12 cities across Europe, with the final taking place at **Wembley Stadium**, London. This is to honour the 60th anniversary of the tournament.

Despite not qualifying for the 1992 UEFA European Championship, Denmark won the competition. They were drafted into the tournament late, after Yugoslavia pulled out, after the outbreak of a civil war in the country.

ENGLAND

England is where football began; the country where the game was first developed, which saw the creation of the game's first Football Association and the first organised league, and which now plays host to the richest domestic league in the world.

Joined FIFA: 1905

Biggest win:
13-0 vs. Ireland, 1882

Highest FIFA ranking: 1

Home Stadium: Wembley Stadium, London

Honours: 1 World Cup (1966)

NATIONAL LEGEND
NEW SOUTHGATE, NEW HOPE

England enjoyed their best FIFA World Cup performance since 1990 in Russia in 2018. Their manager was **Gareth Southgate**, who as a former England defender had missed the decisive penalty in the 1996 UEFA European Championship semi-final against Germany. In 2018 England enjoyed their biggest victory at a FIFA World Cup when beating Panama 6-1 in the second first-round match and went on to finish fourth, losing 2-1 to Croatia after extra-time in their semi-final and then 2-0 to Belgium in the third-place play-off. Southgate's squad was the second-youngest in Russia and became the first England team to win a FIFA World Cup penalty shoot-out, at the fourth time of asking.

GARETH **SOUTHGATE**

201cm
Peter Crouch is England's tallest ever player at 201cm, or 6 foot 7 inches.

NATIONAL LEGEND
CAPTAINS COURAGEOUS

The international careers of Billy Wright and **Bobby Moore**, who both captained England a record 90 times, very nearly overlapped. Wright, from Wolves, played for England between 1946 and 1959 and Moore, from West Ham, between 1962 and 1973, including England's FIFA World Cup win on home soil in 1966. Moore remains England's youngest captain, having been 22 years and 47 days old when appointed against Czechoslovakia on 29 May 1963. He also remains the only man to lift the FIFA World Cup for England, after West Germany were beaten 4-2 at Wembley on 30 July 1966.

41
The oldest player to make his debut for England remains Alexander Morten, who was 41 years and 114 days old when facing Scotland on 8 March 1873 in England's first home game.

BOBBY **MOORE**

HISTORIC MOMENT
IN THE BEGINNING

The day it all began... 30 November 1872, when England played their first official international match, against Scotland, at Hamilton Crescent, Partick. The result was a 0-0 draw in front of a then massive crowd of 4,000, who each paid an admission fee of one shilling (5p). In fact, teams representing England and Scotland had played five times before, but most of the Scottish players had been based in England and the matches are considered unofficial. England's team for the first official game was selected by Charles Alcock, the secretary of the Football Association. His one regret was that, because of injury, he could not pick himself to play.

DISCIPLINARY
NAUGHTY BOYS

Raheem Sterling's red card against Ecuador in June 2014 was the 15th for an England player in a full international. Alan Mullery was England's first player to be dismissed, against Yugoslavia in June 1968. **David Beckham** and Wayne Rooney have both been sent off twice – both picked up controversial red cards in FIFA World Cup knockout matches for England – and Paul Scholes was the only England player to be sent off at the old Wembley Stadium, against Sweden in June 1999.

5

Five sons of former England Internationals have earned caps for their country. The last was Alex Oxlade-Chamberlain, 28 years after the last of his father Mark Chamberlain's eight appearances.

DAVID
BECKHAM

MOST APPEARANCES:

1. **Peter Shilton**, 125
2. **Wayne Rooney**, 120
3. **David Beckham**, 115
4. **Steven Gerrard**, 114
5. **Bobby Moore**, 108

6-3
Hungary's 6-3 win at Wembley in 1953 was the first time England had lost at home to continental opposition.

SCORING RECORD
SPURRED TO GLORY

Right wing-back Kieran Trippier's free-kick goal against Croatia in the 2018 FIFA World Cup semi-final made him the eleventh Tottenham Hotspur player to score for England at a major tournament, more than any other club. Clubmates Harry Kane (six) and Dele Alli (one) also scored in Russia, following in the footsteps of England and Spurs goalscoring legends Jimmy Greaves and **Gary Lineker**. Greaves holds the England record for hat-tricks, with six, while 1986 Golden Boot winner Lineker is England's leading FIFA World Cup goalscorer, with 10 across the 1986 and 1990 tournaments. Tottenham have also provided the country with more players than any other club: midfielder Harry Winks became the 78th in October 2017.

GARY
LINEKER

STAR PLAYER
FAST STARTS

Bryan Robson holds the record for fastest England goal in the FIFA World Cup, after 27 seconds in a 3-1 win against France in 1982, and for his country at the old (since rebuilt) Wembley Stadium, netting after 38 seconds in a 2-1 victory over Czechoslovakia. Another Manchester United player, striker Teddy Sheringham, scored more quickly than any other England player after coming on to the field. He struck with his first touch, a header 15 seconds into a substitute appearance, against Greece in a 2002 FIFA World Cup qualifier at United's Old Trafford ground in October 2001.

SCORING RECORD
GAME OF STONES

No England defender had ever scored more than one FIFA World Cup goal until Manchester City centre-back **John Stones** managed two in 32 first-half minutes against Panama in Nizhny Novgorod, Russia, in 2018. He was joined on the scoresheet, two games later, by fellow centre-back **Harry Maguire**, who gave England the lead in a 2-0 quarter-final victory over Sweden. Neither defender had scored for England before the tournament and Leicester City man Maguire had only received his first international call-up in August 2017. Maguire had gone to the 2016 UEFA European Championship in France but as an England fan, with friends.

JOHN
STONES

HARRY
MAGUIRE

NATIONAL LEGEND
GRAND OLD MAN

Stanley Matthews became England's oldest-ever player when he lined up at outside-right against Denmark on 15 May 1957 at the age of 42 years 104 days. That was 22 years and 229 days after his first appearance. Matthews was also England's oldest marksman. He was 41 years eight months old when he scored against Northern Ireland on 10 October 1956. In stark contrast to Matthews's longest England career, full-back Martin Kelly holds the record for the shortest – a two-minute substitute appearance in a 1-0 friendly win over Norway in 2012.

STAR PLAYERS
THE KIDS ARE ALL RIGHT

England's youngest debutant remains then-Arsenal winger Theo Walcott, who was just 17 years and 75 days old when he faced Hungary on 30 May 2006. Chelsea forward Callum Hudson-Odoi became the youngest man to make his debut in a competitive match for England, coming on as a substitute in a 5-0 victory over the Czech Republic in a March 2019 qualifier for the 2020 UEFA European Championship - aged just 18 years and 135 days. This made him 40 days younger than Duncan Edwards had been when he debuted against Scotland in the British Home Championship on 2 April 1955.

TOP SCORERS:

1. Wayne Rooney, 53
2. Bobby Charlton, 49
3. Gary Lineker, 48
4. Jimmy Greaves, 44
5. Michael Owen, 40

England have hit double figures five times: beating Ireland 13-0 and 13-2 in 1882 and 1899, thrashing Austria 11-1 in 1908, crushing Portugal 10-0 in Lisbon in 1947 and then the United States 10-0 in 1964 in New York.

TOURNAMENT TRIVIA
ROON AT THE TOP

When **Wayne Rooney** scored against Macedonia in September 2003, he became England's youngest goalscorer at the age of 17 years and 317 days – and it long seemed only a matter of time before he broke Sir Bobby Charlton's record 49-goal haul. He drew level thanks to a penalty against San Marino in September 2015, then reached his half-century with another spot-kick, against Switzerland, three days later. Rooney's 100th cap in November 2014, aged 29 years and 22 days, made him the youngest man to reach a century of appearances for England. He retired from international football in August 2017 but made a brief return as a substitute on 15 November 2018, against the United States, for a farewell 120th appearance.

WAYNE
ROONEY

SCORING RECORD
SHARED RESPONSIBILITY

Substitutions meant the captain's armband passed between four different players during England's 2-1 friendly win over Serbia and Montenegro on 3 June 2003. Regular captain David Beckham was missing, so Michael Owen led the team out, but was substituted at half-time. England's second-half skippers were Owen's then-Liverpool team-mates Emile Heskey and Jamie Carragher, and Manchester United's Philip Neville. The first time three different players captained England in one FIFA World Cup finals match was a goalless draw against Morocco in 1986, when first-choice skipper Bryan Robson went off injured, his vice-captain Ray Wilkins was then sent off, and goalkeeper Peter Shilton took over leadership duties.

TOURNAMENT TRIVIA
ROLL UP, ROLL UP

The highest attendance for an England game came at Hampden Park in Glasgow on 17 April 1937, when 149,547 spectators saw Scotland win 3-1 in the British Home Championship. By contrast, only 2,378 turned up in Bologna, Italy, to see San Marino stun England and take the lead after just seven seconds on 17 November 1993. A 7-1 victory by Graham Taylor's side was not enough to secure England a place at the 1994 FIFA World Cup.

7-1
England's biggest defeat came against Hungary in 1954. They lost 7-1.

STAR PLAYER
NEW KING KANE

Centre-forward **Harry Kane** went into the 2018 FIFA World Cup as England's new permanent captain; he ended it as the nation's first Golden Boot winner since Gary Lineker in 1986. His six goals, including a hat-trick in a 6-1 first round victory over Panama, made him only the third England player to score a FIFA World Cup treble, after Sir Geoff Hurst in the 1966 final and Lineker in 1986, and he ended the tournament with 19 England goals from 30 appearances. Kane scored a late winner to beat Croatia 2-1 at Wembley in November 2018, ending a mini-drought and securing England a place among the first four UEFA Nations League finalists the following summer.

HARRY **KANE**

1

Claude Ashton, the Corinthians centre-forward, set a record when he captained England on his only international appearance. This was a 0-0 draw against Northern Ireland in Belfast on 24 October 1925.

35

Striker Jermain Defoe has come on as a substitute 35 times for England – more often than any other player in history – between his debut in 2004 and his final appearance in 2017.

NATIONAL LEGEND
WONDERFUL WALTER

Walter Winterbottom was England's first full-time manager and remains both the longest-serving (with 138 games in charge) and the youngest, aged just 33 when he took the job in 1946. The former teacher and Manchester United player led his country to four FIFA World Cups, from their first appearance in 1950, to the 1962 tournament in Chile.

WALTER **WINTERBOTTOM**

FRANCE

With two world titles and a rich history of helping to develop the game, "Les Bleus" are footballing heavyweights and current FIFA World Cup holders

Joined FIFA: 1907

Biggest Win:
10-0 vs. Azerbaijan,
6 September 1995

Highest FIFA Ranking: 1

Home Stadium:
Stade De France

Honours:
2 World Cup wins (1998, 2018), 2 European Championships (1984, 2000)

KYLIAN
MBAPPE

FRANCE AND FIFA
Jules Rimet – FIFA president from 1921 to 1954 – was the driving force behind the creation of the FIFA World Cup and the first version of the trophy was named in his honour.

STAR PLAYER
IN FOR THE KYL

France won their second FIFA World Cup in July 2018, 20 years after their first. 19-year-old **Kylian Mbappe** scored their last goal in the 4-2 final triumph over Croatia, and was named the best young player of tournament. Mbappe became the second teenager to score in the final of the FIFA World Cup, following Pele against Sweden in 1958, and with his strike against Peru in the group stage, he also became France's youngest scorer at a major tournament, aged just 19 years and 183 days. Mbappe moved from AS Monaco to Paris Saint-Germain in summer 2017, in deal worth £166m.

6

Six France players have won the FIFA World Cup, UEFA European Championship and UEFA Champions League: Didier Deschamps, Marcel Desailly, Christian Karembeu, Bixente Lizarazu, Thierry Henry and Zinedine Zidane.

ANTOINE
GRIEZMANN

STAR PLAYER
GRIEZ LIGHTNING

Atletico Madrid and France striker **Antoine Griezmann** won both the Golden Boot as the six-goal top scorer and Golden Ball for best player at the 2016 UEFA European Championship. France lost 1-0 to Portugal, but Griezmann made amends two years later, when his four goals helped France win the 2018 FIFA World Cup. His tally included three penalties, with one in the final giving his team a 2-1 lead over Croatia. Griezmann's FIFA World Cup triumph came just weeks after he scored twice in Atletico's 3-0 defeat of Marseille in the UEFA Europa League final.

MANAGER RECORD
WORLD CUP COMEDOWN

France have enjoyed mixed fortunes since winning their second FIFA World Cup in the summer of 2018. They became the sixth consecutive world champions to fail to win their first game since lifting the trophy, held to a goalless draw away to Germany in their opening UEFA Nations League clash in September 2018. France did at least go four matches without defeat, the best record of any world champions after the final since the French team of 20 years earlier. These included 2-1 victories in the UEFA Nations League over both the Netherlands and Germany. The Dutch won 2-0 in the return game in Rotterdam to clinch a place at the UEFA Nations League finals.

KOPA – FRANCE'S FIRST SUPERSTAR

Born on 13 October 1931, **Raymond Kopa** was France's first international superstar. Born into a family of Polish immigrants (his family name was Kopaszewski), he was instrumental in Reims's championship successes of the mid-1950s. He later joined Real Madrid and became the first French player to win a European Cup winner's medal, in 1956. He was the playmaker of the France team that finished third in the 1958 FIFA World Cup finals and his performances for his country that year earned him the European Footballer of the Year award. Kopa's death, aged 85, on 3 March 2017 was met with sadness around the world.

RAYMOND **KOPA**

UMTITI BOOM

In 2016, Samuel Umtiti became the first outfield player to make his French international debut at a major tournament since Gabriel De Michele at the 1966 FIFA World Cup. He came on in Les Bleus' 5-2 victory against Iceland.

STAR PLAYER VICTOR HUGO

Hugo Lloris has worn the captain's armband more than any other Frenchman, lifting the FIFA World Cup trophy in June 2018 in his 104th appearance for his country and his 80th as skipper. Yet it took some time for Lloris to be given the national honour. After Patrice Evra lost the captaincy for his role in France's 2010 FIFA World Cup fiasco, when the players briefly went on strike and Nicolas Anelka was sent home for insulting manager Raymond Domenech, new coach Laurent Blanc tried three captains during qualification for the 2012 UEFA European Championship before turning to Lloris, and he was given the job permanently in February 2012.

HUGO **LLORIS**

STAR PLAYER POGBA POWER

France's triumph at the 2013 FIFA U-20 World Cup in Turkey made them the first country to complete a grand slam of FIFA 11-a-side international men's titles, having previously won the FIFA World Cup, the FIFA U-17 World Cup and Olympic Games gold medal. The star of the show in 2013 was dynamic midfielder and captain **Paul Pogba**, who was among those scoring from the spot as Uruguay were beaten 4-1 on penalties in the final after a goalless draw. Pogba was awarded the Golden Ball as the tournament's best player. He shone again five years later for the senior side, scoring France's third goal as they beat Croatia 4-2 in the FIFA World Cup final.

PAUL **POGBA**

ZINEDINE **ZIDANE**

17

DESAILLY: JE SUIS UN ROCK STAR

Despite having been born in the Ghanaian capital Accra, **Marcel Desailly** always insisted he only ever wanted to play for France – the country he moved to as a four-year-old – and became the nation's most-capped player in 2003. He retired the following year with a then-record of 116 international appearances, although this was later passed by frequent team-mate Lilian Thuram. Desailly, a commanding presence at either centre-back or in midfield that saw him dubbed "The Rock", not only won both the 1998 FIFA World Cup and 2000 UEFA European Championship with his country, but was also the first player to win the UEFA Champions League in successive seasons with different clubs – with Marseille in 1993, and then AC Milan the following year.

MARCEL DESAILLY

DIDIER DESCHAMPS

NATIONAL LEGEND
DESCHAMPS THE MULTIPLE CHAMP

Didier Deschamps is only the third man to have won the FIFA World Cup both as a player and a manager, after Brazil's Mario Zagallo in 1958 and 1970 and Franz Beckenbauer with West Germany in 1974 and 1990. Deschamps captained France both in 1998 and in 2000 for France's UEFA European Championship triumph, and retired after winning 103 caps, 55 as captain. Defensive midfielder Deschamps won trophies at club level too, including the FA Cup with Chelsea in 2000. He became national head coach in 2012, leading France to the Euro 2016 final, where they lost 1-0 to Portugal. Two years later, France and Deschamps won the 2018 FIFA World Cup. He has since taken the record for most managerial victories, with 57 wins in 90 games by April 2019.

LILIAN THURAM

17

Fabien Barthez holds his country's record for most FIFA World Cup finals appearances, 17 between 1998 and 2006.

EARNING THEIR STRIPES

France are the only country to play at a FIFA World Cup wearing another team's kit. In Argentina in 1978, Les Bleus were forced to wear the green and white stripes of a local club side, Atletico Kimberley, after a clash of white with Hungary.

NATIONAL LEGEND
LILIAN IN THE PINK

Lilian Thuram made his 142nd and final appearance for France in their defeat by Italy at Euro 2008. The defender's international career had spanned nearly 14 years, since his debut against the Czech Republic in August 1994. Thuram was played club football for Monaco, Parma, Juventus and Barcelona before retiring in the summer of 2008 because of a heart problem and was one of the stars of France's 1998 FIFA World Cup-winning side. He scored both goals in their semi-final victory over Croatia: the only international goals of his career.

The first six players to earn 100 caps for France were in the winning squads at the 1998 FIFA World Cup and 2000 UEFA European Championship: Lilian Thuram, Thierry Henry, Marcel Desailly, Zinedine Zidane, Patrick Vieira and Didier Deschamps.

STAR PLAYER
GIROUD AWAKENING

In June 2017 against Paraguay, Olivier Giroud's became the first Frenchman to hit an international hat-trick since winger Dominique Rocheteau, in a 6-0 win against Luxembourg 32 years earlier. Giroud joined Zinedine Zidane as France's joint fourth top scorer scoring against Colombia and the Republic of Ireland in early 2018. Giroud finished the 2016 UEFA European Championship as joint second top scorer with three goals, but at the 2018 FIFA World Cup, Giroud was not credited with a single shot on target, despite completing all seven games en route to picking up a winner's medal.

NATIONAL LEGEND
HENRY BENCHED

Thierry Henry did not play in the 1998 FIFA World Cup final because of Marcel Desailly's red card. Henry, France's leading goalscorer in the finals with three, was a substitute and coach Aime Jacquet planned to use him late in the game. But Desailly's sending-off forced a re-think: Jacquet instead reinforced his midfield with future Arsenal team-mate Patrick Vieira going on instead, leaving Henry as an unused substitute. But Henry does have the distinction of being the only Frenchman to play at four different FIFA World Cups (1998, 2002, 2006 and 2010). He passed Michel Platini's all-time goal-scoring record for France with a brace against Lithuania in October 2007.

SO NEAR YET SO VAR

Antoine Griezmann became the first man to have an international goal disallowed through the intervention of a video assistant referee when he was deemed offside after finding the net against Spain in March 2017, a match Spain won 2-0.

THIERRY HENRY

STAR PLAYER
KANTE CAN DO IT

Despite being just 1.68m tall, N'Golo Kante has proved a big midfield prescence. He won back-to-back English Premier League titles, with Leicester City in 2016 and Chelsea the following year – the first outfielder to do so with different clubs since compatriot Eric Cantona triumphed with Leeds United in 1992 and Manchester United 12 months later. Kante's magic touch continued as he helped motor France to FIFA World Cup glory in 2018. The 4-2 win meant France extended to 18 games their record of never losing with Kante and fellow midfielder Paul Pogba in the starting line-up.

JUST FONTAINE

NATIONAL LEGEND
NO TIME FOR FONTAINE

Former striker **Just Fontaine** spent the shortest ever spell in charge of the French team. He took over on 22 March 1967 and left on 3 June after two defeats in friendlies. More happily, he still holds the record for most goals at a single FIFA World Cup - 13 across six games he played at the 1958 tournament, including four in France's 6-3 victory over West Germany to finish third. He remains the only Frenchman to score a FIFA World Cup hat-trick.

GERMANY

1993
Germany ended 2014 top of the FIFA world rankings – the first time they had occupied this position in December since 1993, when the rankings were originally introduced.

German footballers are almost ever-presents in the closing stages of major tournaments. The 2014 success had ended an 18-year trophy drought and was their first World Cup success as a reunified nation, after winning in 1954, 1974 and 1990 as West Germany.

Joined FIFA: 1908

Biggest Win:
16–0 vs. Russia, 1912

Highest FIFA Ranking: 1

Home Stadium:
(Rotation)

Honours:
4 World Cups (1954, 1974, 1990, 2014),
3 European Championships (1972, 1980, 1996)

SCORING RECORD
KLOSE ENCOUNTERS

Miroslav Klose became the third player, after Uwe Seeler and Pele to score in four FIFA World Cup finals. His first goal in 2014, an equalizer against Ghana, put him alongside Ronaldo at the top of the all-time FIFA World Cup scoring charts. And it was against Ronaldo's Brazil that Klose pushed ahead on his own. His 24 appearances left him behind only compatriot Lothar Matthaus (25) and Klose's 17 wins were one more than previous record-holder Cafu, of Brazil. Klose retired in 2014 as Germany's all-time leading scorer, with 71 goals in 137 matches – and his team-mates never lost an international in which he found the net.

MIROSLAV **KLOSE**

TOP SCORERS:

1. Miroslav Klose, 71
2. Gerd Muller, 68
3. Lukas Podolski, 49
4. Jurgen Klinsmann, 47
   = Rudi Voller, 47

FRANZ **BECKENBAUER**

NATIONAL LEGEND
DER KAISER

Franz Beckenbauer is widely regarded as the greatest player in German football history. He defined the role of attacking sweeper, first in the 1970 FIFA World Cup finals, and then as West Germany won the 1972 UEFA European Championship and the 1974 FIFA World Cup. Beckenbauer later delivered a FIFA World Cup final appearance in 1986 as an inexperienced coach, and the 1990 trophy in his final game in charge. He later became president of Bayern Munich, the club he captained to three consecutive European Cup victories between 1974 and 1976. He also led Germany's successful bid for the 2006 FIFA World Cup finals and headed the organizing committee.

30

Phillip Lahm shocked the international football world when he retired aged just 30 after winning the FIFA World Cup in 2014.

TOURNAMENT TRIVIA
SAMBA SILENCED

Germany's 1-0 win over Argentina in 2014 came in their record eighth FIFA World Cup Final, this coming after they were the first side to reach four consecutive semi-finals. But the 7-1 semi-final humiliation of Brazil may live longest in the memory – and the record books. Germany led 5-0 at half-time in what became the biggest FIFA World Cup semi-final win and the hosts' heaviest defeat. Other FIFA World Cup finals records include: Toni Kroos's two goals in 69 seconds were the fastest brace and Germany were the first team to score four goals in six minutes. Also Thomas Muller's opening goal was Germany's 2,000th.

STAR PLAYER
KROOS CONTROL

Attacking midfielder **Toni Kroos** became in 2014 the only man born in East Germany to win the FIFA World Cup. He was born in Greifswald in January 1990, nine months before Germany's reunification. He scored twice in the semi-final against Brazil, played the full final against Argentina and ended the tournament on FIFA's ten-man Golden Ball shortlist. At the 2018 FIFA World Cup, Kroos scored Germany's latest-ever regulation-time goal – excluding extra-time – to clinch a 2-1 Group F victory over Sweden. It was timed at 94 minutes and 42 seconds.

NATIONAL LEGEND
KEEPING A LOW PROFILE

In 2014, **Joachim Low** became the 19th coach to win the FIFA World Cup, but the first German coach to do so without having played for his country. After a respectable career as a midfielder for a number of clubs, including Freiburg, and coaching spells in Germany, Austria and Turkey, Low was appointed as Jurgen Klinsmann's assistant in 2004, before taking the top job after the 2006 FIFA World Cup. He led Germany to the 2008 UEFA European Championship final and the semi-finals of Euro 2012, as well as third-place at the 2010 FIFA World Cup.

JOACHIM LOW

11 HOURS AND 19 MINUTES

Germany went a national record of 11 hours and 19 minutes without conceding a goal, between Antoine Griezmann scoring for France in the 2016 UEFA European Championship semi-final and a 31st-minute equalizer by Azerbaijan's Dimitrij Nazarov on 26 March 2017, in a 2018 FIFA World Cup qualifier, a match Germany went on to win 4-1.

100

Ulf Kirsten is one of eight players to have played for both the old East Germany and the reunified Germany after 1990. He managed 100 appearances: 49 for East Germany and 51 for Germany.

NATIONAL LEGEND
YOUNGEST CENTURION LUKAS

Lukas Podolski was briefly Europe's youngest footballer to reach 100 caps when, aged 27 years and 13 days old, he appeared in Germany's third first-round game of the 2012 UEFA European Championship, against Denmark. He marked the occasion by scoring the opener in a 2-1 win. He was voted best young player of the tournament when Germany hosted and finished third at the 2006 FIFA World Cup. He bowed out of international football in March 2017 with the only goal – his 49th – of what he said in advance would be his 130th and final game for Germany, a 1-0 friendly win over England in Dortmund.

TONI KROOS

MANUEL NEUER

Germany went into the 2018 FIFA World Cup as defending champions – and 2017 FIFA Confederations Cup holders, which they had won in Russia. Yet Joachim Low's side finished bottom of Group F, ensuring their first first-round exit for 80 years – they did not compete in 1950 – and only their second ever. Germany were eliminated in 1938, a straight knock-out tournament, after losing 4-2 to Switzerland in a first-round replay following a 1-1 draw. That German team featured several Austrian players, following the Anschluss (German annexation of Austria) earlier in the year.

1-0
East and West Germany met only once at senior national team level. That was on 22 June 1974, in the FIFA World Cup finals. Drawn in the same group, East Germany produced a shock 1-0 win in Hamburg, but both teams advanced.

STAR PLAYER
NEUER RECORD

Manuel Neuer has the longest run between conceding international tournament goals for Germany. There were 557 minutes between Brazil's late goal in the 7-1 2014 FIFA World Cup semi-final rout before Italy's Leonardo Bonucci scored in the 2016 UEFA European Championship quarter-final. Germany won 6-5 on penalties, helped by two spot-kick saves by Neuer. The previous best had been Sepp Maier's 481-minute sequence in the 1970s. Neuer – renowned for his ease with the ball at his feet, as a so-called "sweeper keeper" – was appointed Germany captain in September 2016 after Bastian Schweinsteiger retired.

MARIO GOTZE

ANDRE SCHURRLE

NATIONAL LEGEND
OZIL'S AWARDS

Mesut Ozil – Germany's player of the year 2011–13 and 2015–16 – was almost ever-present as the team won the 2014 FIFA World Cup – and at the end of the final handed his shirt to then-UEFA president Michel Platini. He was man of the match when Germany beat England 4-0 in the 2009 UEFA U21 European Championship final and was among ten nominees for the 2010 FIFA World Cup Golden Ball. Ozil, however, missed Germany's first tournament penalty for 40 years at the 2016 UEFA European Championship, when he missed against Slovakia.

MESUT OZIL

Bayern Munich's **Mario Gotze** was the hero when Germany finally overcame Argentina's resistance in the 2014 FIFA World Cup final. His 113th-minute volley was the first winner hit by a substitute. It seemed apt that Germany's first FIFA World Cup triumph since the reunification of East and West Germany in 1990 was secured by Gotze, set up by **Andre Schurrle**. They had jointly become the first German football internationals born post-reunification, when making their debuts as 79th-minute substitutes against Sweden in November 2010.

5
Lothar Matthaus is Germany's most-capped player. He appeared in five FIFA World Cup finals – 1982, 1986, 1990, 1994 and 1998 – a record for an outfield player he shares with Mexico's Rafael Marquez.

▼ STAR PLAYER
ⓩ PRESSURE ON JULIAN

World champions Germany won their first FIFA Confederations Cup in Russia in 2017, despite coach Joachim Low resting many of his senior stars, including Thomas Muller, Mesut Ozil and Toni Kroos. Lars Stindl scored the only goal of the final, against Chile, while goalkeeper Marc-Andre ter Stegen was named man of the match. The Golden Ball for the tournament's best player went to 23-year-old captain **Julian Draxler** – Germany's youngest skipper at a tournament since Max Breunig at the 1912 Summer Olympics – and the Golden Boot went to three-goal team-mate Timo Werner. Germany also had the youngest average age for any FIFA Confederations Cup-winning squad: 24 years and four months.

JULIAN
DRAXLER

22

Sepp Herberger (1897–1977) was Germany's longest-serving coach (22 years at the helm) and his legendary status was assured after West Germany surprised odds-on favourites Hungary to win the 1954 FIFA World Cup final – a result credited with dragging the country out of a post-war slump.

NATIONAL LEGEND
BASTIAN THE BASTION

No-one has played more matches at the FIFA World Cup and UEFA Euro finals than the 38-game tally of Germany's **Bastian Schweinsteiger** and Portugal's Cristiano Ronaldo. "Schweini" reached the mark at Euro 2016. However the occasion – a semi-final against France – was not a happy one. A handball by German captain Schweinsteiger conceded an opening penalty in a 2-0 defeat. Happier times followed, however. A week later he married Serbian tennis star Ana Ivanovic.

0

Germany are renowned as penalty specialists, but they needed no shoot-outs when winning the 2014 FIFA World Cup, unlike their previous two titles, the 1990 FIFA World Cup and the 1996 UEFA European Championship. These both involved semi-final victories on penalties against England.

BASTIAN
SCHWEINSTEIGER

NATIONAL LEGEND
DER BOMBER

Gerd Muller was the most prolific scorer of Germany's modern era. Neither tall nor graceful, he was quick, strong and had a predator's eye for the net. He also had the temperament to score decisive goals in big games, including the winner in the 1974 FIFA World Cup final, the winner in the semi-final against Poland and two goals in West Germany's 1972 UEFA European Championship final victory over the USSR. He netted 68 goals in 62 appearances for West Germany and remains the leading scorer in the Bundesliga and all-time record scorer for his club, Bayern Munich.

NATIONAL LEGEND
GRAND SAMMER

Matthias Sammer is not only one of eight men to play for both East Germany and the reunified Germany, he also holds the honour of captaining and scoring both goals in East Germany's final game, a 2-0 away win over Belgium on 12 September 1990, 21 days before the official reunification. His powerhouse midfield performances later drove Germany to glory at the 1996 UEFA European Championship, where he was voted the official player of the tournament.

ITALY

Only Brazil (with five victories) can claim to have won the FIFA World Cup more times than Italy. The Azzurri became the first nation to retain the trophy (winning in 1934 and 1938), were surprise champions in Spain in 1982 and collected football's most coveted trophy for a fourth time in 2006.

Joined FIFA: 1910
Biggest Win:
9-0 vs. USA, 1948
Highest FIFA Ranking: 1
Home Stadium:
Stadio Olimpico, Rome
Honours:
4 World Cups (1934, 1938, 1982, 2006), 1 European Championship (1968)

ANDREA
PIRLO

18

Italy have made 18 appearances at FIFA World Cup finals, and won on four occasions.

NATIONAL LEGEND
PEERLESS PIRLO

Deep-lying playmaker **Andrea Pirlo** – Italy's fifth most-capped player with 116 – is one of the finest passers of a football in the modern era. He was one of the stand-out performers when Italy won the 2006 FIFA World Cup and the only player to win three man-of-the-match prizes at the 2012 UEFA European Championship. Pirlo came to the tournament having gone through the Italian league season unbeaten, helping Juventus lift the Serie A title after joining them in 2011 from AC Milan on a free transfer.

TOURNAMENT TRIVIA
SHARE AND SHARE ALIKE

Manager Marcelo Lippi used all his outfield squad members when winning Italy's fourth FIFA World Cup in Germany in 2006 – and all six of his named strikers found the net once apiece, apart from Luca Toni who scored twice. He might have had a third, but his 61st-minute header against France in the final was disallowed for a marginal offside. The other forwards to score were Alessandro Del Piero, Francesco Totti, Alberto Gilardino, Vincenzo Iaquinta and Filippo Inzaghi. Toni retired from football at the end of the 2015–16 season at the age of 39, having a year earlier become the oldest man to finish as Serie A's top scorer.

NATIONAL LEGEND
ZOFF THE SCALE

Goalkeeper **Dino Zoff** set an international record by going 1,142 minutes without conceding a goal between September 1972 and June 1974. Zoff was Italy's captain when they won the 1982 FIFA World Cup – emulating the feat of another Juventus goalkeeper, Gianpiero Combi, who had been the victorious skipper in 1934. Zoff coached Italy to the final of the 2000 UEFA European Championship, which they lost 2-1 to France thanks to an extra-time "golden goal" – then quit a few days later, unhappy following the criticism levelled at him by Italy's then Prime Minister, Silvio Berlusconi.

DINO
ZOFF

2

Vittorio Pozzo is the only man to have won the FIFA World Cup twice as manager – both times with Italy, in 1934 and 1938 (only two players, Giuseppe Meazza and Giovanni Ferrari, were selected in both finals).

STAR PLAYER
THE YOUNG ONES

Juventus striker **Moise Kean** marked his first senior start for Italy by becoming his country's youngest scorer for 60 years and the second youngest ever, finding the net in March 2019 in a 2-0 UEFA European Championship qualifier win over Finland. He was aged just 19 years 23 days old. The other goal was scored by Fabio Quagliarella, who – at 36 years 54 days old – became Italy's oldest ever scorer. The youngest, albeit in a non-competitive match, remains Bruno Nicole who was 18 years and 258 days when hitting a brace in a 2-2 draw against France on 9 November 1958. Nicole later became Italy's youngest captain, aged 21 years 61 days, in April 1961.

MOISE
KEAN

19 SECONDS

Emanuele Giaccherini scored Italy's fastest goal, just 19 seconds into their June 2013 friendly against Haiti – one second quicker than Salvatore Bagni's strike against Mexico 29 years earlier.

NATIONAL LEGEND
HAPPY CENTENARY

After captaining Italy to the 2006 FIFA World Cup title, **Fabio Cannavaro** was named FIFA World Player of the Year – at 33, the oldest winner of the prize, as well as the first defender. Cannavaro, born in Naples in 1973, played every minute of the 2006 tournament and the final triumph against France was the ideal way to celebrate his 100th international appearance. Cannavaro is widely considered one of the greatest defenders of the 21st Century and played for Juventus, Internazionale and Real Madrid.

NATIONAL LEGEND
APPETITE FOR SUCCESS

The stadium shared by AC Milan and Internazionale is popularly known as San Siro, after the district in which it is located. Its official title is Stadio Giuseppe Meazza, named after the star inside-forward who played for both clubs, as well as Italy's 1934 and 1938 FIFA World Cup-winning sides. Meazza, born in Milan on 23 August 1910, was spotted by an Inter scout while playing keepy-uppy in the street with a ball made of rags. He was so thin he had to be fattened up with a diet of steaks. His last goal for Italy was a penalty in the 1938 FIFA World Cup semi-final against Brazil – taken while using one hand to hold up his shorts, whose elastic had broken.

FABIO
CANNAVARO

MOST APPEARANCES:

1 **Gianluigi Buffon**, 176

2 **Fabio Cannavaro**, 136

3 **Paulo Maldini**, 126

4 **Daniele De Rossi**, 117

5 **Andrea Pirlo**, 116

NATIONAL LEGEND
KEEPING IT IN THE FAMILY

Cesare and **Paolo Maldini** are the only father and son to have hoisted the European Cup as winning captains – both with AC Milan and both for the first time in England. Cesare lifted the trophy after his team beat Benfica at Wembley, London, in 1963. Paolo repeated the feat 40 years later, when Milan defeated Juventus at Old Trafford, Manchester. Although he retired as Italy's second most-capped player, Paolo never managed to win an international tournament – he played for Italy sides that finished third and runners-up at the FIFA World Cup and runners-up in the UEFA European Championship.

PAOLO
MALDINI

TOURNAMENT TRIVIA
IN SAFE KEEPING

During World War Two, the Jules Rimet Trophy, the FIFA World Cup – won by Italy in 1938 – was hidden in a shoebox under the bed of football official Ottorino Barassi. He preferred to keep it there, rather than at its previous home – a bank in Rome. The trophy was handed back to FIFA, safe and untouched, only when the FIFA World Cup resumed in 1950. Barassi helped organise the 1934 FIFA World Cup, which was played in his native Italy.

NATIONAL LEGEND
WHEN THE GOING GETS BUFF

Gianluigi Buffon has not only been one of the finest modern-day goalkeepers in the world but has also even surpassed some of the achievements of legendary Italian predecessor Dino Zoff. Buffon emulated 1982 world champion Dino Zoff by being part of Italy's 2006 FIFA World Cup-winning side – only conceding two goals during the tournament, one an own goal and the other a penalty. Buffon became only the third footballer selected for five different FIFA World Cups when he made two appearances in Brazil in 2014, only missing the opening match against England due to a late ankle injury.

GIANLUIGI
BUFFON

NATIONAL LEGEND
COMEBACK KID

Paolo Rossi was the unlikely hero of Italy's 1982 FIFA World Cup triumph, winning the Golden Boot with six goals – including a memorable hat-trick against Brazil in the second round, and the first of Italy's three goals in their final win over West Germany. But he only just made it to the tournament at all, having completed a two-year ban for his alleged involvement in a betting scandal only six weeks before the start of the tournament.

PAOLO
ROSSI

NO. 3
No Internazionale footballer will ever wear the No.3 shirt after it was retired in tribute to the legendary full-back Giacinto Facchetti, following his death in 2006 at the age of 64.

21

No team have drawn more FIFA World Cup matches than Italy, who took their tally to 21 with 1-1 draws against both Paraguay and New Zealand in Group F at the 2010 competition in South Africa.

3

Only England and Spain have lost as many FIFA World Cup penalty shoot-outs as Italy – three apiece. Roberto Baggio, nicknamed "The Divine Ponytail", was involved in all three of Italy's spot-kick defeats, in 1990, 1994 and 1998.

NATIONAL LEGEND
MEDAL COLLECTORS

Giovanni Ferrari not only won both the 1934 and 1938 FIFA World Cup with Italy, he also held the record for the most Serie A titles until 2018. He won it eight times, five with Juventus, two with Internazionale and one with Bologna. Five other players have won eight Serie A titles: Virginio Rosetti, Giuseppe Furino, Andrea Barzagli, Giorgio Chiellini and Leonardo Bonucci. Gianluigi Buffon holds the record, with nine. In fact, Buffon has 11 titles, but the ones in 2004–05 and 2005–06 were rescinded in light of the *Calciopoli* scandal.

ANDREA
BARZAGLI

NATIONAL LEGEND
BOSSI DE ROSSI

Central midfielder Daniele de Rossi was roundly condemned when he was sent off for elbowing Brian McBride of the USA in a 2006 FIFA World Cup group match. His suspension finished in time for him to be a substitute in the final, which Italy won against France. However, in March 2006, De Rossi had won widespread praise for his honesty. During a Serie A match his club AS Roma were awarded a goal against Messina when he diverted the ball into the net with his hand and he persuaded the referee to disallow the goal (Roma still won 2–1).

NATIONAL LEGEND
VENTURA'S MISADVENTURE

The 2018 FIFA World Cup in Russia was the first since 1958 not to feature Italy, after they lost a qualifying play-off 1-0 on aggregate to Sweden. Players and supporters were left visibly distraught at this unexpected failure, which cost both manager Gian Piero Ventura and Italian football association president Carlo Tavecchio their jobs. Four of Italy's star players also announced their international retirements following the November 2017 playoff: goalkeeper Gianluigi Buffon, defenders Giorgio Chiellini and **Andrea Barzagli** and midfielder Daniele De Rossi. However, caretaker manager Luigi Di Biagio selected both Buffon and Chiellini for friendlies in March 2018.

1000

Christian Vieri's first goal for Italy was not just just on his debut in 1997, it marked the Azzuri's 1000th goal scored in all internationals.

NETHERLANDS

Patrick Kluivert's son Justin made his Dutch international debut as a 78th-minute substitute against Portugal in March 2018, aged 18 – the same age at which Patrick first appeared for his country.

The walled banks of orange-shirted Netherlands fans have become a regular feature at the world's major football tournaments, thanks to Johan Cruyff and his team's spectacular brand of "Total Football".

Joined FIFA: 1905

Biggest win:
11–0 vs. San Marino, 2011

Highest FIFA ranking: 1

Home Stadium: Johann Cruyff Arena, Amsterdam

Honours: 1 European Championship (1988)

JOHAN **CRUYFF**

NATIONAL LEGEND
CRUYFF THE MAGICIAN

Johan Cruyff was not only a genius with the ball at his feet but also an inspirational football philosopher, who spread the concept of "Total Football" not only with Ajax Amsterdam and the Netherlands in the 1970s but also in Spain where he played and managed Barcelona and acted as a mentor to those who followed him there, such as Pep Guardiola and Xavi Hernandez. He also gave the world the much-imitated "Cruyff turn", after managing to push the ball with the inside of his foot behind his standing leg before swivelling and surging past bemused Swedish defender Jan Olsson.

100
Midfielder Davy Klaassen's first international appearance, a 2–0 defeat to France in March 2014, meant he was the 100th player to make his Netherlands debut as an Ajax Amsterdam player, having been brought up in the club's famed youth academy.

NATIONAL LEGEND
THE WINNING CAPTAIN

With his distinctive dreadlocks, Ruud Gullit cut a swathe through world football through the 1980s and '90s. Twice a European Cup winner with AC Milan and a former European Footballer of the Year, he will always be remembered fondly by the Dutch fans as being the first man in a Netherlands shirt to lift a major trophy – the 1988 UEFA European Championship. In 1996, Gullit signed for Chelsea and a year later was appointed the club's player-manager.

NATIONAL LEGEND
MICHELS THE MASTER

Rinus Michels (1928–2005) was named FIFA's Coach of the Century in 1999 for his achievements with the Netherlands and Ajax. The former Ajax and Netherlands striker took over the manager's job at his old club in 1965 and built the team around Johan Cruyff – as he later did with the national side, introducing "Total Football". He moved to Barcelona after Ajax's 1971 European Cup victory, but he was called back to mastermind the Netherlands' 1974 FIFA World Cup bid. Nicknamed "The General", he was known as a disciplinarian who took over national team again for their victorious 1988 UEFA European Championship campaign.

RINUS **MICHELS**

NATIONAL LEGEND
DIFFERENT SIDES OF SNEIJDER

In 2017, **Wesley Sneijder** not only became his country's most-capped footballer but also marked his 131st international appearance with his 31st goal. He enjoyed an almost perfect 2010 as he won the treble with Italy's Internazionale – a domestic league and cup double and the UEFA Champions League – but just missed out on adding the FIFA World Cup, as the Netherlands lost 1-0 to Spain in the final. Sneijder also almost won the tournament's Golden Boot; his five goals put him level with Diego Forlan, Thomas Muller and David Villa.

38
Abe Lenstra was Netherlands' oldest goalscorer, aged 38 years and 144 days when he netted in his final game, a 2-2 draw with Belgium, on 19 April 1959.

STAR PLAYER
MEMPHIS SWELL

Substitute Memphis Depay became the youngest FIFA World Cup goalscorer in Dutch history – aged 20 years and 125 days – by netting in the 3-2 Group B victory over Australia at Porto Alegre in 2014. He also scored against Chile five days later, again as a substitute. Depay was one of three nominees for the Best Young Player award, but lost out to France's Paul Pogba. Depay began his career with PSV, where managed by Dutch legend Phillip Cocu, he netted 50 goals in 124 games across all competitions.

WESLEY SNEIJDER

NATIONAL LEGEND
FLYING FEAR DENIED BERGKAMP MORE CAPS

Dennis Bergkamp would have won many more than 79 caps, but for his fear of flying. Bergkamp refused to board aircraft after the Netherlands squad were involved in a bomb hoax incident during the 1994 FIFA World Cup in the United States. He missed every away game for the Netherlands and his clubs unless he could reach the venue by road, rail or boat. His intricately-skilful last-minute winner against Argentina in the quarter-finals of the 1998 FIFA World Cup is seen by many as one of the tournament's finest and most elegant goals.

DENNIS BERGKAMP

STAR PLAYER
VIRGIL RECORD

Virgil van Dijk became the world's most expensive defender in January 2018 after joining Liverpool from Premier League rivals Southampton for a reported £75 million. Two months later, he was named as the Netherlands' new captain, replacing Arjen Robben who had retired from international football the previous October. Robben is one of only two Dutch men to score at three separate FIFA World Cups – he and striker Robin van Persie both found the net in 2006, 2010 and 2014. Van Dijk's first international goal came in his 18th international appearance – second as skipper – in a 3-0 friendly win over European champions Portugal in March 2018.

VIRGIL VAN DIJK

29

NATIONAL LEGENDS
KOEMAN PEOPLE

Brothers Ronald and Erwin Koeman were Netherlands team-mates in winning the 1988 UEFA European Championship and later teamed up in management. Elder brother Erwin served as Ronald's assistant at English clubs Everton and Southampton, but when Ronald was appointed the Netherlands' head coach in February 2018, Erwin opted not to join him. After the Dutch missed out on both the 2016 UEFA European Championship and the 2018 FIFA World Cup, Koeman's reign started encouragingly with his team topping their UEFA Nations League group above France and Germany. New captain Virgil van Dijk scored in both games against Germany, the opener in a 3-0 home win and a stoppage-time equaliser in a 2-2 away draw.

NATIONAL LEGEND
DE BOER BOYS SET RECORD

Twins **Frank** and **Ronald de Boer** hold the record for the most games played by brothers together for the Netherlands. Frank won 112 caps, while Ronald won 67. Ronald missed a crucial spot-kick as the Dutch lost to Brazil in the semi-finals of the 1998 FIFA World Cup, while Frank suffered a similar unfortunate fate at the same stage of the UEFA European Championship two years later. Frank took over as Ajax Amsterdam manager in December 2010, having earlier that year been assistant to Bert van Marwijk to help the Netherlands to the FIFA World Cup final.

RONALD
DE BOER

FRANK
DE BOER

RAFAEL
VAN DER VAART

NATIONAL LEGEND
WORK OF VAART

Rafael van der Vaart became the fifth player to make 100 appearances for the Netherlands, yet for a while it looked as if van der Vaart might just miss out on the milestone: he ended the 2012 UEFA European Championship on 99 caps and coach Bert van Marwijk said he may be left out of future squads. But Van Marwijk's departure after Euro 2012 was a boost for van der Vaart, who made his 100th appearance in a 4-2 friendly loss to Belgium in August 2012. Sadly, a calf injury ruled him out of the 2014 FIFA World Cup three days before Louis van Gaal announced his 23-man squad.

TOURNAMENT TRIVIA
KRUL TO BE KIND

Louis van Gaal pulled a masterstoke when he replaced goalkeeper Jasper Cillessen with Tim Krul in the 119th minute of the Netherlands' quarter-final against Costa Rica in the 2014 FIFA World Cup. He reasoned that the Dutch stood a better chance of winning the resulting shoot-out with Krul as he is two inches taller than Cillessen. Sure enough, Krul saved two penalties and the Dutch went through. Van Gaal could not repeat the trick against Argentina in the semi-final, though third-choice goalkeeper Michel Vorm replaced Cillessen during stoppage-time of the third-place play-off against Brazil, making the Netherlands the first country to field all 23 squad-members during a FIFA World Cup.

Nine Netherlands players were on the losing side in both the 1974 (2-1 to West Germany) and 1978 (3-1 to Argentina) FIFA World Cup finals.

The Netherlands received more cards than any other team in a FIFA World Cup final when they were handed eight yellows, including a lenient one for Nigel de Jong's chest-high challenge on Xabi Alonso, and a red in 2010 against Spain.

Four players have scored five goals in a game for the Netherlands: Jan Vos, Leen Vente, John Bosman and Marco van Basten.

NATIONAL LEGEND
BLIND LEADING THE BLIND

Dutch defender Danny Blind won 42 caps between 1986 and 1996, and appeared at the FIFA World Cups of 1990 and 1994. He was also involved at the 2014 final, this time as an assistant to coach Louis van Gaal. He thus saw his son Daley – like Danny, a defender playing club football for Ajax Amsterdam – not only feature as a regular starter but score his first international goal, in the third-place play-off victory over Brazil. Danny Blind was appointed Guus Hiddink's assistant for the 2016 UEFA European Championship qualifying competition, but was appointed to the top job in May 2015 after Hiddink was sacked.

STAR PLAYER
MATT START

At 17 years and 225 days, centre-back **Matthijs de Ligt** became the Netherlands' youngest player since Mauk Weber in 1931 (17 years and 92 days) when making his international bow against Bulgaria in March 2017. Sixty days later, de Ligt came the youngest player to feature in a UEFA final, but his Ajax side lost to Manchester United in the Europa League final in Stockholm. Another Dutch defender, left-back Jetro Willems is the youngest player in UEFA European Championship finals history. In the Netherlands' Euro 2012 opener against Denmark on 9 June, Willems, aged 18 years and 71 days, was 44 days younger than Belgium's Enzo Scifo had been 1984.

TOP SCORERS:

1. **Robin van Persie**, 50
2. **Klass-Jan Huntelaar**, 42
3. **Patrick Kluivert**, 40
4. **Dennis Bergkamp**, 37
   = **Arjen Robben**, 37

MATTHIJS DE LIGT

Rinus Michels managed the Netherlands in four separate spells between 1974 and 1992, more than any other manager.

NATIONAL LEGEND
SENIOR ADVOCAAT

Dick Advocaat holds two records as Dutch national team coach. When he was re-appointed for his third spell in May 2017, he became, at 69, the oldest man to be national coach – one year older than Guus Hiddick had been when he was fired in 2015. Advocaat also has the most wins as national coach, victories in November 2017 friendlies over Scotland and Romania taking him to 37, one more than Englishman Bob Glendenning, who was in charge between 1925 and his death in 1940. After the Romania victory, however, Advocaat stood down as national coach and former player Ronald Koeman was appointed to replace him.

DICK ADVOCAAT

SPAIN

Spanish clubs have won a record 18 European Cup/ UEFA Champions Leagues between them and the country has produced some of world football's finest players. Spain won their first FIFA World Cup in 2010.

Joined FIFA: 1920
Biggest Win:
13-0 vs. Bulgaria, 1933
Highest FIFA Ranking: 1
Home Stadium:
(Rotation)
Honours:
1 World Cup (2010), 3 European Championships (1964, 2008, 2012)

4-3
When Spain came back from 2-0 and then 3-2 down to win 4-3 in Madrid in May 1929, they became the first non-British team to beat England.

NATIONAL PLAYER
ANDRES THE GIANT

Andres Iniesta left Barcelona in 2018, having won nine La Liga titles, six Copa Del Rey trophies and four UEFA Champions League titles in 17 years at the club. He then bade farewell to international football after the 2018 FIFA World Cup, aged 34, having played 131 times for Spain and scored 13 goals – the most important of which won the 2010 FIFA World Cup. Uniquely, Iniesta has been named man of the match in the UEFA Champions League final (in 2015), UEFA European Championship final (2012) and FIFA World Cup final (2010).

ANDRES INIESTA

70

In 2008, a month short of his 70th birthday, Spain's Luis Aragones became the oldest coach to win the UEFA European Championship.

TOURNAMENT TRIVIA
DOUBLING UP

Spain's 2010 FIFA World Cup triumph made them the first country since West Germany in 1974 to lift the trophy as the reigning European champions. When France combined the two titles, they did it the other way around, by winning the 1998 FIFA World Cup and then the UEFA European Championship two years later. Yet no country had won three major tournaments in a row until Spain won Euro 2012, trouncing Italy 4-0 in the final. This also made Spain the first team to make a successful defence of their UEFA European Championship title.

NATIONAL LEGEND
HAPPY XAVI

When Spain's second most capped outfield player, with 133, retired from international football after the 2014 FIFA World Cup – and La Liga a year later – he was recognized as his country's most-decorated player. Curiously, both the first and final appearances of **Xavi Hernandez**'s international career were defeats to Netherlands sides coached by Louis van Gaal, 2-1 in 2000 and 5-1 in 2014. Triumph was far more familiar to the midfield playmaker, a mainstay of Spain's 2010 FIFA World Cup-winning side as well as the teams lifting the UEFA European Championship trophy in 2008 and 2012.

XAVI
HERNANDEZ

TOURNEMENT TRIVIA
RED ALERT

Spain refused to play in the first UEFA European Championship in 1960, in protest at having to travel to the Soviet Union, a Communist country. But they changed their minds four years later, not only hosting the tournament but also winning it – by beating the visiting Soviets 2-1 in the final. Spain were captained by Fernando Olivella and managed by Jose Villalonga, who had been the first coach to win the European Cup, with Real Madrid in 1956.

ISCO

STAR PLAYER
ISCO INFERNO

Real Madrid attacker **Isco** scored Spain's 37th hat-trick – the first for five years – in a 6-1 friendly victory over Argentina on 27 March 2018. It equalled the South American team's heaviest ever defeat. Isco had helped Spain win the UEFA U21 European Championship in Israel in 2013, his three goals earning him the Bronze Boot. After joining Real Madrid in 2013, he has helped them win four UEFA Champions League titles in five years. Isco was among Spain's most impressive performers at the 2018 FIFA World Cup – but admitted losing to Russia on penalties was "the saddest day of my career".

David Villa and Fernando Torres share Spain's record for most hat-tricks, with three. They even managed one apiece in the same match, the 10-0 crushing of Tahiti at the 2013 FIFA Confederations Cup.

NATIONAL LEGEND
BEST CAS SCENARIO

Spain goalkeeper **Iker Casillas** has long been known to devotees back home as "Saint Iker" – an anointment richly supported by his haul of trophies and medals, both for team and individual. He is one of only three men to lift the FIFA World Cup, the UEFA European Championship and the UEFA Champions League trophies as captain, emulating Germany's Franz Beckenbauer and France's Didier Deschamps. As well as winning the 2008 and 2012 UEFA European Championships and 2010 FIFA World Cup, he is Spain's most capped player and was Europe's joint most-capped.

IKER
CASILLAS

MOST APPEARANCES:

1 Iker Casillas, 167

2 Sergio Ramos, 165

3 Xavi Hernandez, 133

4 Andres Iniesta, 131

5 Andoni Zubizarreta, 126

1 Luis Suarez was named European Footballer of the Year in 1960 – the only Spanish-born player to have taken the prize.

7 Seven players played in Spain's three finals from 2008 to 2012 in the UEFA European Championship and FIFA World Cup.

SCORING RECORD
VILLA FILLS HIS BOOTS

David Villa became Spain's all-time top scorer in FIFA World Cups with his first-round goal against Chile in 2010, his sixth overall across the 2006 and 2010 tournaments. Spain had scored their previous 14 FIFA World Cup penalties, not counting shoot-outs. Villa became Spain's all-time leading scorer with a brace against the Czech Republic in March 2011, but a broken leg ruled him out of the 2012 UEFA European Championship, thus missing out on adding to his Euro 2008 and 2010 FIFA World Cup winners' medals.

DAVID
VILLA

TOP SCORERS:

1 David Villa, 59

2 Raul, 44

3 Fernando Torres, 38

4 David Silva, 35

5 Fernando Hierro, 29

1 Only one Spanish club – Real Madrid – were formally represented at FIFA's first meeting in Paris in 1904. Known only as Madrid FC. The name "Real" is Spanish for "Royal".

TOURNAMENT TRIVIA
HARD TO BEAT

Spain share with Brazil the record for longest international unbeaten run – the Brazilians went 35 games without a defeat between 1993 and 1996, a tally matched by the Spanish from 2007 until losing 2-0 to the United States in a 2009 FIFA Confederations Cup semi-final. That vintage Spain side also became the only country to secure 30 points out of 30 points in a FIFA World Cup qualification campaign, and they went on to lift the trophy in South Africa in 2010.

STAR PLAYER
SILVA SERVICE

Spain entered the 2018 FIFA World Cup finals with an unbeaten qualifying run of 63 matches, the last defeat having been to Denmark in 1993. **David Silva** scored in his fourth consecutive international in a June 2017 qualifying victory over Macedonia and he was also on target in the 8-0 rout of Liechtenstein in September 2017. Other important Silva goals include the last in a 3-0 defeat of Russia in the 2008 UEFA European Championship semi-final, and the opener as Spain defeated Italy 4-0 in the Euro 2012 final to retain their crown. Silva ended the 2018 FIFA World Cup with 35 goals in 125 appearances for his country.

DAVID
SILVA

STAR PLAYER
SURGING SERGIO

Sergio Ramos became the youngest-ever European player to reach 100 international caps, in March 2013, at the age of 26 years and 358 days – and marked the occasion by scoring Spain's goal in a 1-1 draw with Finland. Germany's Lukas Podolski, had been 21 days older when he won his 100th cap. South Korea's Cha Bum-Kun, who was 24 years and 139 days old when he achieved the landmark, holds the global record. Ramos, who can play both at right-back or in central defence, played in Spain's team that won the 2008 and 2012 UEFA European Championships, as well as the 2010 FIFA World Cup.

NATIONAL LEGEND
TORRES! TORRES!

As a child, **Fernando Torres** wanted to be a goalkeeper, but made the wise decision to become a striker instead. He has a penchant for scoring the only goal in the final of a tournament, doing so in the 2008 UEFA European Championship, for Spain against Germany in Vienna, having done the same in the U-16 UEFA European Championship in 2001 and for the Under-19s the following year. Torres became the most expensive Spanish footballer ever when Chelsea paid €58.5million to sign him from fellow English club Liverpool in January 2011.

FERNANDO
TORRES

STAR PLAYER
SUPER PED

Spanish winger Pedro is the only player to have scored in six separate official club tournaments in one calendar year, managing to hit the net for Barcelona in Spain's Primera Liga, Copa del Rey and Super Cup in 2009, as well as the UEFA Champions League, UEFA European Super Cup and FIFA Club World Cup. He was also in the starting line-up for the 2010 FIFA World Cup final – less than two years after being a member of the Barcelona reserve team in Spain's third division and needing new club manager Pep Guardiola's intervention to prevent him being sent home to Tenerife.

NATIONAL LEGEND
THE RAUL THING

Raul Gonzalez Blanco – known as Raul – remains a Spain and Real Madrid icon, despite his record goal tallies being passed, respectively, by David Villa and Cristiano Ronaldo. He was an Atletico Madrid youth-teamer before signing for city rivals Real, where he scored 228 goals in 550 games and captained them from 2003 to 2010. But despite playing at five tournaments between the 1998 and 2006 FIFA World Cups, he was left out of Spain's UEFA Euro 2008 squad – and they won the trophy. After leaving Real, Raul enjoyed further success at Schalke in Germany, Al Sadd in Qatar and New York Cosmos in the United States.

RAUL GONZALEZ
BLANCO

50

Centre-back Carlos Marchena became the first footballer to go 50 internationals in a row unbeaten, when he played in Spain's 3-2 victory over Saudi Arabia in May 2009.

STAR PLAYER
WAITING FOR BUS

Barcelona midfielder **Sergio Busquets** won the FIFA World Cup, UEFA European Championship and two UEFA Champions Leagues before turning 24 in July 2012, but he only broke his scoring duck for Spain in September 2014 – his 68th cap – in a 5-1 win over Macedonia. Since then, he has claimed a third UEFA Champions League, and second international goal. His father, Carles Busquets, was a Barcelona goalkeeper in the 1990s, part of Johan Cruyff's 1992 UEFA European Cup-winning squad, though he was mainly understudy to Andoni Zubizarreta.

SERGIO
BUSQUETS

35

Aritz Aduriz became Spain's oldest goalscorer when finding the net in a 4-0 win over Macedonia on 13 November 2016 in a FIFA World Cup 2018 qualifier. He was aged 35 years and 275 days old – 50 days older than the previous record-holder Jose Maria Pena, who scored the only goal in 30 November 1930 friendly against Portugal.

BELGIUM

Belgium's golden generation has risen: they reached the 2014 FIFA World Cup quarter-finals and the "Red Devils" surpassed any previous achievements by finishing third at the 2018 FIFA World Cup.

Joined FIFA: 1904
Biggest Win: vs. Zambia, 1994
Highest FIFA Ranking: 1
Home Stadium: (Rotation)
Honours: -

STAR PLAYER
BELGIUM'S PERSONAL BEST

Belgium, under Spanish manager Roberto Martinez, enjoyed their most successful FIFA World Cup in Russia in 2018, finishing third. They were the tournament's top scorers with 16 goals and won widespread admiration for such performers as centre-backs Jan Vertonghen and Toby Alderweireld, playmaker Kevin De Bruyne and attacking right-back Thomas Meunier. There were also individual prizes for goalkeeper Thibaut Courtois, who took the tournament's Golden Gloves award for best goalkeeper, and captain Eden Hazard who won the Silver Ball as second best player, behind Croatia's Luka Modric.

Striker Romelu Lukaku's two goals against Ireland at Euro 2016 made him the first Belgian player to score a brace at a tournament since his international manager Marc Wilmots did similarly against Mexico at the 1998 FIFA World Cup.

ROMELU LUKAKU

EDEN HAZARD

STAR PLAYER
HAZ A GO HERO

Eden Hazard is the son of not just one former footballer but two - his mother Carine only retired from the women's game when pregnant with Eden. His father Thierry spent a lot of his career at semi-professional level with La Louviere in the Belgian Second Division, playing mainly as a defensive midfielder. Eden Hazard - and brothers Thorgan, Kylian and Ethan, were all born in La Louviere, the same birthplace as former star Enzo Scifo - once the youngest player at a UEFA European Championship, aged 18 years and 115 days when Belgium beat Yugoslavia in their opening game at the 1984 tournament.

TOP SCORERS:

1	Romelu Lukaku	48
2	Paul Van Himst	30
=	Eden Hazard	30
=	Bernard Voorhoof	30
5	Joseph Mermans	28
=	Marc Wilmots	28

TOURNAMENT TRIVIA
COMEBACK KINGS

Belgium's 3-2 victory over Japan in Rostov at the 2018 FIFA World Cup was the first time since 1970 that a team came back from two goals down to win a knock-out game – and West Germany had needed extra-time to beat England 3-2 in a quarter-final tie. Jan Vertonghen scored Belgium's first goal after 69 minutes, followed by Marouane Fellaini's equalizer five minutes later. Fellow substitute Nacer Chadli got the winner four minutes into stoppage-time. Belgium's 10 different goalscorers in Russia equalled the FIFA World Cup record held by France (1982) and Italy (2006).

MOST APPEARANCES:

1. **Jan Vertonghan**, 114
2. **Axel Witsel**, 103
3. **Eden Hazard**, 102
4. **Jan Ceulemans** , 96
5. **Timmy Simons**, 94

11

Belgium's most-capped footballer, defender **Jan Vertonghen** made his 100th appearance on 2 June 2018 against Portugal – 11 years to the day after his first cap, against the same country. His mother Ria Matthews handed over a commemorative cap to celebrate the 100-match landmark.

JAN **VERTONGHEN**

GUY **THYS**

3

King Baudouin Stadium has hosted the finals of three major European tournaments: the European Cup, the UEFA Cup Winners' Cup, and the UEFA European Championship.

NATIONAL LEGEND
HE'S OUR GUY

Unquestionably Belgium's greatest manager – as well as their longest- serving – was **Guy Thys**. He led them to the final of the 1980 UEFA European Championship and – with a team featuring the likes of Enzo Scifo and Nico Claesen – the semi-finals of the FIFA World Cup six years later. He spent 13 years in the job from 1976 to 1989, then returned for a second spell just eight months after quitting. He stepped down again after managing Belgium at the 1990 FIFA World Cup. During his playing days in the 1940s and 1950s, he was a striker and won two caps for Belgium.

39

Belgium's fifth most-capped player, Timmy Simons, became his country's oldest international when facing Estonia in November 2016 in a 2018 FIFA World Cup qualifier, aged 39 years and 338 days.

STADIUM FACT
TRIUMPH AND TRAGEDY

The largest football venue in Belgium is the 50,000-capacity **King Baudouin Stadium** in Brussels, which opened under its first name, the Jubilee Stadium, on 23 August 1930 and was renamed Heysel in 1946. It was the scene of tragedy in 1985 when a wall collapsed and 39 fans died in disturbances while attending the European Cup final between Liverpool and Juventus. The stadium was rebuilt and given its current name in 1995. When Belgium and the Netherlands co-hosted the 2000 UEFA European Championship, it staged the opening ceremony and first match, Belgium's 2-1 victory over Sweden.

BULGARIA

Regular qualifiers for the game's major competitions, and the birthplace of some of the sport's biggest names, Bulgaria have too often failed to deliver on the big occasions and make a mark on world football.

Joined FIFA: 1922

Biggest Win: 15-0 vs. Ghana, 1968

Highest FIFA Ranking: 3

Home Stadium: Vasil Levski National Stadium, Sofia

Honours: -

6

Defender Aleksandar Shalamanov played for Bulgaria at the 1966 FIFA World Cup, just six years after representing his country as an alpine skier at the Winter Olympics at Lake Placid.

HRISTO
STOICHKOV

NATIONAL LEGEND
HRISTO'S HISTORY

Hristo Stoichkov, born in Plovdiv, Bulgaria, on 8 February 1968, shared the 1994 FIFA World Cup Golden Boot, awarded to the tournament's top scorer, with Russia's Oleg Salenko. Both scored six times, though Stoichkov became the sole winner of that year's European Footballer of the Year award. Earlier the same year, he had combined up-front with Brazilian Romario to help Barcelona reach the final of the UEFA Champions League. He was banned for a year after a brawl earlier in his career, during the 1985 Bulgarian cup final between CSKA Sofia and Levski Sofia.

1994

Yordan Letchkov headed the winning goal against holders and defending champions Germany in the 1994 FIFA World Cup quarter-final in the United States. At the time, he played for German club Hamburg. He later became mayor of Sliven, the Bulgarian town he was born in.

DIMITAR
BERBATOV

NATIONAL LEGEND
MOB RULES

Much-travelled Bulgaria centre-forward **Dimitar Berbatov** claims to have learned English by watching the *Godfather* movies. Berbatov joined Manchester United from Tottenham in 2008 for a club and Bulgarian record fee of £30.75m. Before joining Spurs, he had been a member of the Bayer Leverkusen side who narrowly missed out on a treble in 2002. They lost in the final of both the UEFA Champions League and the German cup and finished runners-up in the German Bundesliga. Berbatov surprised and disappointed fans back home when he announced his international retirement aged just 29, in May 2010, having scored a national-record 48 goals in his 78 appearances for Bulgaria.

TOP SCORERS:

1. **Dimitar Berbatov**, 48
   = **Hristo Bonev**, 48
2. **Hristo Stoichev**, 37
3. **Emil Kostadinov**, 27
4. **Liubomir Angelov**, 26

100

Stiliyan Petrov – nicknamed "Stan" by fans of his English club Aston Villa – was applauded onto the field when he became Bulgaria's first outfield player to reach 100 caps, against Switzerland in March 2011.

STILIYAN
PETROV

NATIONAL LEGEND
BOSSMAN BONEV

Hristo Bonev was out on his own as Bulgaria's leading man both for appearances and goals – and a national hero for his stylish flair on the field. A mainstay of the side at the 1970 and 1974 FIFA World Cups, Bonev scored in Bulgaria's opening game at the 1970 tournament, a 3-2 defeat to Peru, and again four years later in a 1-1 draw against Uruguay. His 48th and final goal came on his last game (his 96th) for his country, a 2-1 loss to Argentina in April 1979. Bonev coached Bulgaria at the 1998 FIFA World Cup in France, the last manager to lead them at the finals, but they were knocked out in the first round.

NATIONAL LEGEND
A NATION MOURNS

Bulgaria lost two of its most popular footballing talents when a June 1971 car crash claimed the lives of strikers Georgi Asparukhov and Nikola Kotkov; Asparukhov was only 28 years old at the time, while Kotkov was 32. Asparukhov scored 19 goals in 50 internationals, including Bulgaria's only goal of the 1966 FIFA World Cup finals in a 3-1 defeat to Hungary. Asparuhov was nominated for the 1965 Ballon d'Or award and finished eighth: over 500,000 people attended his funeral in Sofia.

8

MARTIN
PETROV

Martin Petrov suffered a terrible start to his international career when he was sent off for two yellow cards just eight minutes into his debut as a substitute in a Euro 2000 qualifier against England.

NATIONAL LEGEND
MORE FROM '94

Former centre-back Petar Hubchev was appointed Bulgaria coach in September 2016, making him the second of his country's 1994 FIFA World Cup semi-finalists – after Hristo Stoichkov, 2004–07 – to manage the national side. Lubo Penev – in charge 2011–14 – is the nephew of the 1994 squad coach, Dimitar Penev, but missed that tournament as he was battling testicular cancer. He recovered to play at both Euro 1996 France 1998. Lothar Matthaus, in Germany's team which lost to them in 1994, was Bulgaria's coach 2010–11.

DISCIPLINARY-RELATED
POP OF HORRORS

Bulgaria captain Ivelin Popov has experienced a chequered career with the national side – including several scandals and banishments. He scored twice from the penalty spot in February 2011 in a 2-2 friendly draw with Estonia that was later officially expunged from the records by FIFA amid allegations of match-fixing involving the officials. He had previously been banned from the country's youth ranks in 2008 for allegedly throwing a bottle at a bus driver and then from the senior side in September 2010 for reportedly breaking a curfew to go out drinking with team-mates for striker Valeri Bojinov's birthday.

BORISLAV
MIKHAILOV

MOST APPEARANCES:

1. **Stiliyan Petrov**, 106
2. **Borislav Mikhailov**, 102
3. **Hristo Bonev**, 96
4. **Krasimir Balakov**, 92
5. **Dimitar Penev**, 90
   = **Martin Petrov**, 90

CROATIA

Croatia's distinctive red-and-white chequered jersey has become one of the most recognized in world football. The country hit a new peak in 2018 when reaching their first FIFA World Cup final.

Joined FIFA: 1992
Biggest Win: 10-0 vs. San Marino, 2014
Highest FIFA Ranking: 3
Home Stadium: (Rotation)
Honours: -

NATIONAL LEGEND
SUPER SUKER

Striker **Davor Suker** won the Golden Boot for being top scorer at the FIFA World Cup in 1998, scoring six goals in seven games as Croatia finished third. His strikes included the opening goal in Croatia's 2-1 semi-final defeat to eventual champions France, and the winner in a 2-1 triumph over Holland in the third-place play-off. Suker, by far his country's leading scorer of all time, had hit three goals at the UEFA European Championship in 1996 – including an audacious long-distance lob over Denmark goalkeeper Peter Schmeichel. Suker was named president of the Croatian Football Federation in July 2012.

DAVOR **SUKER**

TOP SCORERS:

1 Davor Suker, 45
2 Mario Mandzukic, 33
3 Eduardo da Silva, 29
4 Ivan Perisic, 23
5 Darijo Srna, 22

LUKA **MODRIC**

STAR PLAYER
MAGICAL MODRIC

Croatia made history by making their first FIFA World Cup final in 2018 – and star of the show was captain and main playmaker **Luka Modric**, who won the Golden Ball prize as the tournament's best player despite their 4-2 final defeat to France. Modric began his career with Dinamo Zagreb before moving to Tottenham Hotspur in England and then winning four UEFA Champions League titles with Spain's Real Madrid. In Russia, Croatia became the first country since Argentina in 1990 to win two penalty shoot-outs at the same FIFA World Cup – beating Denmark in the second round and hosts Russia in the quarter-finals.

DARIJO **SRNA**

4-0
Croatia's second game at the 2014 FIFA World Cup, a 4-0 trouncing of Cameroon, was doubly notable. It was the first time they had scored as many as four goals in a single FIFA World Cup finals match.

5

Darijo Srna is Croatia's fifth top scorer of all time, despite playing many games as a right-back or wing-back.

TOURNAMENT TRIVIA
DALIC'LL DO

Slaven Bilic and Igor Stimac were formidable central defensive partners as Croatia finished third at the 1998 FIFA World Cup and both went on to manage their country – but it was an uncapped player, Zlatko Dalic, who went one better by leading Croatia to the 2018 FIFA World Cup final. Bilic took Croatia to the 2008 and 2012 UEFA European Championships during his six-year spell in charge, but his successor Stimac only lasted 15 matches before being replaced by another former international Niko Kovac. Appointed in place of Ante Cacic in October 2017, Dalic's Croatia qualified for the 2018 finals with a 4-1 aggregate play-off victory over Greece.

STAR PLAYER
UNLUCKY MANDS

Striker **Mario Mandzukic** was Croatia's hero in their 2018 FIFA World Cup semi-final – only to unwittingly turn villain four days later in the final. His goal, 19 minutes into extra-time, beat England 2-1 and sent Croatia to their first ever FIFA World Cup final. In the final, however, he headed an Antoine Griezmann free-kick into his own net after 18 minutes to give France the lead. Mandzukic did pull a goal back to make the score 4-2 to France with 21 minutes left. He thus became the first man to score for both sides in a FIFA World Cup final – only Dutch defender Ernie Brandts, against Italy in 1978 – had done it any FIFA World Cup finals match.

MARIO **MANDZUKIC**

STAR PLAYER
RAK ATTACKS

Only three footballers have won Croatia's Sportsman of the Year prize since Davor Suker in 1998: Mario Mandzukic in 2013, **Ivan Rakitic** two years later and Luka Modric in 2018 – the year Rakitic made history at the 2018 FIFA World Cup. The Barcelona midfielder became the first man to convert the decisive penalty in two different shoot-outs at the same FIFA World Cup: against Denmark and Russia. Rakitic was born in Switzerland but opted to play senior football for Croatia, the land of both his parents. He was named Croatian Footballer of the Year in 2015, the only time since 2013 it has not gone to seven-times winner Luka Modric.

22

Croatia competed in the FIFA World Cup 2018 with only 22 squad players for the majority of the tournament. Coach Zlatko Dalic sent home Nikola Kalinic after the striker allegedly refused to come on as a substitute in their opening game against Nigeria.

2

Croatia's 4-0 victory over Cameroon in the 2014 FIFA World Cup saw striker Ivica Olic become the first player to score for Croatia at two separate FIFA World Cups, having previously found the net in 2002.

3

Three players – Darijo Srna, Stipe Pletikosa and defender Josip Simunic – all reached 100 caps for Croatia in the same game.

IVAN **RAKITIC**

MOST APPEARANCES:

1 Darijo Srna, 134

2 Luka Modric, 122

3 Stipe Pletikosa, 114

4 Josip Simunic, 105

5 Ivica Olic, 104
= Ivan Rakitic, 104

TOURNAMENT TRIVIA
DOUBLE IDENTITY

Robert Jarni and Robert Prosinecki both have the rare distinction of playing for two different countries at different FIFA World Cup tournaments. They both represented Yugoslavia in Italy in 1990, then newly independent Croatia eight years later in France. Full-back Jarni actually played for both Yugoslavia and Croatia in 1990, then only Yugoslavia in 1991, before switching back – and permanently – to Croat colours in 1992 after the country officially joined UEFA and FIFA. He retired with 81 caps for Croatia, seven for Yugoslavia.

ROBERT **JARNI**

CZECH REPUBLIC

The most successful of the former Eastern Bloc countries, as Czechoslovakia, they finished as runners-up in the 1934 and 1962 FIFA World Cups. As Czech Republic, they have failed to qualify for the last three FIFA World Cups.

Joined FIFA: 1994

Biggest Win: 8-1 vs. Andorra, 2005

Highest FIFA Ranking: 2

Home Stadium: (Rotation)

Honours: -

PETR **CECH**

NATIONAL LEGEND
CECH CAP

Goalkeeper **Petr Cech** has worn a protective cap while playing ever since suffering a fractured skull during an English Premier League match in October 2006. He was born as a triplet, along with sister Sarka and brother Michal, who died of an infection at the age of two. Cech served notice of his talents when he was beaten by only one penalty in a shoot-out against France in the 2002 UEFA U-21 European Championship final, helping the Czechs to win the trophy. He claimed winners' medals as Chelsea won the 2012 UEFA Champions League (he was named man of the match) and 2013 UEFA Europa League.

30 MINUTES

Belgium's 1920 victory in the Olympic Games was overshadowed when Czechoslovakia walked off the pitch after only 30 minutes in protest following what they saw as biased refereeing. Czechoslovakia are the only team in the history of Olympic football to have been disqualified.

NATIONAL RECORDS
CZECHS STEP IN

Goalkeepers Tomas Koubek and then Jiri Pavlenka made unwanted history within a year of each other in what became the Czech Republic's heaviest international defeats. Koubek was the unfortunate No.1 in a 4-0 friendly loss to Australia in March 2018 and again in a 5-1 defeat by Russia that September. A further mark was set when England beat the Czech Republic at Wembley in March 2019 in their first 2020 UEFA European Championship qualifier. This time Pavlenka wore the gloves.

PAVEL **NEDVED**

NATIONAL LEGEND
THE CANNON COLLECTS

Pavel Nedved's election as European Footballer of the Year in 2003 ended an impatient wait for fans in the Czech Republic who had seen a string of outstanding players overlooked since Josef Masopust had been honoured back in 1962. Masopust, a midfield general, had scored the opening goal in the FIFA World Cup final that year before Brazil hit back to win 3-1 in the Chilean capital of Santiago. Years later, Masopust was remembered by Pele and nominated as one of his 125 greatest living footballers. At club level, Masopust won eight Czechoslovak league titles with Dukla Prague, the army club.

MOST APPEARANCES:

1 **Petr Cech**, 124
2 **Karel Poborsky**, 118
3 **Tomas Rosicky**, 105
4 **Jaroslav Plasil**, 104
5 **Milan Baros**, 93

34

Antonin Puc was Czechoslovakia/the Czech Republic's top international scorer with 34 goals when he retired in 1938 until he was passed, first by Jan Koller, 67 years later, and, latterly, by Milan Baros.

NATIONAL LEGEND
MOSTLY MOZART

The last Czech player to score at a FIFA World Cup was **Tomas Rosicky**, a double in a 3-0 victory over the United States in 2006. Despite an injury-plagued career, he became only the third Czech to reach a century of caps, in a 2-1 2016 European Championship qualifier defeat to Iceland in June 2015. The midfielder, nicknamed "The Little Mozart" for the way he orchestrates play, retired from international football after the Czech Republic were eliminated from Euro 2016 in the first round, during which he became the oldest Czech player to appear in a UEFA Euro finals, aged 35. He had also been their youngest, aged 19, in 2000.

TOMAS ROSICKY

NATIONAL LEGEND
PLASIL'S PLACE

Midfielder **Jaroslav Plasil** went into the 2016 UEFA European Championship having just become only the fourth Czech player to reach a century of caps, reaching the landmark in a 2-1 friendly defeat to South Korea. He had been part of the side which reached the semi-finals of the 2004 UEFA European Championship, scored against Turkey at the tournament four years later and also played every minute of his side's progress to the second round at Euro 2012. He was also a mainstay in helping reach the 2016 UEFA European Championship, although the 14 goals the Czechs conceded in qualifying were more than any other side to make the finals.

1934
The final of the 1934 FIFA World Cup was the first to go into extra-time, with Czechoslovakia ultimately losing 2-1 to hosts Italy.

JAROSLAV PLASIL

TOP SCORERS:
1. Jan Koller, 55
2. Milan Baros, 41
3. Vladimir Smicer, 27
4. Tomas Rosicky, 23
5. Pavel Kuka, 22 (plus 7 for Czechoslovakia)

1976
In 1976, Antonin Panenka invented the calmly chipped penalty style that is still performed to this day. It's commonly known as "a Panenka".

NATIONAL LEGEND
TEN OUT OF TEN

Jan Koller is Czech football's all-time leading marksman with 55 goals in 91 appearances. Koller scored on his debut against Belgium and struck ten goals in ten successive internationals. He scored six goals in each of the 2000, 2004 and 2008 UEFA European Championship qualifying campaigns. He began his career with Sparta Prague, who converted him from goalkeeper to goalscorer. Then, in Belgium, he was top scorer with Lokeren, before scoring 42 goals in two league title-winning campaigns with Anderlecht. Later, with Borussia Dortmund in Germany, he once went in goal after Jens Lehmann had been sent off and kept a clean sheet – having scored in the first half.

JAN KOLLER

1

Vladimir Smicer won 80 caps for the Czech Republic, having won one for Czechoslovakia.

DENMARK

They've been playing football since 1908 but Denmark's crowning moment came in 1992 when they walked away with the UEFA European Championship crown in one of the biggest ever International football shocks.

Joined FIFA: 1908

Biggest Win: 17-1 vs. France, 1908

Highest FIFA Ranking: 3

Home Stadium: Parken Stadium, Copenhagen

Honours: 1 UEFA European Championship (1992)

CHRISTIAN
ERIKSEN

STAR PLAYER
CHRISTIAN AID

A T-shirt produced as Denmark approached the 2018 FIFA World Cup summed up their tactics as passing the ball to **Christian Eriksen** and waiting for him to score. The playmaker's hat-trick had secured his side's place at the finals, in a 5-1 qualification play-off win away to the Republic of Ireland in November 2017 – 32 years after Denmark had beaten the same country 4-1, also in Dublin, to reach the 1986 FIFA World Cup. Tottenham Hotspur midfielder Eriksen top-scored for Denmark with 11 goals in the 2018 qualification campaign – having previously only hit nine goals for his country since making his international debut in March 2010 against Austria.

16 SECONDS
Ebbe Sand scored the fastest FIFA World Cup goal ever scored by a substitute, when he netted a mere 16 seconds after coming onto the pitch in Denmark's clash against Nigeria at the 1998 FIFA World Cup.

2
Midfielder Morten Wieghorst is the only player to be sent off twice while playing for Denmark – yet has also received a special award for fair play after deliberately missing a wrongly awarded penalty.

TOURNAMENT TRIVIA
DANES ON THE DRAW

Denmark have become draw specialists, with nine in 16 games from the start of 2018. They mounted late comebacks to share the spoils twice in five days in March 2019. Trailing 2-0 to Kosovo in a friendly they got a stoppage-time equaliser from Pierre-Emile Hojbjerg. Then, in their opening 2020 UEFA European Championship qualifier, Denmark trailed Switzerland 3-0 with just six minutes left, but they secured a point with goals from Mathias Jorgensen, Christian Gytkjaer and **Henrik Dalsgaard**.

HENRIK
DALSGAARD

STAR PLAYER
IF THE SHIRT FITS

Danish striker Yussuf Poulsen had an eventful 2018 FIFA World Cup. In Denmark's opening game, he conceded a first-half penalty which was missed by Peru's Carlos Cueva, then scored the game's only goal and was officially voted man of the match. But he was booked in Denmark's first two games so missed their third against France. He wore his favoured middle name "YURARY" on the back of his Denmark shirt, despite wearing "POULSEN" for his German club Leipzig, because the club had already printed shirts with that name on them.

102

Morten Olsen captained Denmark at the 1986 FIFA World Cup and later became the first Dane to reach a century of caps, retiring in 1989 with four goals from 102 appearances.

MORTEN OLSEN

MOST APPEARANCES:

1 Peter Schmeichel, 129
2 Dennis Rommedahl, 126
3 Jon Dahl Tomasson, 112
4 Thomas Helveg, 108
5 Michael Laudrup, 104

PETER SCHMEICHEL

NATIONAL LEGEND
GOLDEN GLOVES

Peter Schmeichel, a European champion with Denmark in 1992, was rated as the world's best goalkeeper in the early 1990s. His son Kasper Schmeichel emulated his father by enjoying club success in England and becoming Denmark's first-choice keeper. Peter was a very animated fan in the stands at the 2018 FIFA World Cup as Kasper saved three spot-kicks when Denmark lost a second round match against Croatia, 3-2 on penalties. He saved from Luka Modric in extra-time, and twice more in the shoot-out.

TOURNAMENT TRIVIA
THE UNEXPECTED IN 1992

Few Danish football fans will forget June 1992, their national team's finest hour, when they won the UEFA European Championship, despite not qualifying for the finals in Sweden. Ten days before the tournament opened UEFA asked the Danes – who had finished second to Yugoslavia in their qualifying group – to take Yugoslavia's place, following their exclusion in the wake of international sanctions over the Balkan War. Expectations were minimal, but then the inconceivable happened. Relying heavily on goalkeeper Peter Schmeichel, his defence, and the creative Brian Laudrup, Denmark crafted one of the biggest shocks in football history by winning the tournament, culminating in a 2-0 victory over world champions Germany.

NATIONAL LEGEND
TOMASSON'S JOINT TOP

Jon Dahl Tomasson, Denmark's joint-top goalscorer with 52, became his national side's assistant manager in 2016, working with Norwegian-born head coach Age Hareide. His final goal for Denmark came in a 3-1 defeat to Japan in the first round of the 2010 FIFA World Cup – tucking away the rebound after his penalty was saved by Eiji Kawashima. Tomasson won 112 caps, while Poul "Tist" Nielsen's 52 strikes came in just 38 appearances between 1910 and 1925. Pauli Jorgensen was also prolific, scoring his 44 goals in just 47 games 1925-39.

JON DAHL TOMASSON

18

Christian Eriksen was the youngest player at the 2010 FIFA World Cup, aged 18 years and four months.

TOP SCORERS:

1 Poul Nielsen, 52
= Jon Dahl Tomasson, 52
3 Pauli Jorgensen, 44
4 Ole Madsen, 42
5 Preben Elkjaer Larsen, 38

6-1

Denmark's 6-1 defeat of Uruguay in the 1986 FIFA World Cup first-round group stage in Neza ranks among the country's finest performances; sadly, their adventure was ended by Spain in the last 16 as they lost 5-1.

GREECE

There is no argument about Greece's proudest footballing moment – their shock triumph at the 2004 UEFA European Championship, one of the game's greatest international upsets. It was only the Greeks' second appearance at a UEFA Euro finals.

Joined FIFA: 1929
Biggest Win: 8-0 vs. Syria, 1949
Highest FIFA Ranking: 8
Home Stadium: Olympic Stadium, Athens
Honours: 1 UEFA European Championship (2004)

17

Goalkeeper Stefanos Kapino became Greece's youngest international when he made his debut in November 2011 in a friendly against Romania, at the age of 17 years and 241 days – 80 days younger than previous record-holder, striker Thomas Mavros, had been when facing the Netherlands in February 1972.

GEORGIOS SAMARAS

3
Konstantinos "Kostas" Mitroglou played a crucial role as Greece qualified for the 2014 FIFA World Cup, scoring three goals in a 4-2 aggregate victory over Romania in a play-off.

TOURNAMENT TRIVIA
GORGEOUS GEORGE

Georgios Samaras won and converted the last-minute penalty that sent Greece through to the knock-out stages of a FIFA World Cup for the first time, clinching a dramatic 2-1 victory over Group C opponents Ivory Coast at the 2014 tournament in Brazil. The goal, following a foul by Giovanni Sio, was former Celtic striker Samaras's ninth goal for his country – his first coming on his debut against Belarus in February 2006. Samaras could actually have played international football for Australia, because his father, Ioannis, was born in Melbourne and moved to Greece aged 13. Ioannis won 16 caps for Greece between 1986 and 1990, but he is a long way behind his son, who made 81 appearances.

38

Greece's oldest player was another goalkeeper, Kostas Chalkias – 38 years and 13 days old – when playing his final international, against the Czech Republic in June 2012.

NATIONAL LEGEND
SIMPLY THEO BEST

Theodoros "Theo" **Zagorakis** – born near Kavala on 27 October 1971 – was captain of Greece when they won the UEFA European Championship in 2004 and the defensive midfielder was also given the prize for the tournament's best player. He is the second most-capped Greek footballer of all time, with 120 caps. But it was not until his 101st international appearance – 10 years and five months after his Greek debut – that he scored his first goal for his country, in a FIFA World Cup qualifier against Denmark in February 2005. He retired from international football after making a 15-minute cameo appearance against Spain in August 2007.

THEODOROS ZAGORAKIS

TOURNAMENT TRIVIA
GREEK LEGEND SOKRATIS

Greece missed out on a place at the 2018 FIFA World Cup after losing a UEFA qualifying play-off 4-1 on aggregate to eventual runners-up Croatia. Two mainstays of the side were long-serving centre-back Sokratis Papastathopoulos and six-goal leading scorer Kostas Mitroglou. Both had starred in Greece's run to the final of the 2007 UEFA U-19 European Championship. They lost then 1-0 to Spain, but it was the country's best tournament performance apart from winning the 2004 UEFA European Championship. Mitroglou ended the 2007 competition as the Golden Boot winner with three goals.

TOP SCORERS:

1 **Nikos Anatopoulos**, 29
2 **Angelos Charisteas**, 25
3 **Theofanis Gekas**, 24
4 **Dimitris Saravakos**, 22
5 **Mimis Papaioannou**, 21

ANGELOS
CHARISTEAS

2004
The UEFA Euro 2004 triumph was the first time a country coached by a foreigner had triumphed at either the UEFA European Championship or FIFA World Cup.

NATIONAL LEGEND
KING OTTO

German coach Otto Rehhagel became the first foreigner to be voted "Greek of the Year" in 2004, after leading the country to glory at that year's UEFA European Championship. He was also offered honorary Greek citizenship. His nine years in charge, after being appointed in 2001, made him Greece's longest-serving international manager. Rehhagel was aged 65 at UEFA Euro 2004, making him the oldest coach to win the UEFA European Championship – though that record was taken off him four years later, when 69-year-old Luis Aragones lifted the trophy with Spain.

NATIONAL LEGEND
HIT AND MISS

Full-back **Vasilios Torosidis**, later Greece captain, scored the winner against Nigeria in 2010 to secure his country's first ever victory at a FIFA World Cup – having earlier in the game been kicked by Sani Kaita, for which the Nigeria midfielder was sent off. He was also in Greece's squad for the 2008 and 2012 UEFA European Championships and 2014 FIFA World Cup. There was no third Euro for Torosidis as Greece finished bottom of the qualification group for Euro 2016, despite being the group's top seed. Their disastrous campaign included home and away defeats to the Faroe Islands.

VASILIOS
TOROSIDIS

1

Only one team – Greece – have beaten both the holders and the hosts on the way to winning either a UEFA European Championship or FIFA World Cup. In fact, they beat hosts Portugal twice – in both the tournament's opening game and the final, with a quarter-final victory over defending champions France in between.

NATIONAL LEGEND
GRIEF AND GLORY FOR GIOROS

It was a bittersweet day for captain **Giorgos Karagounis** when he equalled the Greek record for international appearances, with his 120th cap against Russia in their final Group A game at the UEFA Euro 2012. The midfielder scored the only goal of the game, giving Greece a place in the quarter-finals at Russia's expense – but a second yellow card of the tournament ruled him out of the next match, in which the Greeks lost to Germany. Karagounis was one of three survivors from Greece's Euro 2004 success, along with fellow midfielder Kostas Katsouranis and goalkeeper Kostas Chalkias.

MOST APPEARANCES:

1 **Giorgos Karagounis**, 139
2 **Theodoros Zagorakis**, 120
3 **Kostas Katsouranis**, 116
4 **Angelos Basinas**, 100
  = **Vasilios Torosidis**, 100

GIORGOS
KARAGOUNIS

HUNGARY

For a period in the early 1950s, Hungary possessed the most talented football team on the planet. They claimed Olympic gold at Helsinki in 1952 but finished runners-up in the 1954 FIFA World Cup.

Joined FIFA: 1902

Biggest win: 13-1 vs. France, 1927

Highest FIFA ranking: 18

Home Stadium:
Budapest, Hungary

Honours: -

NATIONAL LEGEND
DZSUDZSAK'S NO DUD

Hungary captain **Balazs Dzsudzsak** became only the third Hungarian man to win 100 caps in March 2019 and marked the occasion in style - not only by being presented with a framed shirt, but by leading his team to a 2-1 victory in Budapest over FIFA World Cup runners-up Croatia, at the start of Euro 2020 qualifiers. Winger Dzsudzsak had led Hungary at the 2016 UEFA European Championship, the country's first tournament since the 1986 FIFA World Cup. He also scored their second and third goals in a 3-3 draw with eventual champions Portugal that helped Hungary reach the second round.

BALAZS
DZSUDZSAK

5.4
Hungary's average of 5.4 goals per game at the 1954 FIFA World Cup remains an all-time high for the tournament.

37
Aged 37 years and 62 days, Zoltan Gera became the second oldest UEFA European Championship finals goalscorer – behind only Austria's Ivica Vastic, who was 38 years and 257 days old when he netted at Euro 2008.

SCORING RECORD
YEARS OF PLENTY

Hungary's dazzling line-up of the early 1950s was known as the "Aranycsapat" – or "Golden Team". They set a record for international matches unbeaten, going 31 consecutive games without defeat between May 1950 and their July 1954 FIFA World Cup final loss to West Germany – a run that included clinching Olympic gold at Helsinki in Finland in 1952. That 31-match tally has been overtaken since only by Brazil and Spain.

73
Hungary in the 1950s also set a record for most consecutive games scoring at least one goal: 73 matches.

NATIONAL LEGEND
GALLOPING MAJOR

In Hungarian football history, no one can compare with **Ferenc Puskas**, who netted 84 goals in 85 international matches for Hungary and 514 goals in 529 matches in the Hungarian and Spanish leagues. Possessing the most lethal left-foot shot in the history of football, he was known as the "Galloping Major" – by virtue of his playing for the army team Honved before joining Real Madrid and going on to play for Spain. During the 1950s, he was top scorer and captain of the legendary "Mighty Magyars" (the nickname given to the Hungarian national team), as well as of the army club Honved.

TOP SCORERS:

1 Ferenc Puskas, 84
2 Sandor Kocsis, 75
3 Imre Schlosser, 59
4 Lajos Tichy, 51
5 Gyorgy Sarosi, 42

FERENC PUSKAS

TOURNAMENT TRIVIA
HUNGARY FOR IT

Hungary's 6-3 win over England at Wembley in 1953 remains one of the most significant international results ever. They became the first team from outside the British Isles to beat England at home – a record that had stood since 1901. The Hungarians had been undefeated for three years and were reigning Olympic champions, while England were the so-called "inventors" of football. The British press dubbed it "The Match of the Century". In the event, the match revolutionized the game in England, Hungary's unequivocal victory exposing England's naïve football tactics.

1

Only one Hungarian footballer has won the Ballon d'Or prize for footballer of the year: Florian Albert in 1967, when it was organized by the magazine *France Football*, rather than FIFA.

66

Hungary reached a big low during qualifying for the 2018 FIFA World Cup: a 1-0 defeat to Andorra in June 2017, ending Andorra's 66-match winless run.

NATIONAL LEGEND
NERVES AND STEEL

Gabor Kiraly may now have won more caps, and earned more attention for his customary tracksuit bottoms – often compared to pyjama trousers – but Gyula Grosics is still recognized as Hungary's greatest goalkeeper. Unusual for a goalkeeper of his era, he was comfortable with the ball at his feet and was willing to rush out of his area. The on-field confidence was not always displayed off it, however – and he was thought to be a nervous character, a hypochondriac and a loner. He allegedly asked to be substituted before the end at Wembley in 1953.

GABOR KIRALY

MOST APPEARANCES:

1 Gabor Kiraly, 108
2 Balazs Dzsudzsak, 102
3 Jozsef Bozsik, 101
4 Zoltan Gera, 97
5 Ronald Juhasz, 95

NATIONAL LEGEND
GOLDEN HEAD

Sandor Kocsis, top scorer in the 1954 FIFA World Cup finals with 11 goals, was so good in the air that he was known as "The Man with the Golden Head". In 68 internationals, he scored an incredible 75 goals, including a record seven hat-tricks. His tally included two decisive extra-time goals in the 1954 FIFA World Cup semi-final against Uruguay, when Hungary had appeared to be on the brink of defeat.

NORTHERN IRELAND

Northern Ireland have played as a separate country since 1921 – before that, there had been an all-Ireland side. They last appeared at a major tournament in 2016, at the UEFA European Championship.

Joined FIFA: 1921
Biggest Win: 7-0 vs. Wales, 1930
Highest FIFA Ranking: 20
Home Stadium:
Windsor Park, Belfast
Honours: –

NATIONAL LEGEND
GEORGE IS BEST

One of the greatest players never to grace a FIFA World Cup, **George Best** (capped 37 times by Northern Ireland) nevertheless won domestic and European honours with Manchester United – including both a European Champions Cup medal and the European Footballer of the Year award in 1968. He also played in the United States, Hong Kong and Australia before his "final" retirement in 1984.

GEORGE BEST

17

Norman Whiteside became the then-youngest player at a FIFA World Cup finals (beating Pele's record) when he represented Northern Ireland in Spain in 1982 aged 17 years and 41 days.

STEVEN DAVIS

STAR PLAYER
THE BOY DAVIS

Midfielder **Steven Davis** became Northern Ireland's youngest post-war captain when he led out the side against Uruguay in May 2006, aged just 21 years, five months and 20 days. He remained captain for more than a decade and maybe his finest moment came in October 2015 when his two goals in a 3–1 defeat of Greece helped to secure Northern Ireland's place at the 2016 UEFA European Championship finals.

2 MINUTES

Peter Watson is thought to have had the shortest Northern Ireland international career, spending two minutes on the pitch in a 5-0 UEFA European Championship qualifying win over Cyprus in April 1971.

77

Aaron Hughes ranks second all-time among Northern Ireland players, with 112 caps. The defender, however, has not been celebrated as a goalscorer. In fact, it took until his 77th appearance, in August 2011, for him to register a goal – it was against the Faroe Islands.

David Healy endured a four-year, 24-game scoring drought between October 2008 and November 2012, before hitting his 36th and final international goal against Israel in March 2013 and retiring from international football later that year, aged 34.

24

NATIONAL LEGEND
GIANT JENNINGS

Pat Jennings's record 119 appearances for Northern Ireland also stood as an international record at one stage. The former Tottenham Hotspur and Arsenal goalkeeper made his international debut, aged just 18, against Wales on 15 April 1964, and played his final game in the 1986 FIFA World Cup, against Brazil, on his 41st birthday. On 26 February 1983, Jennings became the first player in English football to make 1,000 senior appearances, and marked the occasion with clean sheet in a 0–0 draw for Arsenal at West Bromwich Albion.

1958
Northern Ireland's captain at the 1958 FIFA World Cup was Tottenham Hotspur's cerebral Danny Blanchflower – the first twentieth-century captain of an English club to win both the league and FA Cup in the same season, in 1960–61.

PAT **JENNINGS**

NATIONAL LEGEND
HERO HEALY

Northern Ireland's record goalscorer **David Healy** got off to the ideal start, scoring a brace on his international debut against Luxembourg in February 2000. But perhaps his two greatest days for his country came when he scored the only goal against Sven-Goran Eriksson's England in September 2005 – Northern Ireland's first victory over England since 1972 – and then, 12 months later, scoring a hat-trick to beat eventual champions Spain 3–2 in a 2008 UEFA European Championship qualifier.

DAVID **HEALY**

MOST APPEARANCES:
1. Pat Jennings, 119
2. Aaron Hughes, 112
3. Steven Davis, 111
4. David Healy, 95
5. Mal Donaghy, 91

TOURNAMENT TRIVIA
HOSTILE HOSTS

Northern Ireland topped their first- round group at the 1982 FIFA World Cup, thanks to a 1–0 win over hosts Spain at a passionate Mestalla Stadium in Valencia. Watford striker Gerry Armstrong scored the goal and the Irish held on despite defender Mal Donaghy being sent off. A 4–1 second-round loss to France denied Northern Ireland a semi-finals place. Armstrong moved to Spain, joining Mallorca the following year and, predictably, was regularly booed by rival fans.

TOP SCORERS:
1. David Healy, 36
2. Kyle Lafferty, 20
3. Colin Clarke, 13
   = Billy Gillespie, 13
5. Gerry Armstrong, 12
   = Joe Bambrick, 12
   = Iain Dowie, 12
   = Jimmy Quinn, 12

NATIONAL LEGENDS
EVANS ABOVE

Belfast-born brothers Jonny and Corry Evans came through Manchester United's youth ranks and have each passed the 50-caps landmark. Centre-back Jonny had 78 by April 2019, and midfielder Corry had 52. They were also united by individual despair when Northern Ireland missed out on a place at the 2018 FIFA World Cup after a 1–0 aggregate defeat to Switzerland in a play-off. The only goal came from a penalty for handball after a shot struck Corry, who insisted the ball hit his shoulder, not his hand. Corry was booked and missed the second leg, which ended with Johnny's stoppage-time header being cleared off the line by first-leg goalscorer Ricardo Rodriguez.

NORWAY

Although they played their first international, against Sweden, in 1908 and qualified for the 1938 FIFA World Cup, it would take a further 56 years, and the introduction of a direct brand of football, before Norway reappeared at a major international tournament.

Joined FIFA: 1908
Biggest Win: 12-0 vs. Finland, 1946
Highest FIFA Ranking: 2
Home Stadium: Ullevaal Stadion, Oslo
Honours: -

JON ARNE
RIISE

NATIONAL LEGEND
LONG-DISTANCE RIISE

Fierce-shooting ex-Liverpool, AS Monaco and AS Roma left-back **Jon Arne Riise** marked the game in which he matched Thorbjorn Svenssen's Norwegian appearances record, against Greece in August 2012, by getting onto the scoresheet, albeit in a 3-2 losing cause. He was also on the losing side when claiming the record for himself, a 2-0 loss in Iceland the following month, before scoring his 16th international goal in his 106th match four days later as Norway beat Slovenia 2-1. Midfielder Bjorn Helge Riise, Jon Arne's younger brother, joined him at English club Fulham, and made 35 full international appearances.

NATIONAL LEGENDS
DOUBLE JEOPARDY

Sharing joint fifth place in Norway's scoring ranks are a pair who often led the line together in the late 1990s and early 21st century. Tore Andre Flo scored Norway's opener in a 2-1 defeat of Brazil at the 1998 FIFA World Cup, and Ole Gunnar Solskjaer who, despite numerous injuries, scored his 23 goals in only 67 appearances, including one on his 1995 debut against Jamaica. In 2008, he became the youngest person to be given Norway's equivalent of a knighthood, aged 35.

15

Egil Olsen, one of Europe's most eccentric coaches, was signed up for a surprise second spell as national manager with Norway in 2009, 15 years after he had led the unfancied Scandinavians to the 1994 finals.

EGIL
OLSEN

0

Norway are the only country in the world to have played Brazil and never lost. Their record stands at won two, drawn two, lost zero.

15

Attacking midfielder **Martin Odegaard** became Norway's youngest international when he made his debut against the United Arab Emirates in August 2014, at the age of 15 years and 253 days.

THORBJORN SVENSSEN

NATIONAL LEGEND
ROCK STAR

Defender **Thorbjorn Svenssen** did not score a single goal in his 104 games for Norway between 1947 and 1962, but did become the first Norwegian to reach a century of caps and, at the time, only the second footballer ever, behind only England's Billy Wright. Svenssen – nicknamed "Klippen", or "The Rock" – made his last appearance in May 1962, aged 38 years and 24 days. He died, aged 86, in January 2011.

93

He no longer holds Norway's record for international appearances but Thorbjorn Svenssen captained the country more than any other player, leading them out 93 times

MARTIN ODEGAARD

2

After beating Brazil in the first round in France in 1998, Norway made it to an incredible No. 2 in FIFA's official rankings.

STAR PLAYER
NEW GAARD

Martin Odegaard became, aged 15 years and 300 days, the youngest player to feature in a UEFA European Championship qualifier, when he came on as a substitute against Bulgaria in October 2014, He broke a 31-year-old record held by Iceland's Siggi Jonsson. In March 2015, in a 5-1 loss to Croatia, Odegaard, now aged 16 years and 101 days, became the youngest European player to start in a competitive international. He was 164 days younger than Liechtenstein goalkeeper Peter Jehle, who played in a Euro 98 qualifier.

NATIONAL LEGEND
JUVE DONE IT ALL

Jorgen Juve netted his national record 33 international goals in 45 appearances between 1928 and 1937. He did not score as Norway claimed bronze at the Berlin 1936 Olympics, but was playing when Norway beat Germany 2-0 in the quarter-finals, prompting spectators Adolf Hitler and other Nazi leaders to storm out in fury. After retiring in 1938, he worked as a legal scholar, sports journalist and author of books about the Olympics and football.

JORGEN JUVE

TOP SCORERS:

1 Jorgen Juve, 33

2 Einar Gundersen, 26

3 Harald Hennum, 25

4 John Carew, 24

5 Tore Andre Flo, 23
= Ole Gunnar Solskjaer, 23

TOURNAMENT TRIVIA
LONG-STAY TRAVELLERS

Norway's best finish at an international tournament was the bronze medal they clinched at the 1936 Summer Olympics in Berlin, having lost to Italy in the semi-finals but beaten Poland 3-2 in a medal play-off thanks to an Arne Brustad hat-trick. That year's side has gone down in Norwegian football history as the "Bronselaget", or "Bronze Team". However, they had entered the tournament with low expectations and were forced to alter their travel plans ahead of the semi-final against Italy on 10 August – Norwegian football authorities had originally booked their trip home for the previous day, not expecting their team to get so far.

POLAND

Poland first qualified for the UEFA European Championship in 2008 and co-hosted the tournament with Ukraine in 2012, making first-round exits both times. At Euro 2016, however, they were quarter-finalists.

Joined FIFA: 1921
Biggest Win: 10-0 vs. San Marino, 2009
Highest FIFA Ranking: 5
Home Stadium: Stadion Narodowy, Warsaw
Honours: -

⭐ STAR PLAYER
LOVING LEWANDOWSKI

Although **Robert Lewandowski** made his World Cup finals debut in Russia, he didn't score and Poland finished bottom of Group H. Lewandowski, however, remains a feared striker – despite being rejected by Legia Warsaw aged 16 and as a 20-year-old failing to impress future Poland coach Franciszek Smuda, who chided the man who recommended him: "You owe me petrol money." Lewandowski eventually broke through with Lech Poznan, helped Borussia Dortmund to two Bundesliga titles in Germany and won five more after joining Bayern Munich in 2014, on his way to becoming Poland's all-time top scorer.

ROBERT
LEWANDOWSKI

🌐 NATIONAL LEGEND
PEERLESS PRESIDENTS

Grzegorz Lato is Poland's fourth most-capped player and third highest scorer, the only Polish winner of the Golden Boot with his seven goals at the 1974 FIFA World Cup, and a member of the gold medal-winning team at the 1972 Summer Olympics. He was also a leading figure in Poland's co-hosting with Ukraine of the 2012 UEFA European Championship, having become president of the country's football federation in 2008. He vowed: "I am determined to change the image of Polish football, to make it transparent and pure." He was succeeded as federation president in 2012 by **Zbigniew Boniek**, arguably Poland's finest ever player.

ZBIGNIEW
BONIEK

16

Prolific striker **Robert Lewandowski** set a European record for goals in a FIFA World Cup qualifying competition with 16 for the 2018 FIFA World Cup – a tally which included three hat-tricks.

🌐 NATIONAL LEGEND
MILIK DELIVERY

Arkadiusz Milik was the hero as Poland finally won a game at a UEFA European Championship in 2016, after three draws and three defeats in their two previous tournaments, in 2008 and 2012. Milik struck in an opening win against Northern Ireland, kicking off what proved to be a run to the quarter-finals when only a penalty shoot-out defeat to Portugal ended Polish hopes. In fact, Poland did not trail for a single minute throughout the tournament until that 5-3 loss on spot-kicks.

TOP SCORERS:
1 **Robert Lewandowski**, 57
2 **Wlodzimierz Lubanski**, 48
3 **Grzegorz Lato**, 45
4 **Kazimierz Deyna**, 41
5 **Ernest Pohl**, 39

4

Ernest Wilimowski wrote his name into FIFA World Cup history in 1938 when he scored four goals but still finished on the losing side. Poland went down 6-5 after extra-time to Brazil in a first-round tie in Strasbourg, France.

TRIUMPH AND TRAGEDY

Jakub Blaszczykowski was one of his country's few players to come out of Euro 2012 with credit, despite going into the tournament in testing circumstances. He joined the rest of the squad only after attending the funeral of his father. As a 10-year-old, Blaszczykowski had witnessed his mother being stabbed to death by his father, who served 15 years in prison. Blaszczykowski was encouraged to pursue football by his uncle Jerzy Brzeczek, a former Poland captain and 1992 Olympic Games silver medalist. Blaszczykowski became the third Pole to reach 100 caps, doing so against Senegal in Poland's 2018 FIFA World Cup opener.

JAKUB BLASZCZYKOWSKI

NATIONAL LEGEND
STAYING ON LATER THAN LATO

Record-breaking Polish stalwart **Michal Zewlakow** bowed out of international football on familiar turf, even though his country were playing an away game. The versatile defender's 102nd and final appearance for his country was a goalless friendly in Greece in March 2011, at the Karaiskakis stadium in Piraeus where he used to play club football for Olympiacos. Zewlakow had overtaken **Grzegorz Lato**'s appearances record for Poland in his previous match, an October 2010 friendly against Ecuador.

16

Aged just 16 years and 188 days, and on his debut, Wlodzimierz Lubanski scored Poland's third goal in a 9-0 victory over Norway in 1963 to become their youngest-ever scorer.

5

Poland had five different goalscorers when they beat Peru 5-1 at the 1982 FIFA World Cup: Wlodzimierz Smolarek, Grzegorz Lato, Zbigniew Boniek, Andrzej Buncol and Wlodzimierz Ciolek.

MICHAL ZEWLAKOW

2000
Michal Zewlakow and brother Marcin became the first twins to line up together for Poland, against France in February 2000.

NATIONAL LEGEND
PIATEK TAKES HIS CHANCES

Uncapped **Krzysztof Piatek** was one of 10 players dropped from Poland's preliminary squad for the 2018 FIFA World Cup. He nonetheless earned a club move to Italy, where he enjoyed much succcess. Piatek finally made his Poland debut in September 2018 in a friendly against the Republic of Ireland. A month later, he marked his competitive debut with a goal in a 3-2 defeat to Portugal, then appeared as a substitute to fire Poland's Euro 2020 qualifying winner away to Austria, 2-0.

MOST APPEARANCES:

1 Jakub Blaszczykowski, 106
= Robert Lewandowski, 106
3 Michal Zewlakow, 102
4 Grzegorz Lato, 100
5 Kazimierz Deyna, 97

GRZEGORZ LATO

PORTUGAL

Cristiano Ronaldo became the first Portuguese player – and fourth ever – to score at four different FIFA World Cups in 2018 in Russia.

Despite producing some of Europe's finest ever players, Portugal's international history was one of near misses — until they triumphed at the 2016 UEFA European Championship and the inaugural UEFA Nations League.

Joined FIFA: 1921

Biggest win:
8-0 vs. Lichtenstein, 1994 & 1999,
8-0 vs. Kuwait, 2003

Highest FIFA ranking: 2

Home Stadium:
Estadio de Luz, Benfica

Honours: 1 European Championship (2016), 1 Nations League (2019)

STAR PLAYER
PRESIDENTIAL POWER

Cristiano Ronaldo dos Santos Aveiro was given his second name because his father was an admirer of United States President Ronald Reagan. The five-time FIFA World Player of the Year is Real Madrid and the UEFA Champions League's all-time leading goalscorer – he has lifted that trophy five times. Already Portugal's top scorer, he became his country's most-capped player at the 2016 UEFA European Championship – and ended the competition lifting the trophy, despite going off injured 25 minutes into the final against France.

$93.9M
Real Madrid paid a then-world record fee of $93.9m in 2009 for Cristiano Ronaldo. He moved to Juventus in July 2018 for a fee of $117m.

CRISTIANO RONALDO

TOURNAMENT TRIVIA
HAPPY EDER AFTER

Substitute striker **Eder** was the unlikely hero when Portugal finally ended their long wait for an international trophy to triumph at the 2016 UEFA European Championship. The forward – who spent the 2015-16 season on loan at French club Lille – scored the only goal of the final in Paris, in the 109th minute, to defeat host nation France. It was the latest opening goal scored in any UEFA European Championship final. Portugal, coached by Fernando Santos, drew their three first-round games to qualify as one of the best third-place teams.

EDER

TOP SCORERS:

1. Cristiano Ronaldo, 88
2. Pauleta, 47
3. Eusebio, 41
4. Luis Figo, 32
5. Nuno Gomes, 29

1 **Cristiano Ronaldo**, 158
2 **Luis Figo**, 127
3 **Joao Moutinho**, 116
4 **Nani**, 112
5 **Fernando Couto**, 110

LUIS
FIGO

STAR PLAYER
NICE ONE, SAN

Renato Sanches is Portugal's youngest player at an international tournament, he was 18 years and 301 days for their 2016 UEFA European Championship opener against Iceland. He was one of the stars of the tournament, and was voted UEFA Euro 2016's best young player. His superb long-range strike against Poland in the quarter-finals made him the youngest scorer at any UEFA European Championship knock-out round, aged 18 years and 316 days. Ten days later, he was the youngest man to play in a UEFA European Championship final.

SCORING RECORD
SILVA LINING

Striker **Andre Silva** missed a 14th-minute penalty in Portugal's 2-1 third-place play-off victory against Mexico at the 2017 FIFA Confederations Cup. Yet Silva can claim several Portuguese football milestones, having scored four goals in a 6-1 victory over Hungary at the 2014 UEFA European U–19 Championship – Portugal would finish as runners-up – then marking his debut for the Under-21s with a hat-trick against Albania. After graduating to the senior side, Silva became the youngest Portuguese man to score a hat-trick in a 6-0 victory over the Faroe Islands in a 2018 FIFA World Cup qualifier in October 2016 at the age of 20 years 339 days.

ANDRE
SILVA

320

A phenomenal striker, Eusebio scored 320 goals in 313 Portuguese league matches, won the first European Golden Boot in 1968 (and earned a second in 1973).

1000

In a May 2018 FIFA World Cup warm-up friendly against Tunisia, Andre Silva scored Portugal's 1,000th international goal in a 2-2 draw.

NATIONAL LEGEND
THE FAMOUS FIVE

Eusebio, Mario Coluna, Jose Augusto, Antonio Simoes, and Jose Torres were the "Fabulous Five" in Benfica's 1960s Dream Team, who made up the spine of the Portuguese national side at the 1966 FIFA World Cup. Coluna (the "Sacred Monster"), scored the vital third goal in the 1961 European Cup final and captained the national side in 1966. Jose Augusto, who scored two goals in the opening game against Hungary, went on to manage the national side and later the Portuguese women's team.

NATIONAL LEGEND
THE BLACK PANTHER

Born in Mozambique, **Eusebio da Silva Ferreira** was named Portugal's "Golden Player" to mark UEFA's 50th anniversary in 2004. Signed by Benfica in 1960 at the age of 18, he scored a hat-trick in his second game – against Santos in a friendly tournament in Paris – outshining their young star, Pele. He helped Benfica win a second European Cup in 1962, was named European Footballer of the Year in 1965 and led Portugal to third place in the 1966 FIFA World Cup, finishing as top scorer with nine goals.

EUSEBIO
DA SILVA FERREIRA

REPUBLIC OF IRELAND

Ever since Jack Charlton took the team to UEFA Euro 88, Ireland have remained one of Europe's most dangerous opponents.

Joined FIFA: 1924

Biggest Win: 8-0 vs. Malta, 1983

Highest FIFA Ranking: 6

Home Stadium: Aviva Stadium, Dublin

Honours: -

MICK McCARTHY

NATIONAL LEGEND
RETURN OF THE MICK

Mick McCarthy was both the first man to captain the Republic of Ireland at a FIFA World Cup – in Italy in 1990 – and the last to manage them at the finals – in Japan and South Korea in 2002. In 2018, he also became the only man given the permanent job twice. His first spell in charge went from 1996 to 2004. The Yorkshireman, whose father is Irish, began his second term with successive 1-0 victories over Gibraltar and Georgia. McCarthy played in all three games at the 1988 UEFA European Championship and was the captain, assistant coach and head coach at the FIFA World Cups of 1990, 1994 and 2002, respectively.

STAR PLAYER
BRADY BUNCH

Irish eyes were smiling again at Italy's expense in their final first-round group game at the 2016 UEFA European Championship, when **Robbie Brady** headed a late winning goal. It gave Martin O'Neill's team a place in the second round, where they took the lead through a Brady penalty against France, but succumbed 2-1. Brady was the first Republic of Ireland player to score in consecutive UEFA European Championship games; Robbie Keane achieved the feat in the 2002 FIFA World Cup.

PACKIE BONNER

64

Martin O'Neill, who played 64 times for Northern Ireland between 1971 and 1984, succeeded Italian veteran Giovanni Trapattoni as manager, who resigned after failing to qualify for the 2014 FIFA World Cup finals.

TOURNAMENT TRIVIA
IS WINNING JERSEY MISSING IN ACTION?

Irish fans' memories of their past FIFA World Cup adventures were reawakened in June 2017 when rapper MIA appeared to be wearing one of goalkeeper **Packie Bonner**'s shirts in a photoshoot. Bonner starred at the 1988 European Championship and the 1990 and 1994 FIFA World Cups, and suggested one of several red-and-yellow patterned jerseys he gave away for charity after USA 94 may have ended up with one of MIA's stylists. Bonner enhanced his national hero status by saving Daniel Timofte's penalty in the second-round shoot-out victory against Romania at Italia 90, before David O'Leary's winning spot-kick clinched their place in the quarter-finals where they lost 1-0 to hosts Italy.

ROBBIE BRADY

MOST APPEARANCES:

1. Robbie Keane, 146
2. Shay Given, 134
3. John O'Shea, 118
4. Kevin Kilbane, 110
5. Steve Staunton, 102

JACK **CHARLTON**

NATIONAL LEGEND
CHAMPION CHARLTON

Jack Charlton became a hero after he took Ireland to their first major finals in 1988, defeating England 1-0 in their first game at the UEFA European Championship. Things got even better at their first FIFA World Cup finals two years later, where the unfancied Irish lost out only to hosts Italy in the quarter-finals. Charlton quit the Irish team in 1996 after failing to qualify for the 1996 UEFA European Championship in England. "In my heart of hearts, I knew I'd wrung as much as I could out of the squad I'd got," he later claimed.

4

Paddy Moore was the first player ever to score four goals in a FIFA World Cup qualifier when Ireland came from behind to draw 4-4 with Belgium on 25 February 1934.

ROBBIE **KEANE**

NATIONAL LEGEND
ROBBIE KEEN

Much travelled striker **Robbie Keane** broke the Republic of Ireland's scoring record in October 2004 and added to it right up to 31 August 2016, when he marked his 146th and final appearance with his 68th goal, this in a 4-0 friendly victory against Oman. His most famous goals were last-minute equalizers against Germany and Spain at the 2006 FIFA World Cup. He marked the final game at the old Lansdowne Road with a hat-trick against San Marino in November 2006 and, four years later, won his 100th cap in the inaugural game at its replacement, the Aviva Stadium.

118 SECONDS
A spot-kick given for Ireland against France in 2016, after 118 seconds, was the earliest in the UEFA European Championship finals.

23

Robbie Keane's brace against Gibraltar in August 2016, took him to 23 goals in UEFA European Championship qualifiers: more than any other player.

TOP SCORERS:

1. Robbie Keane, 68
2. Niall Quinn, 21
3. Frank Stapleton, 20
4. John Aldridge, 19
   = Tony Cascarino, 19
   = Don Givens, 19

66

Only England's Billy Wright, with 70, has played more consecutive internationals than **Kevin Kilbane**, whose 109th Republic of Ireland cap against Macedonia in March 2011 was also his 66th in a row, covering 11 years and five months.

KEVIN **KILBANE**

NATIONAL LEGEND
KEANE CARRY ON

Few star players have walked out on their country with quite the dramatic impact as Republic of Ireland captain **Roy Keane** in 2002 at their FIFA World Cup training camp in Saipan, Japan. The midfielder quit before a competitive ball had been kicked, complaining about a perceived lack of professionalism in the Irish preparations – and his loss of faith in manager Mick McCarthy. Ireland reached the second round without him, losing on penalties to Spain, but his behaviour divided a nation. When McCarthy stepped down, Keane and the Irish football federation brokered a truce, and he returned to international duty in April 2004 under new boss Brian Kerr.

ROY **KEANE**

MARTIN **O'NEILL**

ROMANIA

Since 1938, Romania have qualified for the finals of the FIFA World Cup only four times in 14 attempts. The country's football highlight came in 1994 when, inspired by Gheorghe Hagi, they reached the quarter-finals.

Biggest Win:
9-0 vs. Finland, 1973

Highest FIFA Ranking: 3

Home Stadium: Arena Naţională, Bucharest

Honours: -

Romania conceded just two goals throughout the qualifying competition for the 2016 UEFA European Championship (the fewest of any team) – but then let in that same number in the tournament's opening match, a 2-1 defeat to hosts France.

NATIONAL LEGEND
HAPPY AS LADISLAU

The first Romanian to win 100 caps was midfielder **Ladislau Boloni**. His century was completed in a 2-0 away defeat to the Republic of Ireland in March 1988. Seven days later, he scored the last of his 23 international goals – in his penultimate game – a 3-3 draw with East Germany. He bowed out in a 2-0 loss to the Netherlands. One of Boloni's most notable displays came when he scored the winning goal against world champions Italy in 1983 to help Romania qualify for the 1984 UEFA European Championship.

LADISLAU BOLONI

NATIONAL LEGEND
CENTURY MAN

Gheorghe Hagi, Romania's "Player of the [twentieth] Century", scored three goals and was named in the Team of the Tournament at the 1994 FIFA World Cup in the United States, at which Romania lost out on penalties to Sweden after a 2-2 draw in the quarter-finals. Hagi made his international debut in 1983, aged just 18, scored his first goal aged 19 (in a 3-2 defeat to Northern Ireland) and remains Romania's joint-top goalscorer with 35 goals in 125 games. Farul Constanta, in Hagi's hometown, named their stadium after him in 2000 – but fans stopped referring to it as such after he took the manager's job at rivals Timisoara.

GHEORGHE HAGI

TOP SCORERS:

1 Gheorghe Hagi, 35
= Adrian Mutu, 35

3 Iuliu Bodola, 31

4 Viorel Moldovan, 25
= Ciprian Marica, 25

TOURNAMENT TRIVIA
FAMOUS FOURSOME

Gheorghe Hagi, Florin Raducioiu, Ilie Dumitrescu and Gheorghe "Gica" Popescu helped Romania light up the FIFA World Cup in the USA in 1994. Raducioiu (four), Dumitrescu (three) and Hagi (two) scored nine of their country's ten goals that summer and also the trio converted their penalties in a quarter-final shoot-out against Sweden, only for misses by Dan Petrescu and Miodrag Belodedici to send the Romanians home. As well as being team-mates, Popescu and Hagi are also brothers-in-law – their wives, Luminiya Popescu and Marlilena Hagi, are sisters.

2

Romania only scored two goals in the 2016 UEFA European Championship: both from the penalty spot, scored by striker Bogdan Stancu.

CHRISTOPH
DAUM

NATIONAL LEGEND
ENDURING DORINEL

Dorinel Munteanu has played for Romania more times than any other, although at one point his former team-mate Gheorghe Hagi's 125-cap record looked safe. Versatile defensive midfielder Munteanu was stuck on 119 appearances throughout an 18-month absence from the international scene before being surprisingly recalled at the age of 37 by manager Victor Piturca in February 2005. He ended his Romania career two years later, having scored 16 times in 134 games. Yet many Romanians believe he was wrongly denied a goal against Bulgaria at the 1996 UEFA European Championshipn. The match ended 1-0 to Bulgaria and Romania were eliminated in the first round following three straight defeats.

DORINEL
MUNTEANU

2

German coach **Christoph Daum** became only the second foreigner to take charge of Romania's national side when succeeding Anghel Iordanescu in July 2016 – the first was Austrian Josef Uridil, who worked alongside Constantin Radulescu at the 1934 FIFA World Cup.

TOURNAMENT TRIVIA
RUDOLF BY ROYAL APPOINTMENT

Romania played in the inaugural FIFA World Cup, in Uruguay in 1930, where they beat Peru 3-1 before being eliminated 4-0 by the hosts. Coach Constantin Radulescu filled in as a linesman for some games not featuring his own side. It is reputed the squad was picked by King Carol II and its captain was Rudolf Wetzer, the only Romania player to score five goals in a game. It was in a pre-tournament 8-1 victory over Greece in May 1930.

6

Sadly, two yellow-card offences in six minutes in the quarter-final against Italy in 2000 meant Georghe Hagi's final bow on the international stage saw him receive a red card, and leave the field to take an early bath.

16
Right-back Cristian Manea became Romania's youngest international when making his debut against Albania in May 2014, aged 16 years, nine months and 22 days, having played only five senior matches for his club Viitorul Constanta.

TOURNAMENT TRIVIA
YELLOW PERIL

Despite topping Group G ahead of England, Colombia and Tunisia at the 1998 FIFA World Cup, Romania's players of that tournament might perhaps be best remembered for their collective decision to dye their hair blond ahead of their final first-round game. The newly bleached Romanians struggled to a 1-1 draw against Tunisia, before being knocked out by Croatia in the second round, 1-0.

RUSSIA

Before the break-up of the Soviet Union (USSR) in 1992, the team was a world football powerhouse. Playing as Russia since August 1992, the good times have eluded them – apart from being UEFA Euro 2008 semi-finalists.

Joined FIFA: 1992

Biggest Win:
7–0 vs. San Marino, 1995,
7–0 vs. Lichtenstein, 2015

Highest FIFA Ranking: 3

Home Stadium: Luzhniki Stadium, Moscow

Honours: –

SCORING RECORD
ARTEM'S TIME

Artem Dzyuba scored his first international goal for Russia on 8 September 2014, in a 4–0 victory over Liechtenstein – and he enjoyed a happy anniversary precisely a year later in a 7–0 thrashing of the same opponents, scoring four of his side's strikes. The win equalled the biggest in Russia's history: 7–0 against San Marino in June 1995. Dzyuba was Russia's top scorer, with eight, during qualification for the 2016 UEFA European Championship but failed to score in the finals as Russia finished bottom of their group. However, Dzyuba came good at the 2018 FIFA World Cup, scoring three goals, including the equalizer against Spain in the second round.

17
The youngest Soviet-era debutant was Eduard Streltsov, who hit a hat-trick on his debut against Sweden in June 1956, at the age of 17 years and 340 days, and then scored another treble in his second game, against India.

TOURNAMENT TRIVIA
HAPPY HOSTS

Expectations on the field for 2018 FIFA World Cup hosts Russia, at 70th the lowest team in the FIFA World Football Rankings, were not great. In the opening game of the finals, they beat Saudi Arabia 5–0 and then downed Egypt 3–1 to guarantee a second-round place. Once there, Russia beat Spain on penalties before losing, again in a shoot-out, to Croatia in the last eight. Manager Stanislav Cherchesov, a former Russia goalkeeper, spoke of the pride felt nationwide by their unexpected progress.

4

Winger **Denis Cheryshev** scored four goals at the 2018 FIFA World Cup; he replaced Alan Dzagoev against Saudi Arabia and scored – making him the first ever substitute to score in a FIFA World Cup opening game.

DENIS CHERYSHEV

MOST APPEARANCES:

1 **Sergei Ignasevich**, 127
2 **Igor Akinfeev**, 111
3 **Viktor Onopko**, 109
4 **Vasili Berezutskiy**, 101
5 **Aleksandr Kerzhakov**, 91

18

Igor Akinfeev became post-Soviet Russia's youngest international footballer when he made his debut in a friendly against Norway on 28 April 2004. The CSKA Moscow goalkeeper was just 18 years and 20 days old.

NATIONAL LEGEND
YURI WANTED AGAIN

Russia went out on the road after their better-than-expected performance as 2018 FIFA World Cup hosts. Home games were played away from Moscow - including a 5-1 UEFA Nations League trouncing of the Czech Republic in Rostov and a goalless draw against Sweden in Kaliningrad. No squad member had won more than 50 caps, until the March 2019 recall of 35-year-old wing-back Yuri Zhirkov, who had announced his international retirement after the FIFA World Cup. It came more than 14 years after his debut against Italy in 2005.

IGOR AKINFEEV

2

Although born in what is now Ukraine, Viktor Onopko played most of his club career in Russia and Spain and was twice named Russian Footballer of the Year – in 1993 and 1994.

NATIONAL LEGEND
KERZH LIFTS THE CURSE

Only one man was in Russia's squads for the 2002 FIFA World Cup finals and the next time they qualified, in 2014: **Aleksandr Kerzhakov**. He made his international debut as a 19-year-old a teenager in March 2002, and he played just eight minutes of the finals three months later. With five goals, he was Russia's leading scorer in qualifying for the 2014 finals, and Kerzhakov scored his 26th international goal to earn a 1-1 draw in Russia's opener against South Korea in Cuiaba. This goal equalled Russia's all-time scoring record set by a team-mate in 2002: Vladimir Beschastnykh.

LEV YASHIN

TOP SCORERS:

1 **Aleksandr Kerzhakov**, 30
2 **Vladimir Beschastnykh**, 26
3 **Roman Pavlyuchenko**, 21
4 **Artem Dzyuba**, 20
5 **Andrei Arshavin**, 17
= **Valeri Karpin**, 17

ALEKSANDR KERZHAKOV

NATIONAL LEGEND
SUPER STOPPER

Lev Yashin made it into FIFA's Century XI team. In a career spanning 20 years, Yashin played 326 league games for Dynamo Moscow - the only club side he ever played for - and won 78 caps for the Soviet Union, conceding, on average, less than a goal a game (only 70 in total). With Dynamo, he won five Soviet championships and three Soviet cups, the last of which came in his final full season in 1970. He saved around 150 penalties in his career, and kept four clean sheets in his 12 FIFA World Cup matches.

1

Only one goalkeeper has ever been named European Footballer of the Year: Lev Yashin in 1963 - the same year in which he won his fifth Soviet championship.

SCOTLAND

A country with a vibrant domestic league and a rich football tradition – it played host to the first ever international football match, against England, in November 1872 – Scotland have never put in the performances on the international stage to match their lofty ambitions.

Joined FIFA: 1910

Biggest Win:
11-0 vs. Ireland, 1901

Highest FIFA Ranking: 13

Home Stadium:
Hampden Park, Glasgow

Honours: -

KENNY
DALGLISH

TOP SCORERS:

1	Kenny Dalglish, 30	
=	Denis Law, 30	
3	Hughie Gallacher, 23	
4	Lawrie Reilly, 22	
5	Ally McCoist, 19	

2
Kenny Dalglish joined Herbert Chapman and Brian Clough as one of the few managers to lead two different sides to the league title, guiding Blackburn Rovers to the summit of English football in 1994–95.

NATIONAL LEGEND
KING KENNY

Kenny Dalglish is Scotland's joint-top international goalscorer (with Denis Law) and remains the only player to have won more than a century of caps for the national side, with 102 in total – 11 more than the next highest cap-winner, goalkeeper Jim Leighton. Dalglish made his name spearheading Celtic's domestic dominance in the 1970s, winning four league titles, four Scottish Cups and one League Cup. He then went on to become a legend at Liverpool, winning a hat-trick of European Cups (1978, 1981 and 1984) and leading the side as player-manager to their first ever league and cup double in 1986.

DENIS
LAW

4

Denis Law twice scored four goals in a match for Scotland, the first against Northern Ireland on 7 November 1962 – helping the Scots to win the British Home Championships – and then against Norway in a friendly on 7 November 1963.

DAVID
WEIR

40

Rugged Rangers centre-back **David Weir** became Scotland's oldest international footballer when he faced Lithuania in a 2012 UEFA European Championship qualifier on 3 September 2010, aged 40 years and 111 days, for his 66th appearance.

TOURNAMENT TRIVIA
UNOFFICIAL WORLD CHAMPIONS

One of the victories most cherished by Scotland fans is the 3-2 triumph over arch-rivals and reigning world champions England in April 1967 at Wembley – the first time Sir Alf Ramsey's team had lost since clinching the 1966 FIFA World Cup. Scotland's man of the match that day was ball-juggling left-half/midfielder Jim Baxter, while it was also the first game in charge for Scotland's first full-time manager, Bobby Brown. Less fondly recalled is Scotland's 9-3 trouncing by the same opposition at the same stadium in April 1961.

Steven Fletcher ended Scotland's 46-year wait for a hat-trick and his own six-year international goal drought when scoring three in his country's 6-1 victory over Gibraltar at Hampden Park in March 2015.

46

MOST APPEARANCES:

1 **Kenny Dalglish**, 102
2 **Jim Leighton**, 91
3 **Darren Fletcher**, 80
4 **Alex McLeish**, 77
5 **Paul McStay**, 76

STAR PLAYER
UPPER TIERNEY

Celtic defender **Kieran Tierney** was appointed Scotland's fifth-youngest ever captain by temporary national coach Malky Mackay, who succeeded Gordon Strachan following Scotland's failure to qualify for the 2018 FIFA World Cup. In February 2018, former defender Alex McLeish was made manager for a second spell. McLeish's first spell lasted only 10 months in 2007, but saw seven wins in 10 games. No such luck second time around. In 14 months before being sacked in April 2019, his Scotland lost seven times in 12 matches, including an embarrassing 3-0 reverse in Kazakhstan.

NATIONAL LEGEND
DIVIDED LOYALTIES

Scottish-born winger Jim Brown played and scored for the USA side which lost to Argentina in the first FIFA World Cup in 1930. He had moved to New Jersey three years earlier and qualified through his US-citizen father. Two of his brothers also played professionally: younger brother John, a goalkeeper, was capped by Scotland, but Tom did not play at international level. Jim's son, George, appeared once for the USA, in 1957, while two of John's sons, Peter and Gordon, both played rugby for Scotland.

17

The youngest ever Scotland captain is John Lambie, who led the team aged 17 years and 92 days, against Ireland in March 1886; the youngest since 1900 is Darren Fletcher, aged 20 years and 115 days, against Estonia in May 2004.

KIERAN TIERNEY

NATIONAL LEGEND
HOW GEMILL DANCED TO THE MUSIC OF SCOTLAND'S WORLD CUP TIME

Archie Gemmill scored Scotland's greatest goal on the world stage in the surprise 3-2 victory over the Netherlands at the 1978 FIFA World Cup. He jinked past three defenders before chipping the ball neatly over Dutch goalkeeper Jan Jongbloed. Amazingly, in 2008, this magical moment was turned into a dance in the English National Ballet's "The Beautiful Game", and was referenced in cult in 1990s film, *Trainspotting*, which is set in Edinburgh.

ARCHIE GEMMILL

STAR PLAYER
TRUST IN LEIGH

In his 13th appearance for his country, Celtic striker **Leigh Griffiths** hit the back of the net for the first time with an 87th-minute free-kick against old enemies England in a June 2017 FIFA World Cup qualifier – and repeated the trick with another magnificent set-piece strike three minutes later. This put Scotland 2-1 ahead and they seemed set for a first home win against their neighbours since centre-back Richard Gough's sole goal in a 1985 Hampden Park clash. Scottish hearts were broken, however, when England captain Harry Kane volleyed an injury-time equaliser.

LEIGH GRIFFITHS

65

SERBIA

The former Yugoslavia was one of the strongest football nations in eastern Europe. Serbia broke from Montenegro in 2006 and last featured at a major tournament in 2018 at the FIFA World Cup.

Joined FIFA: 2006
Biggest Win:
5-0 vs. Romania, 2009
Highest FIFA Ranking: 6
Home Stadium: Rajko Mitić Stadium, Belgrade
Honours: -

NATIONAL LEGEND
STJEP UP

Yugoslavia/Serbia's all-time top goalscorer remains **Stjepan Bobek**, with 38 in 63 appearances. He also holds the record for most goals in a Yugoslavia/Serbia top-flight game – in June 1948 he got nine for Partizan Belgrade in a 10-1 rout of 14 Oktobar. Although Partizan won the title that season, his 24 goals were four fewer than Franjo Wolfl of second-placed Dinamo Zagreb. Wolfl scored six goals in 12 international appearances and the pair combined to help Yugoslavia win the silver medal at the London 1948 Olympic Games. Bobek also was in Yugoslavia's squad that again won silver at the 1952 Games.

STJEPAN BOBEK

TOP SCORERS:

1. Stjepan Bobek, 38
2. Milan Galic, 37
   = Blagoje Marjanovic, 37
   = Savo Milosevic, 37
5. Rajko Mitic, 32

1930
The first man to captain and then coach his country at the FIFA World Cup was Milorad Arsenijevic, who captained Yugoslavia to the semi-finals at the inaugural tournament in Uruguay in 1930 and then managed their squad in Brazil 20 years later.

17
Andrija Zivkovic became Serbia's youngest senior international at the age of 17 years 92 days against Japan at the 2013 UEFA European U19 Championship.

STAR PLAYER
HITMAN MIT

Fiery striker **Aleksandar Mitrovic** was named player of the tournament at the 2013 UEFA European U19 Championship when Serbia beat France 1-0 in the final and he set up Andrija Lukovic for the goal. Mitrovic was Serbia's focal point at the 2018 FIFA World Cup, scoring six goals in qualifying and their goal in the 2-1 loss to Switzerland, his sixth of 2018 and 17th overall. Aleksandar Kolarov scored the only goal in Serbia's Group E opener against Costa Rica, but a 2-0 loss to Brazil saw them go home after the group stage.

ALEKSANDAR **MITROVIC**

TOURNAMENT TRIVIA
A TAD SPECIAL

In September 2012 Serbia matched their record victory margin, crushing Wales 6-1 in a 2014 FIFA World Cup qualifier, with both Branislav Ivanovic and Aleksandr Kolarov scoring. Other five-goal wins included 6-1 over Azerbaijan in 2007 and 5-0 against Romania two years later. The victory over Wales was also a notable occasion for forward Dusan Tadic, who scored his first goal in his eighth appearance in four years. He went on to win more than 60 caps including influential performances and four goals on the way to the 2018 FIFA World Cup in Russia.

STAR PLAYER
BRAN POWER

Versatile defender **Branislav Ivanovic**, who became Serbia's most-capped player with two appearances at the 2018 FIFA World Cup, has enjoyed scoring significant late goals against Portuguese opposition. His first goal for his country was an 88th-minute equalizer in a UEFA European Championship qualifier away to Portugal in September 2007. His stoppage-time header gave Chelsea victory over Benfica in the final of the 2013 UEFA Europa League, a year after suspension ruled him out of the club's UEFA Champions League triumph over Bayern Munich.

BRANISLAV **IVANOVIC**

2

Two players have been named Serb Footballer of the Year in consecutive years since 2005: first was Branislav Ivanovic, in 2012 and 2013, and he was followed by his Chelsea team-mate Nemanja Matic in 2014 and 2015.

3

Midfielder Dejan Stankovic is the only man to have represented three different countries at separate FIFA World Cups, playing for Yugoslavia in 2002, Serbia and Montenegro in 2006, and Serbia in 2010.

TOURNAMENT TRIVIA
GOING IT ALONE

After Serbia and Montenegro competed at the 2006 FIFA World Cup, the 2010 tournament was the first featuring Serbia alone following Montenegro's independence. Topping their qualifying group ahead of France, Radomir Antic's Serbian side failed to make it through to the knockout stages in South Africa, despite beating Group D rivals Germany. A Serbian working for an opposing team was partly to blame – Milovan Rajevac was coach of the Ghana side that beat Serbia 1-0 in their opening first-round match. A mainstay in the Serbian defence was dominating centre-back **Nemanja Vidic**, a 2008 UEFA Champions League-winner and hero at Manchester United, who retired from international duty in 2011.

NEMANJA **VIDIC**

NATIONAL LEGEND
STAN'S THE MAN

Dejan Stankovic scored twice on his international debut for Yugoslavia in 1998. He has also twice scored memorable volleyed goals from virtually on the halfway line – once for Internazionale against Genoa in 2009–10, with a first-time shot from the opposing goalkeeper's clearance, and an almost identical finish against German club FC Schalke 04 in the UEFA Champions League the following season. Stankovic tied Savo Milosevic's Serbian appearances record with his final competitive international in October 2011, but went one better in October 2013 when playing the first 10 minutes of a 2-0 friendly defeat of Japan at Novi Sad.

DEJAN **STANKOVIC**

100

Savo Milosevic was the first Serbian player to reach a century of international appearances – and he can claim to have played for his country in four different guises, representing Yugoslavia before and after it broke up, Serbia & Montenegro and finally Serbia alone.

SAVO **MILOSEVIC**

SLOVAKIA

Slovakia have finally begun claiming bragging rights over their neighbours, the Czech Republic. Slovakia qualified for their first FIFA World Cup in 2010, at which they upset defending champions Italy 3-2 and reached the second round.

Joined FIFA: 1994

Biggest Win:
9-0 vs. San Marino, 2007 & 2009, vs. Liechtenstein, 2004

Highest FIFA Ranking: 14

Home Stadium:
Tehelné pole, Bratislava

Honours: -

MOST APPEARANCES:

1. **Marek Hamsik**, 114
2. **Miroslav Karhan**, 107
3. **Martin Skrtel**, 103
4. **Jan Durica**, 91
5. **Peter Pekarik**, 88

MARTIN **SKRTEL**

THREE AND A HALF
Adam Nemec had to wait more than three and a half years between his Slovakia debut against Luxembourg in February 2011 and his first international goal, the only one of the game as his side beat Malta in September 2014.

Slovakia's qualification campaign for Euro 2016 included a national record six straight victories, including a surprise 2-1 win against defending champions Spain.

STAR PLAYER
COOL DUDA

Slovakia made it to the second round when reaching their first ever UEFA European Championship finals in 2016, only then going out 3-0 to reigning world champions Germany. **Ondrej Duda** became the first man to score for Slovakia at a UEFA European Championship, with an equalizer in their opening game against Wales just 52 seconds after coming on – the fastest Euros goal by a substitute since Spain's Juan Carlos Valeron needed just 36 seconds against Russia in 2004.

ONDREJ **DUDA**

TOURNAMENT TRIVIA
MAREK OFF THE MARK

Slovakia's biggest win is 7-0, a result they have achieved three times – with wing-back Marek Cech the only man to play in all three games: against Liechtenstein in September 2004 and twice versus San Marino, in October 2007 and June 2009. He scored twice in the most recent match and, in fact, four of his five international goals since his 2004 debut came against San Marino – he also scored a brace in a 5-0 victory in November 2007.

STAR PLAYERS
SKRTEL POWER

Martin Skrtel and Marek Hamsik have shared many special moments together, including Slovakia's run to the last 16 of the 2010 FIFA World Cup and the 2016 UEFA European Championship. The pair also won every Slovak Footballer of the Year prize since 2007: Skrtel winning four times and Hamsik eight. Hamsik became Slovakia's most capped player with his 108th appearance in October 2018, scoring in a 2-1 home defeat to the Czech Republic in the UEFA Nations League. In that game Skrtel also became only the third Slovakian player to win 100 caps.

ROBERT
VITTEK

MAREK
HAMSIK

Playmaker **Marek Hamsik** has been named Slovakia's Player of the Year for six consecutive seasons – 2013–18. He has eight overall.

TOP SCORERS:

1 **Marek Hamsik**, 24
2 **Robert Vittek**, 23
3 **Szilard Nemeth**, 22
4 **Miroslav Karhan**, 14
= **Marek Mintal**, 14

 NATIONAL
LEGEND
ROBERT THE HERO

Slovakia's **Robert Vittek** became only the fourth player from a country making their FIFA World Cup debut to score as many as four goals in one tournament, at the 2010 event in South Africa. He hit one against New Zealand, two against defending champions Italy, and a late penalty in a second-round defeat to Holland. The previous three players to have done so were Portugal's Eusebio in 1966, Denmark's Preben Elkjaer Larsen in 1986 and Croatia's Davor Suker in 1998.

STAR PLAYER
CUTTING EDGE HAMSIK

It wasn't a happy story for Marek Hamsik and Slovakia when it came to qualifying for the 2014 FIFA World Cup. Slovakia finished a disappointing third behind Greece and group G winners Bosnia & Herzegovina. Hamsik scored twice in eight appearances, but missed the final two games. The Mohawk was back at the 2016 UEFA European Championship where Hamsik helped to inspire Slovakia to advance to the second round and he scored in a 2-1 group win over Russia. He became the second Slovakia player to reach 100 appearances in a 1–0 defeat to Scotland in September 2017 in a FIFA World Cup qualifier.

NATIONAL LEGEND
VLAD ALL OVER

Three relatives named Vladimir Weiss – different generations of the same family – have represented their country in international football, with two of them featuring at the 2010 FIFA World Cup. The first Vladimir made three appearances for Czechoslovakia, including the 1964 Olympics final in which he scored an own goal as Hungary triumped 2-1. The second Vladimir won 19 caps for Czechoslavakia and 12 for Slovakia, and the third, then aged only 20, ended the 2010 FIFA World Cup with 12.

8

Eight Slovakia players played in Czechoslovakia's triumphant 1976 UEFA European Championship final against West Germany, including captain Anton Ondrus and both their scorers in the 2–2 draw: Jan Svehlik and Karol Dobias.

107

Miroslav Karhan became the first Slovakia player to pass 100 caps and he retired in 2011 with 107 to his name.

MIROSLAV
KARHAN

SWEDEN

Twelve appearances at the FIFA World Cup finals (with a best result of second, as tournament hosts, in 1958) and three Olympic medals (including gold in London in 1948) bear testament to Sweden's rich history on the world football stage.

Joined FIFA: 1908
Biggest Win: 12-0 vs. Latvia, 1927, vs. South Korea 1948
Highest FIFA Ranking: 2
Home Stadium: Friends Arena, Stockholm
Honours: -

Centre-back Olof Mellberg became the first Swedish man to play in four UEFA European Championship finals when he appeared at Euro 2012.

NATIONAL LEGEND
ONE MORE ENCORE AGAIN

One of the most famous and decorated Swedish footballers of modern times, **Henrik Larsson** (a star on the club scene with both Celtic and Barcelona), quit international football after the 2002 FIFA World Cup and again after the 2006 FIFA World Cup in Germany. He then made a further comeback in the 2010 FIFA World Cup qualifiers. With 37 goals in his 106 appearances, including five in his three FIFA World Cups, fans and officials clamoured for his return each time he tried to walk away.

HENRIK LARSSON

Alexander Isak became Sweden's youngest international scorer on 12 January 2017 when he netted the opener in a 6-0 friendly defeat of Slovakia in Abu Dhabi, aged 17 years and 113 days old.

SCORING RECORD
ANDERS KEEPERS

Midfielder **Anders Svensson** celebrated equalling Thomas Ravelli's Sweden appearances record by scoring in both his 142nd and 143rd games for his country: a long-range strike as Norway were beaten 4-2 and then the winning goal against the Republic of Ireland in a qualifier for the 2014 FIFA World Cup. He then became his country's most capped player in a 1-0 victory over Kazakhstan, but he didn't score. Svensson retired from international football in 2013, aged 37, after Sweden lost to Portugal in the qualifying play-off. He made 148 appearances, and scored 21 goals.

ANDERS SVENSSON

MOST APPEARANCES:

1. Anders Svensson, 148
2. Thomas Ravelli, 143
3. Andreas Isaksson, 133
4. Kim Kallstrom, 131
5. Olof Mellberg, 117

NATIONAL LEGEND
IBRA-CADABRA

Few modern footballers can claim such consistent success – or boast such an unrepentant ego – as Swedish forward **Zlatan Ibrahimovic**. His proclamations have included "There's only one Zlatan", "I am like Muhammad Ali" and – in response to criticism from Norway's John Carew – "What Carew does with a football, I can do with an orange". He christened the newly built Friends Arena in Solna with all four goals as hosts Sweden beat England 4-2 in a November 2012 friendly – his final strike topping the lot, a 30-yard overhead kick which won the FIFA Ferenc Puskas goal of the year award.

ZLATAN IBRAHIMOVIC

TOP SCORERS:

1. **Zlatan Ibrahimovic**, 62
2. **Sven Rydell**, 49
3. **Gunnar Nordahl**, 43
4. **Henrikh Larsson**, 37
5. **Gunnar Gren**, 32

His clubs have included Ajax Amsterdam, Juventus, both Milan giants, Barcelona, Paris Saint-Germain and Manchester United, but Zlatan Ibrahimovic never won a UEFA Champions League.

STAR PLAYERS
NEW GOALDEN BOYS

Sweden's new goalscoring heroes have been not only centre-forward Marcus Berg, but also centre-backs Andreas Granqvist and Victor Lindelof. Berg scored a record seven goals in hosts Sweden's run to the 2009 UEFA European U-21 Championship semi-finals and top-scored with eight in 2018 FIFA World Cup qualifiers. Granqvist top-scored in Sweden's run to the World Cup quarter-finals and he then added a vital penalty in their UEFA Nations League Group B match against Turkey. Sweden secured promotion with a 2–0 defeat of Russia with Lindelof and Berg scoring the goals.

4 Substitute Jakob Johansson scored his first international goal four minutes after coming on, in the second leg of the FIFA 2018 World Cup qualifying play-off against Italy, the only score of the tie.

2ND Sweden's best result at a FIFA World Cup is runners-up. Englishman George Raynor, who led them to Olympic gold in London in 1948, steered Sweden to third place and the runners-up spot in the 1950 and 1958 FIFA World Cups, respectively.

NATIONAL LEGEND
GRE-NO-LI OLYMPIC AND ITALIAN GLORY

Having conquered the world by leading Sweden to gold in the 1948 Olympics in London, Gunnar Gren, Gunnar Nordahl and **Nils Liedholm** were snapped up by AC Milan. Their three-pronged "Gre-No-Li" forward line led the Italian giants to their 1951 scudetto win. Nordahl, who topped the Serie A scoring charts five times between 1950 and 1955, remains Milan's all-time top scorer with 221 goals in 268 games. Gren and Liedholm went on to appear for the Swedish national team in the 1958 FIFA World Cup, where they finished runners-up.

NILS LIEDHOLM

STAR PLAYER
SUPER GRANQVIST

Sweden saw off the Netherlands and Italy to qualify for the 2018 FIFA World Cup, where they lost 2-0 to England in the quarter-finals. Their top scorer at the 2018 finals was centre-back and captain **Andreas Granqvist** – the successor to Zlatan Ibrahimovic as both captain and Swedish player of the year. He netted two penalties in Russia, the only goal against South Korea and the second strike in their 3-0 victory over Mexico that secured top spot in Group F. In between Sweden's two wins, they had lost 2-1 to Germany, the defending champions' only victory.

ANDREAS GRANQVIST

SWITZERLAND

Switzerland may not be an international football powerhouse, but they are the home of both FIFA and UEFA. Switzerland co-hosted the 2008 UEFA European Championship, with Austria, and reached the semi-finals of the inaugural UEFA Nations League in 2019.

Joined FIFA: 1905
Biggest win:
9-0 vs. Lithuania, 1924
Highest FIFA ranking: 3
Home Stadium:
Stade de Suisse Wankdorf, Bern
Honours: -

NATIONAL LEGEND
FREI-S AND LOWS

Citing abuse from his own fans during recent matches, **Alexander Frei** announced his retirement from international football in April 2011, following a string of underwhelming results with the national side. He left as Switzerland's all-time leading goalscorer with 42 in 84 games. Frei was joined in international retirement by strike partner Marco Streller, who had scored 12 goals in 37 games.

TOURNAMENT 🏆 TRIVIA
CLEAN SHEET WIPE OUT

Switzerland remain the only team to exit the FIFA World Cup without conceding a goal in regulation time, which they did in 2006. However, in the shoot-out defeat to Ukraine in the second round, following a goalless 120 minutes, they failed to score a single penalty and lost 3-0. Despite being beaten three times in the shoot-out, goalkeeper Pascal Zuberbuhler's performances in Germany earned him a Swiss record for consecutive clean sheets at an international tournament.

YANN **SOMMER**

2004
After being compared to a llama by an angry Swiss sports press for spitting at Steven Gerrard at UEFA Euro 2004, Alexander Frei, Switzerland's all-time top scorer, adopted a llama at Basel zoo as part of his apology to the nation.

3

Yann Sommer is only the third goalkeeper to score a FIFA World Cup own goal, after Spain's Andoni Zubizarreta in 1998 and Noel Valladeres of Honduras in 2014. Sommer deflected a penalty from Costa Rica off his head into the net in 2018.

ALEXANDER **FREI**

TOP SCORERS:

1. **Alexander Frei**, 42
2. **Max Abegglen**, 34
   = **Kubilay Turkyilmaz**, 34
3. **Andre Abegglen**, 29
   = **Jacques Fatton**, 29

MOST APPEARANCES:

1. **Heinz Hermann**, 118
2. **Alain Geiger**, 112
3. **Stephan Lichtsteiner**, 105
4. **Stephane Chapuisat**, 103
5. **Johann Vogel**, 94

4

Karl Rappan, who pioneered pressurising defending and positional fluidity, managed Switzerland in four separate spells between 1937 and 1963.

STAR PLAYER
SHAQIRI LOYALTY TEST

Playmaker **Xherdan Shaqiri** scored one of the most spectacular goals of the 2016 UEFA European Championship, an overhead kick from outside the penalty area to give Switzerland a 1–1 draw in their second-round match with Poland – the Poles, however, prevailed on penalties. Two years earlier he had scored the 50th hat-trick in FIFA World Cup history during his side's 3–0 triumph over Honduras in Manaus. Kosovo-born Shaqiri indicated he would be prepared to switch international allegiance to his native land – which became a full UEFA and FIFA member in 2016 – if permitted.

XHERDAN SHAQIRI

JOSEF HUGI

2–1
The Swiss were the first team at the 2018 FIFA World Cup to come from behind to win, after beating Serbia 2-1.

NATIONAL LEGEND
WHO'S HUGI

Only two men have scored more than three goals in one game for Switzerland and **Josef Hugi** leads the way with a five-timer. His 23 goals in 34 games for his country included five on 12 October 1960 as France were beaten 6–2 in Basel. Hugi found the net six times at the 1954 FIFA World Cup including a hat-trick in a 7–5 quarter-final defeat to Austria, as he finished second top scorer at the tournament. His six FIFA World Cup finals goals remains a national record. In the 1924 Paris Olympic Games, Paul Sturzenegger netted four in a 9–0 win over Lithuania.

STAR PLAYER
LEADING LIGHT LICHTSTEINER

Captain Stephan Lichtsteiner went into the 2018 FIFA World Cup as only the fourth Swiss player to reach a century of caps. The attacking right-back - who won 14 titles with Italian giants Juventus before joining English club Arsenal in summer 2018 - went on to skipper Switzerland as they clinched top spot in the UEFA Nations League group they shared with Belgium and Iceland in late 2018. The Schweizer Nati scored 14 goals across their four games, emphatically more than fellow semi-finalists the Netherlands (eight), England (six) and Portugal (five).

STAR PLAYER
ADMIR ADDS MORE

Switzerland reached the knock-out stages of the UEFA European Championship for the first time in 2016, and their 1–0 Group A victory over Albania - thanks to a goal by centre-back Fabian Schar - was the first time they had ever won their Euro tournament opener. In their next match they managed a 1–1 draw against Romania, courtesy of a second-half equalizer by Admir Mehmedi. Mehmedi thus became the first Swiss player to score in both FIFA World Cup and UEFA European Championship finals, after his strike against Ecuador in Brazil two years earlier. Ten days later, Xherdan Shaqiri emulated Mehmedi, equalizing against Poland in the round of 16.

22

Legendary Swiss international player and manager, **Jakob "Kobi" Kuhn**, was only 22 years old when he was sent home from the 1966 FIFA World Cup for missing a curfew.

JAKOB "KOBI" KUHN

TURKEY

MOST APPEARANCES:

1 **Rustu Recber**, 120
2 **Hakan Suker**, 112
3 **Bulent Korkmaz**, 102
4 **Arda Turan**, 100
5 **Emre Belozoglu**, 99

Turkey had qualified for the FIFA World Cup only twice in the 20th Century. Since 2000, however, Turkish fans have had plenty to cheer about, including a third-place finish at the 2002 FIFA World Cup in Japan and South Korea.

Joined FIFA: 1923
Biggest Win:
7-0 vs. Syria, 1949, vs. South Korea, 1954, vs. San Marino, 1996
Highest FIFA Ranking: 5
Home Stadium:
Atatürk Olympic Stadium
Honours: -

RUSTU
RECBER

NATIONAL LEGEND
RUSTU TO THE RESCUE

With his distinctive ponytail and charcoal-black warpaint, Turkey's most capped international, **Rustu Recber** has always stood out. But perhaps never more so than as a star mainstay in Turkey's third-place performance at the 2002 FIFA World Cup, as he was named FIFA's Goalkeeper of the Year. He was on the bench by the 2008 UEFA European Championship but played in the quarter-final after first-choice goalkeeper Volkan Demirel was sent off in the final group game and suspended – and Recber became the hero again, saving from Croatia's Mladen Petric in a penalty shoot-out to send Turkey into their first UEFA European Championship semi-final, a narrow defeat to Germany.

FAITH
TERIM

NATIONAL LEGEND
TAKE FAT

It seemed finally to be the end of an epic era when **Fatih Terim**'s third spell as national manager finished abruptly in July 2017, but Terim remains Turkish football history's dominant force. After coaching Galatasaray to the 2000 UEFA Cup – the nation's first European trophy – he led Turkey on their surprise run to the 2008 UEFA European Championship semi-finals. Turkey led in the semi-final only to concede a last-minute winner to Germany. Terim returned to Galatasaray in 2009 but became national manager for the third time in 2013.

STAR PLAYER
WORK HARD, PLAY ARDA

Wing wizard **Arda Turan** – Turkey's captain at the 2016 UEFA European Championship – has survived cardiac arrhythmia, swine flu and a car crash to emerge as one of Turkish football's leading lights. His international achievements include key goals at the 2008 UEFA European Championship, the first a stoppage-time winner against Switzerland, then Turkey's late opener when overturning a two-goal deficit against the Czech Republic in a first-round qualification decider. After leaving Galatasaray, he has enjoyed great success in Spanish club football, winning European and domestic trophies with Atletico Madrid and Barcelona.

3

Fatih Terim has managed Turkey in three separate spells.

★ STAR PLAYER
FROM ONE EMRE TO ANOTHER

Combative midfielder Emre Belozoglu was a key member of the Turkey side who achieved their best ever tournament finish, third at the 2002 FIFA World Cup. He was still there, in March 2019 at 38, captaining his country to a 2-0 win over Albania in a UEFA Euro 2020 qualifier as he earned his 97th international cap. This Emre is not to be confused with **Emre Mor** who became in 2016, at 18, Turkey's youngest player ever at the UEFA European Championship finals.

EMRE MOR

15

Zeki Riza Sporel scored Turkey's first goal in international football, against Romania on 26 October 1923. He actually hit a brace that day in a 2-2 draw – the first of 16 games for Turkey in which he hit 15 goals.

17

Playmaker Nuri Sahin became both Turkey's youngest international and youngest goalscorer, on the same day. Sahin was 17 years and 32 days old when he made his debut against Germany in Istanbul on 8 October 2005, and his goal, one minute from time, gave Turkey a 2-1 win.

🌐 NATIONAL LEGEND
TWIN TURKS

Hamit Altintop (right) was born 10 minutes before identical twin brother **Halil** (left) – and he has been leading the way throughout their professional footballing careers since their birth in December 1982. Both began playing for German amateur side Wattenscheid, before defender-come-midfielder Hamit signed for FC Schalke 04 in the summer of 2006 and striker Halil followed suit shortly afterward. Hamit would stay just a season there, though, before being bought by Bayern Munich. Both helped Turkey reach the semi-finals of the 2008 UEFA European Championship – losing to adopted homeland Germany – though only Hamit was voted among UEFA's 23 best players of the tournament.

HALIL ALTINTOP

HAMIT ALTINTOP

100

Arda Turan came out of international retirement after coach Fatih Terim was succeeded by former Romania coach Mircea Lucescu and he made his 100th appearance for Turkey in a 3-0 defeat against Iceland in October 2017.

⚽ SCORING RECORD
SUPER SUKER

Turkey beat South Korea 3-2 to claim third place at the 2002 FIFA World Cup, their finest ever performance in the competition, after an 11-second strike from **Hakan Suker**. Suker's total of 51 goals (in 112 games) is more than double his nearest competitor in the national team ranking. His first goal came in only his second appearance, as Turkey beat Denmark 2-1 on 8 April 1992. He went on to score four goals in a single game twice – in the 6-4 win over Wales on 20 August 1997 and in the 5-0 crushing of Moldova on 11 October 2006.

HAKAN SUKER

TOP SCORERS:
1 **Hakan Suker**, 51
2 **Burak Yilmaz**, 24
3 **Tuncay Sanlli**, 22
4 **Lefter Kucukandonyadis**, 21
5 **Nihat Kahveci**, 19
= **Metin Oktay**, 19
= **Cemil Turan**, 19

11

Hakan Sukur scored the fastest-ever FIFA World Cup finals goal – taking only 11 seconds to score Turkey's first goal in their third-place play-off match against South Korea at the 2002 FIFA World Cup.

UKRAINE

Ukraine has been a stronghold of football in eastern Europe for many years. Since separating from the Soviet Union in 1991, Ukraine has become a football force in its own right, qualifying for the FIFA World Cup for the first time in 2006, reaching the quarter-finals.

Joined FIFA: 1992
Biggest Win:
9-0 vs. San Marino, 2013
Highest FIFA Ranking: 11
Home Stadium: (Rotation)
Honours: -

TOP SCORERS:

1 Andriy Shevchenko, 48

2 Andriy Yarmolenko, 36

3 Yevchen Konoplyanka, 21

4 Serhiy Rebrov, 15

5 Oleh Husyev, 13

TOURNAMENT TRIVIA
GET ZIN IN

Midfielder or left-back **Oleksandr Zinchenko** promised hope for the future even as Ukraine made a 2016 UEFA European Championship first-round exit. Two weeks before the tournament, he became the country's youngest ever goalscorer in a 4-3 friendly win over Romania before becoming, in Ukraine's tournament opener against Germany aged 19 years, 179 days old, his nation's youngest player at a major finals. After moving from Russia to England, where he won a Premier League title with Manchester City, he continued to thrive for Ukraine, helping them to top their UEFA Nations League B group in 2018. Zinchenko set their promotion campaign off to a perfect start with the stoppage-time winner to seal an opening 2-1 victory away to the Czech Republic.

OLEKSANDR **ZINCHENKO**

14

No one has found the net quicker after kick-off than Andriy Yarmolenko for Ukraine. The winger scored just 14 seconds into the 3-2 friendly defeat against Uruguay in September 2011.

STAR PLAYER
YARMED AND DANGEROUS

Only Andriy Shevchenko has scored more goals for Ukraine than **Andriy Yarmolenko**. He was crucial in helping Ukraine qualify for the 2016 UEFA European Championship, with six goals – including a hat-trick in a 6-0 victory over Luxembourg and strikes in both legs of their play-off victory over Slovenia. He was also leading scorer in Ukraine's 2018 FIFA World Cup qualification bid, again with six goals, but they failed to reach the finals after finishing third in their group. And 2018 ended badly when Yarmolenko ruptured his Achilles tendon in October.

ANDRIY **YARMOLENKO**

NATIONAL LEGEND
REB ALERT

Serhiy Rebrov scored Ukraine's first ever FIFA World Cup goal, giving them a 1-0 win over Northern Ireland in an August 1996 qualifier for the 1998 tournament. He was part of the squad for Ukraine's first FIFA World Cup finals in 2006, scoring against Saudi Arabia to help his side toward the quarter-finals where they lost 3-0 to eventual champions Italy. After spells in England and Turkey, Rebrov returned to Kiev and, in 2014, went into management, steering Dynamo to two Ukrainian league titles.

MOST APPEARANCES:

1. Anatoliy Tymoshchuk, 144
2. Andriy Shevchenko, 111
3. Ruslan Rotan, 100
4. Oleh Husyev, 98
5. Oleksandr Shovkovskyi, 92

ANATOLIY TYMOSHCHUK

NATIONAL LEGEND
ROCKET MAN

Andriy Shevchenko beat team-mate **Anatoliy Tymoshchuk** to become the first Ukrainian footballer to reach a century of international appearances – but the defensive midfielder overtook Shevchenko and retired in 2016 and is the country's most capped player with 144 appearances. He also had the rare honour of seeing his name in space, when Ukrainian cosmonaut Yuri Malenchenko launched into orbit wearing a Zenit St Petersburg shirt with "Tymoshchuk" on the back in 2007.

NATIONAL LEGEND
LEADING FROM THE FRONT

Oleg Blokhin, Ukraine's coach on their first appearance at a major tournament finals, made his name as a striker with his hometown club Dynamo Kiev. Born in 1952, when Ukraine was part of the Soviet Union, Blokhin scored a record 211 goals in another record 432 appearances in the USSR national league. He also holds the goals and caps records for the USSR, with 42 in 112 games. Always an over-achiever, Blokhin managed Ukraine to the finals of the 2006 FIFA World Cup in Germany, where they lost out to eventual winners Italy 3-0 in the quarter-finals after knocking out Switzerland in the second round – also on penalties.

11 SECONDS

Oleg Blokhin was renowned for his speed – when Olympic gold medallist Valeriy Borzov trained the Kiev squad in the 1970s, Blokhin recorded a 100 metres time of 11 seconds, just 0.46 seconds slower than Borzov's own 1972 medal-winning run.

18

Serhiy Rebrov was 18 years and 24 days old when making his debut against the USA in June 1992, becoming Ukraine's youngest international.

3

Three Ukrainians have won the Ballon D'Or, though only Andriey Shevchenko (2006) has done so since Ukraine's independence from the Soviet Union.

8

There were eight different scorers in Ukraine's 9-0 thrashing against San Marino in a FIFA World Cup qualifier in 2013 – it's still the country's biggest ever win.

NATIONAL LEGEND
SUPER SHEVA

Andriy Shevchenko was a promising boxer as a youngster, before deciding to focus on football full time. He has won trophies at every club he's played for and is Ukraine's second-most capped player and leading goalscorer, with 48 goals in 111 games. This includes two at the 2006 FIFA World Cup, where he captained his country in their first ever major finals appearance, and a double to secure a 2-1 comeback win over Sweden in Ukraine's first match co-hosting the 2012 UEFA European Championship. Shevchenko was Ukraine's assistant coach at the 2016 UEFA European Championship and replaced Mykhailo Fomenko as manager after the tournament.

ANDRIY SHEVCHENKO

WALES

In a land where rugby union has long been the main national obsession, recent progress – including a semi-final appearance at the 2016 UEFA European Championship – has inspired unprecedented excitement and optimism.

Joined FIFA: 1906
Biggest Win:
11-0 vs. Ireland, 1888
Highest FIFA Ranking: 8
Home Stadium:
Cardiff City Stadium, Cardiff
Honours: -

100 MILLION

Gareth Bale cost Real Madrid a world record $100 million (£86 million) when he moved from Tottenham Hotspur in August 2013.

GARETH **BALE**

NATIONAL LEGEND
ALL HAIL BALE

It was predictable that Wales' first goalscorer at the 2016 UEFA European Championship – their first finals since the 1958 FIFA World Cup – would be **Gareth Bale**. The Real Madrid man – a four-times UEFA Champions League winner – opened the scoring with a free-kick in a 2-1 first-round win over Slovakia, and repeated the trick in their next game, against England. Before Bale, only France's Michel Platini in 1984 and Germany's Thomas Hassler in 1992, had scored twice from direct free-kicks at one UEFA Euro finals. Once Wales' youngest international, he became their leading goalscorer in style with a hat-trick in a 6-0 rout of China in March 2018.

29

Full-back Chris Gunter was aged only 29 when he won his 93rd cap for Wales and thus passed Neville Southall as his country's most-capped player.

JOHN **CHARLES**

NATIONAL LEGEND
BILLY IDOL

Winger Harry Wilson became Wales' youngest full international when replacing Hal Robson-Kanu in October 2013, in a 2014 FIFA World Cup qualifier. At 16 years and 207 days, he was 108 days younger than previous record-holder Gareth Bale. Wales' oldest international is Billy Meredith, whose 48th and final international came aged 45 years and 229 days in March 1920. Meredith's international career lasted a Welsh record 25 years.

TOURNAMENT TRIVIA
FAMILY MATTERS

Wales's only FIFA World Cup finals came in 1958 when they fell 1-0 to eventual champions Brazil and Pele's first international goal. It was a family affair in more ways than one. Left-winger Cliff Jones was joined in the squad by cousin Ken, a back-up goalkeeper who never played for his country. Their father, Ivor, and uncle, Bryn, both played for Wales too. Mainstays in 1958 were Mel and **John Charles**. John, dubbed "The Gentle Giant", excelled at both centre-back and centre-forward. He scored Wales's first goal in Sweden, a 1-1 draw against Hungary. Mel is one of only four Welshmen to score four times in a full international.

TOP SCORERS:

1. **Gareth Bale**, 31
2. **Ian Rush**, 28
3. **Ivor Allchurch**, 23
= **Trevor Ford**, 23
4. **Dean Saunders**, 22

Welsh striker Robert Earnshaw holds the remarkable record of scoring hat-tricks in all four divisions of English football, the FA Cup and the League Cup. He also grabbed a treble for Wales, against Scotland on 18 February 2004. In full internationals, Wales have registered 15 hat-tricks – each one by a different player.

15

GARY **SPEED**

NATIONAL LEGEND
HEADLINING GIGGS

The most-decorated Welsh player of all-time took over as the country's national coach in 2018 – despite having no previous full-time managerial experience. **Ryan Giggs** scored 12 goals in 64 games for Wales between 1991 and 2007. On a domestic level, with his only senior club Manchester United, he won 13 English league titles, four FA Cups, three League Cups, two UEFA Champions Leagues and one FIFA Club World Cup – and appeared in more than 1,000 first-team matches before retiring, aged 40, in 2014. Following Wales's failure to qualify for the 2018 FIFA World Cup, manager Chris Coleman resigned and Giggs took over.

RYAN **GIGGS**

NATIONAL LEGEND
SHOCK LOSS OF A MODEL PROFESSIONAL

The football world was united in shock and grief at the sudden death of Wales manager **Gary Speed** in November 2011. Former Leeds United, Everton, Newcastle United and Bolton Wanderers midfielder Speed, the country's most capped outfield player, was found at his home in Cheshire, England. The 42-year-old had been manager for 11 months, overseeing a series of encouraging performances that saw a rise in the world rankings from 116th to 48th and a prize for FIFA's "Best Movers" of 2011. An official memorial game was played in Cardiff in February 2012 between Wales and Costa Rica, the country against whom he had made his international debut in May 1990.

18

Ryan Giggs was criticized by some fans for failing to play in friendlies – he missed 18 in a row in one spell – and never represented Wales at a major tournament.

1906
Pioneer movie-makers Sagar Mitchell and James Kenyon captured Wales vs. Ireland in March 1906, making it the first filmed international football match.

NATIONAL LEGEND
BRICKS TO BRILLIANCE

Goalkeeper **Neville Southall** made the first of his then-record 92 appearances for Wales in a 3–2 win over Northern Ireland on 27 May 1982. The former hod-carrier and bin man kept 34 clean sheets in 15 years playing for Wales and won the English Football Writers' Association Player of the Year in 1985 thanks to his performances alongside Welsh captain Kevin Ratcliffe at Everton. In his final match for Wales, on 20 August 1997, he was substituted halfway through a 6–4 defeat against Turkey in Istanbul.

NEVILLE **SOUTHALL**

MOST APPEARANCES:

1. **Chris Gunter**, 95
2. **Neville Southall**, 92
3. **Ashley Williams**, 86
4. **Gary Speed**, 85
5. **Wayne Hennessey**, 84

EUROPE : OTHER TEAMS

For the smaller countries in Europe, the thrill of representing their nation is more important than harbouring dreams of world domination.

Country: Iceland
Joined FIFA: 1947
Most Appearances: Runar Kristinsson, 104
Top Scorer: Eidur Gudjohnsen, 26

Country: San Marino
Joined FIFA: 1988
Most Appearances: Andy Selva, 74
Top Scorer: Andy Selva, 8

Country: Finland
Joined FIFA: 1908
Most Appearances: Jari Litmanen, 137
Top Scorer: Jari Litmanen, 32

Country: Luxembourg
Joined FIFA: 1910
Most Appearances: Mario Mutsch, 102
Top Scorer: Leon Mart, 16

Country: Gibraltar
Joined FIFA: 2016
Most Appearances: Liam Walker, 39
Top Scorer: Liam Walker, Jake Gosling, Joseph Chipolina, Lee Casciaro, 2

Country: Austria
Joined FIFA: 1905
Most Appearances: Andreas Herzog, 103
Top Scorer: Toni Polster, 44

Country: Georgia
Joined FIFA: 1992
Most Appearances: Levan Kobiashvili, 100
Top Scorer: Shota Arveladze, 26

Country: North Macedonia
Joined FIFA: 1994
Most Appearances: Goran Pandev, 103
Top Scorer: Goran Pandev, 33

Country: Azerbaijan
Joined FIFA: 1992
Most Appearances: Rashad Sadygov, 111
Top Scorer: Gurban Gurbanov, 14

Country: Bosnia-Herzegovina
Joined FIFA: 1996
Most Appearances: Edin Dzeko, 103
Top Scorer: Edin Dzeko, 56

Country: Slovenia
Joined FIFA: 1992
Most Appearances: Bostjan Cesar, 101
Top Scorer: Zlatko Zahovic, 35

Country: Armenia
Joined FIFA: 1992
Most Appearances: Sargis Hovsepyan, 132
Top Scorer: Henrikh Mkitaryan, 27

Country: Albania
Joined FIFA: 1932
Most Appearances: Lorik Cana, 93
Top Scorer: Erjon Bogdani, 18

Country: Belarus
Joined FIFA: 1992
Most Appearances: Alyaksandr Kulchy, 102
Top Scorer: Maksim Romaschenko, 20

Country: Andorra
Joined FIFA: 1996
Most Appearances: Ildefons Lima, 123
Top Scorer: Ildefons Lima, 11

Country: Montenegro
Joined FIFA: 2007
Most Appearances: Fatos Beciraj, 63
Top Scorer: Stevan Jovetic, 24

TOURNAMENT TRIVIA
UNDERDOGS HAVE THEIR DAY

Iceland became the smallest nation ever to qualify for a FIFA World Cup, with a 2-0 victory over Kosovo in October 2017 thanks to goals from star midfielder **Gylfi Sigurdsson** and Johann Berg Gudmundsson. Striker Alfred Finnbogason netted their first FIFA World Cup finals goal, in a 1-1 draw with two-time winners Argentina. Unlike in their first UEFA European Championship appearance two years earlier, Iceland missed out on the knock-out stages after going down 2-0 to Nigeria and 2-1 to Croatia. Manager and part-time dentist Heimir Hallgrimsson resigned after the finals.

GYLFI **SIGURDSSON**

NATIONAL LEGEND
LIT'S A KNOCKOUT

Perhaps it's not be too surprising that **Jari Litmanen** should have become a football star – both his parents played for the Lahti-based club Reipas while Litmanen's father Olavi also won five caps for the national team. But Jari's skills and achievements far outstripped them both – and, arguably, any other player the country has produced. It was fitting that Litmanen became the first Finnish player to get his hands on the UEFA European Cup – or Champions League trophy – when his Ajax Amsterdam side beat AC Milan in 1995.

JARI
LITMANEN

330,000
With a population of 330,000 only 182,000 Tahiti (2013 FIFA Confederations Cup) has been a smaller nation at an international finals than Iceland at the 2018 FIFA World Cup and 2016 UEFA European Championship.

137

Georgia became the lowest-ranked side ever to defeat Spain in 2016. Georgia stood 137th in the FIFA rankings – 131 places below their opponents.

MATHIAS
JANISCH

SCORING RECORD
SELVA SERVICE

San Marino, with a population of under 30,000, remain near the bottom of FIFA's world rankings but they finally had something to celebrate in November 2014, thanks to a goalless draw with Estonia – their first ever point in a UEFA European Championship qualifier – and ending a run of 61 successive defeats. They have avoided defeat only five times and have never recorded a competitive victory. In fact, San Marino's only win was a 1-0 friendly triumph over Liechtenstein in April 2004. Andy Selva, who retired in 2016 after making his debut in 1998, is San Marino's top scorer with eight goals.

SCORING RECORD
REBORN BOURG

A long and painful wait finally ended for traditional whipping-boys Luxembourg when they beat Northern Ireland 3-2 in September 2013. It was the "Red Lions" first home win in a FIFA World Cup qualifier for 41 years, since overcoming Turkey 2-0 in October 1972. It was also five years to the day since their last FIFA World Cup qualifying victory, a 2-1 triumph in Switzerland in 2008. Luxembourg's goals came from Aurelien Joachim, Stefano Bensi and **Mathias Janisch**. The winning goal, with three minutes remaining, was the first of Janisch's international career.

NATIONAL LEGEND
SUPER PAN

North Macedonia celebrated 100 years of football in the country with a friendly against future world champions Spain in August 2009 – and striker **Goran Pandev** marked the occasion by becoming his country's all-time leading scorer. His first-half brace gave the hosts a 2-0 lead and although Spain came back to win 3-2, he replaced 16-goal Gorgi Hristov at the top of North Macedonia's scoring charts. Pandev has played the majority of his club career in Italy, after signing for Internazionale from local team FK Belasica as an 18-year-old in 2001.

GORAN
PANDEV

15

The break-up of the Soviet Union in 1990 led to 15 new footballing nations, though initially Russia played on at the 1992 UEFA European Championship as CIS, or the Commonwealth of Independent States – without the involvement of Estonia, Latvia and Lithuania.

STAR PLAYER
HAPPY DAYS FOR ILDEFONS

Andorra's long-serving captain **Ildefons Lima** had double cause for celebration on 9 June 2017. Not only did he equal Oscar Sonejee's record of 106 international appearances, but also Andorra also beat Hungary 1-0 in a 2018 FIFA World Cup qualifier – only their second ever competitive victory and first in 66 matches. The winning goal came from his central defensive partner Marc Rebes, his first for Andorra in his ninth game. Lima made his debut, and scored, in Andorra's second international, a 4-1 defeat to Estonia, on 22 June 1997.

ILDEFONS LIMA

STAR PLAYER
ED BOY

Edin Dzeko became Bosnia-Herzegovina's all-time leading scorer with a second-half hat-trick in an 8-1 2014 FIFA World Cup qualifier victory over Liechtenstein in September 2012. The goals not only took him past previous record-holder Elvir Bolic, but also ahead of Dzeko's international team-mate Zvjedan Misimovic, whose brace earlier in the game had briefly put him in the lead. The pair swapped the lead for a while before Dzeko took over for good. Dzeko then became his country's most-capped international when scoring the only goal to beat Austria in the UEFA Nations League in September 2018.

EDIN DZEKO

5
Iceland picked an unchanged starting eleven for all five of their games at the tournament, making them the first team to do so in the UEFA European Championship.

54

The British Overseas Territory of Gibraltar became UEFA's 54th member state in time to take part in qualifiers for the 2016 UEFA European Championship, but they were deliberately kept apart from neighbours Spain in the draw.

MATTHIAS SINDELAR

NATIONAL LEGEND
BASKET CASE

Captain **Rashad Sadygov** not only secured Azerbaijan's biggest win in their history when he scored the only goal against Turkey in a UEFA Euro 2012 qualifier in October 2010 – he was also delivering a blow against the country in which he was making his living. Having previously played for Turkish top-flight side Kayserispor, he had since moved on to rivals Eskisehirspor. Not every transfer has worked out well for Sadygov: he missed the transfer deadline when signing for Azeri side PFC Neftchi in 2006, so he decided to play basketball for a season to keep himself fit until allowed to resume football.

RASHAD SADYGOV

NATIONAL LEGEND
MORE SIND AGAINST

Austria's star player **Matthias Sindelar** refused to play for a new, merged national team when Germany annexed Austria in 1938. Sindelar, born in modern-day Czech Republic in February 1903, was the inspirational leader of Austria's so-called Wunderteam of the 1930s. He scored 27 goals in 43 games for Austria, who went 14 internationals unbeaten between April 1931 and December 1932, won the 1932 Central European International Cup and silver at the 1936 Olympics.

17 Iceland striker Eidur Gudjohnsen made history on his international debut away to Estonia in April 1996 when he was 17. He was a substitute for his father, Arnor Gudjohnsen, aged 34.

STAR PLAYER
A SEQUEL TO HAMLET

Striker Hamlet Mkhitaryan played twice for post-Soviet state Armenia in 1994, though died two years later from a brain tumour at the age of just 33. His son **Henrikh Mkhitaryan**, seven when his father died, has gone on to become the country's all-time leading scorer – and one who often dedicates his achievements to his late parent. The younger Mkhitaryan became Armenia's joint top scorer, alongside Artur Petrosyan, with a goal against Denmark in June 2013. While Petrosyan's goals came in 69 games, Mkhitaryan's 11 were scored in 39 – and he pulled away on his own, with a 12th international strike, in a 2-2 draw with Italy in October 2012.

HENRIKH MKHITARYAN

STAR PLAYER
BY JOVE

Stevan Jovetic struck seven goals in seven games for Montenegro from September 2016 to June 2017, taking him past strike partner and captain **Mirko Vucinic** as the country's leading scorer with 23. His 2018 FIFA World Cup qualifying hat-trick helped to down Armenia 4-1 in June 2017. Vucinic's 17 goals included a winner against Switzerland in a Euro 2012 qualifier which he celebrated by removing his shorts and wearing them on his head – antics that earned him a yellow card.

MIRKO VUCINIC

NATIONAL LEGEND
KULCHY COUP

Midfielder Alyaksandr Kulchy became the first player to win 100 caps for Belarus, skippering the side against Lithuania in a June 2012 friendly. He also ended ex-Arsenal and Barcelona playmaker Alexander Hleb's run of four successive Belarus footballer of the year awards by claiming the prize in 2009. Hleb, whose younger brother Vyacheslav has also played for Belarus, had previously won the accolade in 2002 and 2003 as well, only for Belarus's all-time top scorer Maksim Romashenko to take it in 2004.

100 Slovenia's Bostjan Cesar made his 100th appearance was against Scotland in October 2017, but it was marred by a late red card and he retired after one more game.

TOURNAMENT TRIVIA
KAZAK JOY, SCOTTISH MISERY

Some 27,000 Kazakhstan fans celebrating a national new year had even more reason for joy in March 2019 with perhaps the country's finest footballing result, a surprise 3-0 trouncing of Scotland in their opening 2020 UEFA European Championship qualifier in Astana - despite being ranked 117th in the world. Yuriy Pertsukh, Yan Vorogovskiy and Baktiyar Zaynutdinov were the goalscoring heroes in the first game in charge for new Kazakhstan coach, forer Czech Republic midfielder and manager Michael Bilek. Kazakhstan had gone without a win in their 10 qualifiers for the 2018 FIFA World Cup.

STAR PLAYER
XHAKA CLAN

Granit and Taulant Xhaka, both born in Swiss city Basel to Kosovo Albanian parents, became the first brothers to face each other on opposing sides at a UEFA European Championship on 11 June 2016 – midfielder Granit, 23, for Switzerland, 25-year-old defender Taulant for Albania. Granit and Switzerland won 1-0, and their mother was seen in the stands that day wearing a half-and-half football shirt, supporting both her sons.

GRANIT & TAULANT XHAKA

SOUTH AMERICA

Football may not have been born in South America, but the passion and enthusiasm that the continent's fans have for the sport is unmatched anywhere in the world. In this spirit, Uruguay, Argentina and Paraguay are bidding to host the centenary World Cup in 2030.

Confederation Founded: 1916

Number of Federations: 10

Headquarters: Luque, Paraguay

Most Continental Championship Wins: Uruguay, 15

12

With the exception of the Centenario tournament in 2016, 12 teams have competed in each Copa America since 1993: the ten CONMEBOL states, along with two invited nations.

The first FIFA World Cup was held in South America: Uruguay hosted and won the tournament in 1930.

21

Brazil have competed at all 21 FIFA World Cups – more than any other nation – and have won five, also a record.

RIVALDO

RONALDO

The first football team established in South America was the Lima Cricket and Football Club, in Peru in 1859.

10

With only ten member states, CONMEBOL has the fewest of any FIFA confederation.

ARGENTINA

Copa America champions on 14 occasions, FIFA Confederations Cup winners in 1992, Olympic gold medallists in 2004 and 2008 and, most treasured of all, FIFA World Cup winners in 1978 and 1986: few countries have won as many international titles as Argentina.

Joined FIFA: 1912

Biggest win:
12-0 vs. Ecuador, 1942

Highest FIFA ranking: 1

Home Stadium:
Estadio Monumental Antonio Vespucio Liberti

Honours: 2 FIFA World Cups (1978, 1986), 14 Copa Americas (1921, 1925, 1927, 1929, 1937, 1941, 1945, 1946, 1947, 1955, 1957, 1957, 1959, 1991, 1993)

Argentina is one of only three countries, alongside France and Brazil, to have won the FIFA World Cup, FIFA Confederations Cup and Olympics Games gold medals.

STAR PLAYER
LEO BRAVO

Lionel Messi was sent off just two minutes into his national debut, against Hungary in August 2005 after coming on as a substitute, but went on to become his Argentina's all-time record goalscorer, youngest FIFA World Cup scorer (against Serbia and Montenegro in 2006, aged 19), their youngest captain (at 23 years old during the 2010 FIFA World Cup) and winner of the Golden Ball for best player at the 2014 FIFA World Cup, where his four Man of the Match awards were a record for one tournament.

LIONEL
MESSI

19

Lionel Messi became only the second substitute to hit a Copa America hat-trick when he came off the bench to score three times in Argentina's 5-0 victory over Panama in the opening round of the 2016 Copa America Centenario. There were just 19 minutes between his first and third goals.

STAR PLAYER
RIGHT ANGEL

Winger **Angel Di Maria** scored the only goal to give Argentina their first Olympic Games football gold medal, beating Nigeria at Beijing in 2008. The match was played in such heat that officials allowed both sides occasional water breaks. Di Maria is much travelled: he was playing in Portugal for Benfica in 2008, having joined Rosario Central in his homeland aged just four. Di Maria later played for Spain's Real Madrid – he was voted man of the match when they won the 2013 UEFA Champions League final against Atletico Madrid – before big-money moves to Manchester United in England and French club Paris Saint-Germain.

ANGEL
DI MARIA

TOP SCORERS:

1 Lionel Messi, 68
2 Gabriel Batistuta, 54
3 Sergio Aguero, 41
4 Hernan Crespo, 35
5 Diego Maradona, 34

SERGIO ROMERO

Only one member of Cesar Menotti's 1978 FIFA World Cup winning Argentina squad was from a foreign club: Mario Kempes, who scored twice in the final and won the Golden Boot.

1

STAR PLAYER
HERO ROMERO

No man has kept goal for Argentina more than **Sergio Romero**. He won an Olympic Games gold medal in 2008 but had to wait until September 2009 for his senior international debut against Paraguay. Romero, who had won 94 caps by summer 2018, was ever-present for Argentina at both the 2010 and 2014 FIFA World Cups, helping them reach the 2014 final with two saves in a semi-final penalty shoot-out victory over the Netherlands. The 1-0 final defeat to Germany denied him the FIFA World Cup winner's medal earned by compatriot 'keepers Ubaldo Fillol (58 caps) in 1978 and Nery Pumpido (36) eight years later.

TOURNAMENT TRIVIA
MESSI ENDINGS

Argentina reached – and lost a final – for a third consecutive year when Chile won a penalty-shoot-out at the 2016 Copa America Centenario. This final – just as in 2015 when the then hosts Chile took the shoot-out 4-1 – ended goalless after 120 minutes before Chile triumphed 4-2. Argentina had also fallen to Germany in the 2014 FIFA World Cup final. In fact, Argentina last won the Copa America in 1993 and the FIFA World Cup in 1986. Messi ended the final in despair, after failing in the shoot-out – missing high and wide – then shocked the sport by announcing his international football retirement, aged just 29. He soon returned, however.

14

Argentina have finished Copa America runners-up more times than any other nation, 14, three more than Brazil, most recently in 2015 and 2016.

NATIONAL LEGEND
BEGINNER'S LUCK

Aged just 27 years and 267 days old, Juan Jose Tramutola became the FIFA World Cup's youngest-ever coach when Argentina opened their 1930 campaign by beating France 1-0. Argentina went on to reach the final, only to lose 4-2 to Uruguay. Top-scorer at the 1930 FIFA World Cup was Argentina's Guillermo Stabile, with eight goals in four games – the only internationals he played. He later won six Copa America titles as his country's longest-serving coach between 1939 and 1960.

2 MINUTES
Midfielder Marcelo Trobbiani played just two minutes of FIFA World Cup football – the last two minutes of the 1986 final, after replacing winning goalscorer Jorge Burruchaga.

DIEGO MARADONA

NATIONAL LEGEND
DIVINE DIEGO

To many, **Diego Maradona** is the greatest footballer ever. The Argentinian legend became famous as a ball-juggling child during half-time intervals at Argentinos Juniors matches, but was distraught to be left out of Argentina's 1978 FIFA World Cup squad and was then sent off for retaliation at the 1982 tournament. Maradona, as triumphant Argentina captain in Mexico in 1986, scored the notorious "Hand of God" goal and then a spectacular individual strike within five minutes of each other in a quarter-final win over England. He again captained Argentina to the final in 1990, in Italy – the country where he inspired Napoli to Serie A and UEFA Cup success.

THE KIDS ARE ALRIGHT

Sergio Aguero struck in the final, and ended the tournament as six-goal top scorer, when Argentina won the FIFA World U-20 Championship for a record sixth time in 2007, in Canada, beating the Czech Republic 2-1. Two years later, Aguero married Giannina Maradona – the youngest daughter of Argentina legend Diego – and in February 2009 she gave birth to Diego's first grandchild, Benjamin. Sergio Aguero is widely known by his nickname of "Kun", after a cartoon character he was said to resemble as a child.

SERGIO
AGUERO

12

Argentina were responsible for the biggest win in Copa America history, when five goals by Jose Manuel Moreno helped them thrash Ecuador 12-0 in 1942.

YELLOW GOODBYE

Some 20 years before France were forced to wear local Argentine club Atletico Kimberly's kit at the 1978 FIFA World Cup, Argentina themselves faced similar embarrassment for their first-round match against West Germany. The Argentines had neglected to bring along a second kit and a colour-clash with their opponents meant borrowing the yellow shirts of Swedish side IFK Malmo. Despite taking a third-minute lead, Argentina lost 3-1 and departed the tournament bottom of Group A.

MARCOS ROJO

MARCOS
ROJO

NATIONAL LEGEND
THE ANGEL GABRIEL

Gabriel Batistuta, nicknamed "Batigol", is the only man to have scored hat-tricks in two separate FIFA World Cups. Argentina's former all-time leading goalscorer grabbed the first against Greece in 1994 and the second against Jamaica four years later. Hungary's Sandor Kocsis, France's Just Fontaine and Germany's Gerd Muller each scored two hat-tricks in the same FIFA World Cup. Batistuta, born in Reconquista on 1 February 1969, also set an Italian league record by scoring in 11 consecutive Serie A matches for his club Fiorentina at the start of the 1994–95 season

GABRIEL
BATISTUTA

TOURNAMENT TRIVIA
WORLD CUP WOES

The last trophy won by Argentina was the Copa America in 1993 and their drought continued at the 2018 FIFA World Cup. They qualified narrowly, needing a Lionel Messi hat-trick against Ecuador in the final round of the qualifying tournament to book their place. In Russia, amid rumours of dressing room rebellion – denied by coach Jorge Sampaoli – they were held 1-1 by minnows Iceland, with Messi missing a penalty, and lost 3-0 to Croatia. Victory over Nigeria thanks to goals from Messi and **Marcos Rojo** saw Argentina sneak through, but their luck ran out against France in the Round of 16, when they lost a 4-3 thriller.

20

Argentina's national stadium, "El Monumental" in Buenos Aires, hosted its first game in 1938. But the original design was not completed until 20 years later – largely thanks to the £97,000 River Plate received for a transfer fee from Juventus for Omar Sivori.

NATIONAL LEGEND
FITTER, JAVIER

Only Javier Mascherano has won more caps for Argentina than **Javier Zanetti**, who made 143 international appearances – despite being surprisingly left out of squads for both the 2006 and 2010 FIFA World Cups. Zanetti, who played at full-back or in midfield, also played more Serie A matches than any other non-Italian – and all for Internazionale of Milan, with whom he won the treble of Italian league, Italian Cup and UEFA Champions League in 2009–10. Despite those achievements, he and Inter team-mate Esteban Cambiasso failed to make Diego Maradona's squad for the 2010 FIFA World Cup.

JAVIER **ZANETTI**

MOST APPEARANCES:

1 Javier Mascherano, 147
2 Javier Zanetti, 143
3 Lionel Messi, 136
4 Roberto Ayala, 114
5 Diego Simeone, 104

NATIONAL LEGEND
SECOND TIME LUCKY

Luisito Monti is the only man to play in the FIFA World Cup final for two different countries. The centre-half, born in Buenos Aires on 15 May 1901 but with Italian family origins, was highly influential in Argentina's run to the 1930 final. They lost the game 4–2 to Uruguay – after Monti allegedly received mysterious pre-match death threats. Following a transfer to Juventus the following year, he was allowed to play for Italy and was on the winning side when the Azzurri beat Czechoslovakia in the 1934 final. Another member of the 1934 team was Raimundo Orsi, who had also played for Argentina before switching countries in 1929.

TOURNAMENT TRIVIA
NUMBERS GAME

Argentina's FIFA World Cup squads of 1978 and 1982 were given numbers based on alphabetical order rather than positions, which meant the No. 1 shirt was worn by midfielders Norberto Alonso in 1978 and Osvaldo Ardiles in 1982. The only member of the 1982 squad whose shirt number broke the alphabetical order was No. 10, Diego Maradona. Italian club Napoli retired the number the number 10 in tribute of Maradona, who starred for the team at his peak.

NATIONAL LEGEND
FRINGE PLAYERS

Daniel Passarella was a demanding captain when he led his country to glory at the 1978 FIFA World Cup. He was the same as coach. After taking over the national side in 1994, he refused to pick anyone unless they had their hair cut short – and ordered striker Claudio Caniggia to get rid of his "girl's hair". Passarella was quite a character: it was alleged once by Maradona that that Passarella, while playing for Fiorentina, would travel to Monaco to have an affair with another player's wife.

DANIEL **PASSARELLA**

Martin Palermo missed all three penalties he took during Argentina's 1999 Copa America clash with Colombia. The first hit the crossbar, the second flew over the bar and the third was saved. Colombia won the match 3-0.

BRAZIL

No country has captured the soul of the game to the same extent as Brazil. The only nation to appear in every FIFA World Cup finals, Brazil are competition winners a record five times.

Joined FIFA: 1923

Biggest win:
10-1 vs. Bolivia, 1949

Highest FIFA ranking: 1

Home Stadium:
Maracana, Rio de Janeiro

Honours: 5 FIFA World Cups (1958, 1962, 1970, 1994, 2002), 9 Copa Americas (1919, 1922, 1949, 1989, 1997, 1999, 2004, 2007, 2019)

26

1970 FIFA World Cup star Tostao retired at the age of 26 in 1973, after an eye injury.

STAR PLAYER
TAKING AIM WITH NEYMAR

Brazil's triumph in the 2013 FIFA Confederations Cup, a record third in a row, was consolation for "only" a silver medal at the London 2012 Olympic Games. **Neymar** scored three goals at London 2012, and later was voted South American Footballer of the Year for the second successive year and then, in 2013, was named player of the FIFA Confederations Cup. Those were his last matches as a Santos player before he joined Spanish giants Barcelona. He was Brazil's undoubted star at the 2014 FIFA World Cup, with four goals in four games before being injured in the quarter-final win against Colombia.

NEYMAR

43

Brazilian legend Rivaldo played until he was 43 – more than a decade after the highlight of his career, helping Brazil win the 2002 FIFA World Cup.

NATIONAL LEGEND
BRAZIL HAVE HAD THEIR BIG PHIL

The return of "Big Phil" **Luiz Felipe Scolari** as Brazil coach in November 2012 was meant to culminate, in 2014, with a repeat of his success spearheading the country to triumph at the 2002 FIFA World Cup. Although his second reign did bring glory at the 2013 FIFA Confederations Cup, the following year's FIFA World Cup on home turf will be remembered for the many unwanted records his team set and the embarrassment with which their efforts ended – most notably, the 7-1 defeat by Germany in their Belo Horizonte semi-final. Scolari was relieved of his role just days after a 3-0 defeat to the Netherlands in the third-place play-off.

LUIZ FELIPE SCOLARI

NATIONAL LEGEND
THE KING

Pele is considered by many as the greatest player of all time, a sporting icon par excellence and not only for his exploits on the pitch. When, for instance, he scored his 1,000th goal, Pele dedicated it to the poor children of Brazil. He began playing for Santos at the age of 15 and won his first FIFA World Cup two years later, scoring twice in the final. Despite numerous offers from European clubs, the economic conditions and Brazilian football regulations at the time allowed Santos to keep hold of their prized asset for almost two decades, until 1974.

All-time leading scorer of the Brazilian national team, Pele is the only footballer to be a member of three FIFA World Cup-winning teams.

TOP SCORERS:

1 **Pele**, 77

2 **Ronaldo**, 62

3 **Neymar**, 60

4 **Romario**, 55

5 **Zico**, 48

PELE

Pele leads the way with seven hat-tricks for Brazil, followed by Zico and Romario on four – but only one-time Flamengo and Barcelona centre-forward Evaristo de Macedo has scored five goals in one game for Brazil, against Colombia in March 1957.

NATIONAL LEGEND
JOY OF THE PEOPLE

Garrincha, one of Brazil's greatest legends, was really Manuel Francisco dos Santos at birth but his nickname meant 'Little Bird' – inspired by his slender, bent legs. Despite the legacy of childhood illness, he was a star right-winger at Botafogo from 1953 to 1965. He and Pele were explosively decisive newcomers for Brazil at the 1958 FIFA World Cup finals. In 1962 Garrincha was voted player of the tournament four years later. He died in January 1983 at just 49. His epitaph was the title often bestowed on him in life: "The Joy of the People."

1954
The world-renowned yellow and blue kit now worn by Brazil was not adopted until 1954, as a replacement for their former all-white strip.

TOURNAMENT TRIVIA
LAND OF FOOTBALL

No country is more deeply identified with football success than Brazil, who have won the FIFA World Cup a record five times – in 1958, 1962, 1970, 1994 and 2002. They are also the only team never to have missed a FIFA World Cup finals and are favourites virtually every time the competition is staged. After winning the trophy for a third time in Mexico in 1970, Brazil kept the Jules Rimet Trophy permanently. Sadly, it was stolen from the federation's headquarters in 1983 and was never recovered.

SOCRATES

TOURNAMENT TRIVIA
CLOSE ENCOUNTERS

Brazil have been involved in many memorable games. Their 3-2 defeat to Italy in 1982 is regarded as one of the classic games in FIFA World Cup finals history. Paolo Rossi scored all three of Italy's goals with Brazil coach Tele Santana much criticized for going all out in attack when only a 2-2 draw was needed. Brazil's 1982 squad, with players such as **Socrates**, Zico and Falcao, is considered one of the greatest teams never to win the tournament. In 1994, a 3-2 win over the Netherlands in the quarter-finals – their first competitive meeting in 20 years – was just as thrilling, with all the goals coming in the second half.

NATIONAL LEGEND
LETTING LUCIO

Elegant centre-back **Lucio** set a FIFA World Cup record during the 2006 tournament by playing for 386 minutes without conceding a foul – only ending in Brazil's 1-0 quarter-final defeat to France. While mostly noted for leadership and control at the back, he also had an eye for goal – heading the late winner that gave Brazil a 3-2 triumph over the USA in the 2009 FIFA Confederations Cup final. The following year he was part of Italian club Internazionale's treble success, clinching the Italian league and cup as well as the UEFA Champions League.

LUCIO

1000

Brazil played their 1,000th match on 14 November 2012, with Neymar's second-half equaliser securing a 1-1 draw against Colombia in New Jersey, United States.

TOURNAMENT TRIVIA
EARLY ARRIVAL ... AND DEPARTURE

Brazil became the first country outside host nation Russia to secure a place at the 2018 FIFA World Cup, after just 14 of South American federation CONMEBOL's scheduled 18 qualification rounds as they beat Paraguay 3-0 on 28 March 2017. They had been sixth of ten South American nations in the group when Tite took over as manager in summer 2016 but he led them to eight consecutive victories and comfortable qualification. Yet despite high hopes for the 2018 tournament – and surpassing Germany as the FIFA World Cup's all-time highest scorers, with 229 goals – they bowed out 2-1 to Belgium in the quarter-finals.

STAR PLAYER
COUTINHO'S SHOOTING BOOTS

Brazil's first two goals at the 2018 FIFA World Cup were scored not by star striker and captain Neymar but by Philippe Coutinho, seen by many as Neymar's replacement at Barcelona after joining for £135m from Liverpool in January that year – six months after Neymar had left for Paris Saint-Germain. Coutinho's goals came in a 1-1 draw with Switzerland and 2-0 victory over Costa Rica. He had previously scored a hat-trick for Brazil when they beat Haiti 7-1 at the 2016 Copa America Centenario, his country's 54th international treble.

STAR PLAYER
SILVA VALUE

Brazil qualified from the first round of a FIFA World Cup for the 13th time running at Russia in 2018. They clinched top place in Group E by winning their third game 2-0 against Serbia – with their second goal scored by veteran centre-back **Thiago Silva**, from a corner by Neymar. Silva's previous FIFA World Cup goal, in a quarter-final victory over Colombia in 2014, was also set up by a Neymar corner. Silva won Olympic Games bronze with Brazil at Beijing in 2008 and silver at London 2012. He was Brazil's captain when they won the 2013 FIFA Confederations Cup triumph on home soil.

THIAGO SILVA

3

Right-back **Djalma Santos** is one of only two players to be voted into the official all-star team of a FIFA World Cup on three different occasions.

DJALMA SANTOS

RONALDO

Ronaldinho became a FIFA World Cup winner in 2002, aged 22. His long-range goal against England gave Brazil victory in the quarter- finals – though he was sent off seven minutes later and had to sit out the semi-final, before returning for the final.

RONALDINHO

NATIONAL LEGEND
WHITHER RONALDO?

Only one person knows exactly what happened to **Ronaldo** in the hours before the 1998 FIFA World Cup final – the man himself. He sparked one of the biggest mysteries in FIFA World Cup history when his name was left off the teamsheet before the game, only for it to reappear just in time for kick-off. It was initially reported that Ronaldo had an ankle injury, and then a upset stomach. Finally team doctor Lidio Toledo revealed the striker had been rushed to hospital after suffering a convulsion in his sleep, but that he had been cleared to play after neurological and cardiac tests.

ROMARIO

NATIONAL LEGEND
ROM NUMBERS

Brazilian goal poacher supreme **Romario** is one of the few footballers to claim more than 1,000 career goals. He is also the last man to win both the FIFA World Cup and the Golden Ball award as the best player at the same tournament, something he achieved in 1994 when his five goals – including the semi-final winner against Sweden – helped Brazil to their fourth title. The former Barcelona and Fluminense forward moved into politics after retiring from playing to become elected as an MP, as did his 1994 FIFA World Cup strike partner Bebeto.

MOST APPEARANCES:

1. **Cafu**, 142
2. **Roberto Carlos**, 125
3. **Dani Alves**, 115
4. **Lucio**, 105
5. **Claudio Taffarel**, 101

MARCELO

STAR PLAYER
INAUPICIOUS START

Left-back/left-winger **Marcelo** achieved the dubious "honour" of being the first player to score the opening goal of a FIFA World Cup finals in his own net. He inadvertently gave Croatia the lead in the 2014 tournament's curtain-raiser in Sao Paulo, but Brazil did come back to win 3-1, thanks to a pair of goals from Neymar and one from Oscar. Marcelo, who a couple of weeks earlier had scored for his club, Real Madrid, as they won the UEFA Champions League final, also became the first Brazil player ever to score past his own goalkeeper in the FIFA World Cup finals.

TOURNAMENT TRIVIA
SUPER POWERS' POWER CUT

There was a new addition to the annual international calendar in 2011: the Superclasico de los Americas, a two-legged event between Brazil and Argentina. Brazil were the first winners, thanks to a goalless draw followed by a 2-0 win. They dramatically retained the crown in 2012. Brazil won the first leg at home, 2-1, but the return game in Chaco was postponed after a power cut – possibly because Brazil's team bus hit an electricity trailer. The rearranged game ended 2-1 to Argentina, but Brazil won 4-3 on penalties.

CHILE

MARCELO SALAS

Chile were one of four founding members of CONMEBOL, South America's football confederation, in 1916. Their greatest glories were hosting and finishing third at the 1962 FIFA World Cup and winning their first two Copa America titles in 2015 and 2016.

Joined FIFA: 1912

Biggest win:
7-0 vs. Venezuela, 1979, vs. Armenia, 1997, vs. Mexico, 2016

Highest FIFA ranking: 3

Home Stadium:
Estadio Nacional Julio Martínez Prádanos

Honours: 2 Copa Americas (2015, 2016)

NATIONAL LEGEND
SALAS DAYS

Chile's third leading scorer **Marcelo Salas** formed a much-feared striking partnership with Ivan Zamorano during the late 1990s and early 21st century. Salas scored four goals as Chile reached the second round of the 1998 FIFA World Cup in France despite not winning a game. The striker spent two years in international retirement, from 2005 to 2007, but returned for the first four games of qualification for the 2010 FIFA World Cup. His scored twice in Chile's 2-2 draw with Uruguay on 18 November 2007, but his international career ended for good three days later, following a 3-0 defeat to Paraguay.

2

Two Argentinians – Marcelo Bielsa and Jorge Sampaoili – coached Chile to consecutive FIFA World Cup knockouts in 2010 and 2014, their first consecutive knockouts ever.

SCORING RECORD
LUCKY LEO

For many years Leonel Sanchez held the Chilean record for international appearances, scoring 23 goals in 84 games. But he was lucky to remain on the pitch for one of them. Sanchez escaped an early bath despite punching Italy's Humberto Maschio in the face during their so-called "Battle of Santiago" clash at the 1962 FIFA World Cup, when English referee Ken Aston could have sent off more than just the two players he did dismiss. Sanchez, a left-winger born in Santiago on 25 April 1936, finished the tournament as one of its six four-goal leading scorers – along with Garrincha, Vava, Valentin Ivanov, Drazan Jerkovic and Florian Albert.

STAR PLAYER
SANCHEZ SETS MORE CHILE RECORDS

The winning spot-kick against Argentina to secure Chile's first Copa America in 2015 was struck by the well-travelled **Alexis Sanchez**, then of Arsenal in England, following spells in Italy with Udinese and in Spain with Barcelona. Sanchez holds the record as Chile's youngest international, having made his debut against New Zealand in April 2006 at the age of 17 years and four months. At the 2017 FIFA Confederations Cup, Sanchez passed Marcelo Salas to become Chile's all-time record goalscorer. Then, in 2018, and now with Manchester United, he took over at the top of the appearances list too.

ALEXIS SANCHEZ

NATIONAL LEGEND
VIDAL ESCAPES TO VICTORY

Hosts Chile's 2015 Copa America campaign nearly careered off the road, literally. Star midfielder **Arturo Vidal** crashed his red Ferrari after over-enjoying a night out, having scored twice in a 3-3 draw with Mexico. Coach Jorge Sampaoli resisted public pressure to drop him for the deciding match of the group after Vidal promised to donate his tournament fee to charity and a 5-0 thrashing of Bolivia – he grabbed another double – sealed Chile's quarter-final place. Vidal was named Man of the Match in the final and was selected for the 2015 Copa America team of the tournament.

ARTURO VIDAL

48

Chile went precisely 48 years between victories at a FIFA World Cup, from a 1-0 third-place play-off success against Yugoslavia on 16 June 1962 to a first-round victory by the same scoreline over Honduras on 16 June 2010.

1930
Chile forward Carlos Vidal – nicknamed "Little Fox" – was the first man to miss a penalty at a FIFA World Cup, seeing his spot-kick saved by France goalkeeper Alex Thepot in 1930.

99
Chile waited 99 years for their first Copa America triumph, winning the tournament in 2015. They won the tournament the following year, too.

MOST APPEARANCES:
1 Alexis Sanchez, 130
2 Gary Medel, 125
3 Claudio Bravo, 119
4 Gonzalo Jara, 115
5 Mauricio Isla, 113
= Arturo Vidal, 113

JEAN BEAUSEJOUR

TOURNAMENT TRIVIA
CONFED UP

Chile made their FIFA Confederations Cup debut in 2017 and reached the final, after beating European champions Portugal 3-0 in a penalty shoot-out after a goalless draw in the semi-final. Goalkeeper and captain Claudio Bravo saved from Ricardo Quaresma, Joao Moutinho and Nani, while Arturo Vidal, **Charles Aranguiz** and Alexis Sanchez all found the net for Chile. Although world champions Germany won the final 1-0, Bravo collected the Golden Glove award as the tournament's best goalkeeper, and Sanchez claimed the Silver Ball as second best player, behind Germany's Julian Draxler..

CHARLES ARANGUIZ

SCORING RECORD
BRAVO, BEAUSEJOUR

Chile's first FIFA World Cup goal for nearly 50 years came in South Africa, 2010, from **Jean Beausejour,** who then hit Chile's third in their opening-game 3-1 triumph over Australia in Brazil four years later. It meant he became the first Chilean player ever to score at more than one FIFA World Cup. Goalkeeper and captain at both tournaments was Claudio Bravo, Chile's third most-capped player of all time.

4
Eduardo Vargas scored four times as Chile matched their record win – and their biggest in a competitive match – by beating Mexico 7-0 in their June 2016 quarter-final at that summer's Copa America Centenario.

EDUARDO VARGAS

URUGUAY

Uruguay was the first country to win a FIFA World Cup, in 1930, and with a population of under four million, they remain the smallest to do so. They claimed the game's greatest prize for a second time in 1950.

Joined FIFA: 1916

Biggest win:
9–0 vs. Peru, 1927

Highest FIFA ranking: 2

Home Stadium: Estadio Centenario, Montevideo

Honours: 2 FIFA World Cups (1930, 1950), 15 Copa Americas (1916, 1917, 102–, 1923, 1924, 1926, 1935, 1942, 1956, 1959, 1967, 1983, 1987, 1995, 2011)

EDINSON **CAVANI**

3

It took just three minutes for Edinson Cavani to score his first international goal, after coming on as a substitute for his Uruguay debut against Colombia in February 2008.

3.4M
Uruguay's population of 3.4 million and area of 176,000 sq km makes it the smallest nation to have lifted the FIFA World Cup trophy. The next smallest in terms of population is Argentina with 43m.

STAR PLAYER
CAV FAITH

Edinson Cavani not only helped Uruguay finish fourth at the 2010 FIFA World Cup and win a record 15th Copa America but the devout Christian won praise when playing for Italian club Napoli from the Archbishop of Naples Crescenzio Sepe, who declared: "God serves himself by having Cavani score goals." Yet his 2015 Copa America ended unhappily with a bizarre sending-off at the end of a quarter-final defeat to hosts Chile after retaliating when opponent Gonzala Jara prodded him in the bottom.

NATIONAL LEGEND
CLASS APART

Oscar Washington Tabarez, a former schoolteacher known as "The Maestro", led Uruguay to the second round of the 1990 FIFA World Cup and returned for a second spell in 2006, taking them back to the tournament in 2010 – and a fourth-place finish. When he took charge of his 168th Uruguay game in 2016, he passed West Germany's Sepp Herberger for the most matches coached for one team. His Uruguay teams set a national record of 18 matches unbeaten between 2011 and 2012 – and won the 2011 Copa America.

OSCAR WASHINGTON **TABAREZ**

16

There were 16 years between Oscar Washington Tabarez's first and second stints in charge of Uruguay. In that time, they didn't win a single FIFA World Cup game.

DIFFERENT BALL GAME

Uruguay were the inaugural hosts – and the first winners – of the FIFA World Cup in 1930, having won football gold at the Olympics of 1924 in Paris and 1928 in Amsterdam. Uruguay beat arch-rivals Argentina 4-2 in the 1930 final, a game in which two different footballs were used – Argentina's choice in the first half, in which they led 2-1, before Uruguay's was used for their second-half comeback. Uruguay declined the chance to defend their title in 1934, refusing to travel to host country Italy in pique at only four European nations visiting in 1930.

CáCeres

MARTIN **CACERES**

MOST APPEARANCES:

1 **Diego Godin**, 131

2 **Maxi Pereria**, 125

3 **Edinson Cavani**, 114

4 **Diego Forlan**, 112
  Fernando Muselera, 112

Forward Hector Scarone, now Uruguay's fourth-top scorer with 31 goals in 52 internationals, won three titles with Uruguay: hte FIFA World Cup in 1930, and football gold at the Olympics of 1924 in Paris and 1928 in Amsterdam.

STAR PLAYER
BITE RETURN

Notoriety has cast many shadows over the career of **Luis Suarez**. He earned infamy with a deliberate goal-line handball in the last minute of extra-time when Uruguay and Ghana were level in their 2010 FIFA World Cup quarter-final – then celebrated wildly when Asamoah Gyan missed – and Uruguay won the resulting shoot-out. Worse followed, however, at the 2014 FIFA World Cup, when he bit into the shoulder of Italian defender Giorgio Chiellini, earning himself a nine-match international ban and a four-month suspension from all football. His scoring instincts, are much more admirable – his international goals total includes four during Uruguay's triumphant 2011 Copa America campaign.

LUIS **SUAREZ**

TOURNAMENT TRIVIA
BOYS IN BLUE

On 20 July 1902 Argentina inflicted Uruguay's heaviest loss, 6-0 in Montevideo. The two countries have played each other a world record 193 times – with Uruguay winning 59, Argentina 89 and there have been 45 draws. Before an agreed kit-swap in 1910, Uruguay would often wear vertical light-blue and white stripes and Argentina would don pale-blue shirts. One of Uruguay's most momentous recent triumphs over their arch rivals came when they defeated hosts Argentina on penalties in the quarter-finals of the 2011 Copa America on the way to lifting the trophy. Defender **Martin Caceres** struck the winning spot-kick.

1901
Uruguay's 3–2 home defeat to neighbours Argentina, in Montevideo on 16 May 1901, was the first official international match outside the UK.

TOURNAMENT TRIVIA
HAPPY ANNIVERSARY

A so-called "Mundialito", or "Little World Cup", was staged in December 1980 and January 1981 to mark the 50th anniversary of the FIFA World Cup – and, as in 1930, Uruguay emerged triumphant. The tournament was meant to involve all six countries who had previously won the tournament, though 1966 champions England turned down the invitation and were replaced by 1978 runners-up Holland. Uruguay beat Brazil 2-1 in the final, a repeat of the scoreline from the final match of the 1950 FIFA World Cup. The Mundialito-winning Uruguay side was captained by goalkeeper Rodolfo Rodriguez and coached by Roque Maspoli, who had played in goal in that 1950 final.

TOP SCORERS:

1 **Luis Suarez**, 58

2 **Edinson Cavani**, 48

3 **Diego Forlan**, 36

4 **Hector Scarone**, 31

5 **Angel Romano**, 28

SOUTH AMERICA: OTHER TEAMS

With only ten nations in South America, CONMEBOL is competitive. Though there are minnows who don't have the history or prowess of Brazil or Argentina, the rest of South America has still produced wonderful stories in football over the years.

Country: Colombia
Joined FIFA: 1938
Most Appearances: Carlos Valderrama, 111
Top Scorer: Radamel Falcao, 34
Honours: 1 Copa America (2001)

Country: Peru
Joined FIFA: 1925
Most Appearances: Roberto Palacios, 128
Top Scorer: Paulo Guerrero, 38
Honours: 2 Copa Americas (1939, 1975)

Country: Bolivia
Joined FIFA: 1926
Most Appearances: Ronald Raldes, 102
Top Scorer: Joaquin Botero, 20
Honours: 1 Copa America (1963)

Country: Paraguay
Joined FIFA: 1925
Most Appearances: Paulo da Silva, 150
Top Scorer: Roque Santa Cruz, 32
Honours: 2 Copa Americas (1953, 1979)

Country: Ecuador
Joined FIFA: 1930
Most Appearances: Ivan Hurtado, 168
Top Scorer: Agustin Delgado, 31
Honours: -

Country: Venezuela
Joined FIFA: 1952
Most Appearances: Juan Arango, 129
Top Scorer: Saloman Rondon, 24
Honours: -

STAR PLAYER
MINA MAKES HIS MARK

Colombian centre-back Yerry Mina surprised even himself at the 2018 FIFA World Cup in Russia when he proved not only a tower of strength in defence but was his team's three-goal leading scorer. That equalled the record tally for a defender at the finals. Colombia lost their opening game to Japan, but Mina scored the first goal of their next game a 3-0 defeat of Poland. He then struck again with the lone goal which beat Senegal and sent Colombia into the second round. Mina headed the last-minute equaliser in a 1-1 draw with England before Colombia lost on penalties.

1-0
Venezuela's best performance in the 2018 FIFA World Cup qualifying competition, when they finished bottom of the 10-team group, was a 1-0 win in Paraguay.

STAR PLAYER
HERO GUERRERO

Veteran playmaker **Paolo Guerrero** had to battle all the way for the right to lead Peru at the 2018 World Cup, their first appearance in the finals for 36 years. Peru's captain was suspended for 12 months during the qualifiers for failing a dope test for what he claimed was coca tea after a tie against Argentina. The ban would have ruled him out of the finals, but it was lifted pending appeal, and Guerrero was allowed to play in the finals. He even scored in a 2-0 win over Australia, but Peru went out at the group stage. That goal was his record-extending 35th for Peru, 14 years after his debut.

PAOLO **GUERRERO**

TOURNAMENT TRIVIA
BOLIVIA LEAVE IT LATE

Bolivia have only ever won the Copa America once, but did so in dramatic and memorable style when playing host in 1963. They were the only team to finish the competition unbeaten in all six matches, topping the league table. But they almost threw away glory on the competition's final day, twice squandering two-goal leads against Brazil. Bolivia led 2-0 before being pegged back to 2-2, then saw a 4-2 advantage turn to 4-4, before Maximo Alcocer scored what proved to be Bolivia's winning goal with four minutes remaining.

44

Peru were coached at the 1982 FIFA World Cup by Tim, who had been waiting an unprecedented 44 years to return to the FIFA World Cup finals – after playing once as striker for his native Brazil in the 1938 tournament.

13

Bolivia's Ronald Raldes, made his international debut in 2001 but had to wait 13 years to score for his country – finally finding the net in a 3-2 November 2014 victory over Venezuela.

ICONIC MOMENT
ECUADOR'S EARTHQUAKE TRIBUTE

Ecuador reached the knock-out stages of the 2016 Copa America Centenario – the first time they had advanced from the opening round since 1987. They drew with Brazil (0-0) and Peru (2-2) and defeated Haiti 4-0. Head coach Gustavo Quinteros dedicated their progress to the more than 600 people killed by an earthquake in the country's Manabi region on 16 April 2016. Ecuador's opening goal against Haiti was scored by West Ham United striker **Enner Valencia**, who had netted three times at the 2014 FIFA World Cup – the first Ecuadorian to score more than once in a FIFA World Cup finals match.

ENNER
VALENCIA

35,742
The smallest national stadium in South America is the Estadio Olimpico Atahualpa, Quito, Ecuador, which holds 35,742.

TEAM TRIVIA
HIGH LIFE

Bolivia and Ecuador play their home internationals at higher altitudes than any other teams on earth. Bolivia's showpiece Estadio Hernando Siles stadium, in the capital La Paz, is 3,637 metres (11,932ft) above sea level, while Ecuador's main Estadio Olimpico Atahualpa, in Quito, sits 2,800 metres (9,185ft) above sea level. Opposing teams have complained that the rarefied nature of the air makes it difficult to breathe, let alone play, but a FIFA ban on playing competitive internationals at least 2,500 metres (8,200ft) above sea level, first introduced in May 2007, was suspended entirely in May 2008.

CARLOS
VALDERRAMA

NATIONAL LEGEND
TALKING HEAD

Colombia's record international remains frizz-haired midfielder **Carlos Valderrama** who played 111 times for the Cafeteros, scoring 11 goals, between 1985 and 1998. Valderrama stood out for both his hairstyle and his playmaking talent when he captained Colombia in a golden era for the national team. He was voted South American Footballer of the Year in 1987 and 1993 while appearing in the finals of the FIFA World Cup on three successive occasions in 1990, 1994 and 1998. Valderrama was a hugely popular figure at the 2018 finals in Russia when he undertook television pundit duties, still parading his famous hairstyle.

IVAN HURTADO

168

With 168 caps, **Ivan Hurtado** of Ecuador is the most capped South American footballer of all time.

Paraguay's two most-capped players, centre-back Paulo da Silva (148 appearances, first against Bolivia on 27 July 2000) and goalkeeper Justo Villar (120 caps, debut v Guatemala, 3 March 1999) were mainstays in their country's most successful FIFA World Cup performance: topping their group in 2010 and reaching the quarter-finals, only losing to eventual champions Spain. Both were still in the side in October 2016, helping Paraguay win a FIFA World Cup qualifier in Argentina for the first time – thanks to a Derlis Gonzalez strike.

SCORING RECORD
NOT SO FAB

Colombia full-back Frank Fabra endured a bittersweet Copa America first at the 2016 Centenario tournament when he scored for both teams in one match – no other player had done this in the competition's 100-year history. He found the net at both ends as his side lost 3-2 to Costa Rica in the first round, although Colombia did recover to qualify for the next stage and ultimately reached the semi-finals.

NATIONAL LEGEND
WINNING RON

Bolivia's most-capped player, centre-back **Ronald Raldes**, scored just his second ever international goal against Ecuador at the 2015 Copa America, helping secure Bolivia's first Copa America victory since 1997. Their failure to qualify for the 2018 FIFA World Cup means 1994 remains their only finals – but the 2018 campaign did include back-to-back wins for the first time since 1998, including a surprise 2-0 victory over Argentina thanks to a brace from Marcelo Moreno – who had gone ten internationals without a goal beforehand.

RONALD RALDES

JUAN ARANGO

10 MILLION
Yerry Mina became the first Colombian to join Barcelona in 2018, costing them £10m from Brazil's Palmeiras.

TEAM TRIVIA
GOING CARACAS FOR FOOTBALL

Baseball and boxing may have held more sway with Venezuelans in recent decades but football fever has been on the rise in the twenty-first century – given a big boost by the country staging its first Copa America in 2007. This not only saw extravagant investment in new stadia but also Venezuela's first Copa America victory since 1967 – and unprecedented progress into the knock-out stages. **Juan Arango**, a popular success in Spain with La Liga club RCD Mallorca, scored Venezuela's goal in a 4-1 quarter-final loss to Uruguay. However Venezuela have yet to qualify for the FIFA World Cup.

SCORING RECORD
FALCAO BITES BACK

Colombia captain **Radamel Falcao** made a remarkable recovery to play at the 2018 FIFA World Cup finals in Russia. Four years earlier it had been feared a knee injury might bring his goal-hungry career to a premature end. In 2009, FC Porto bought Falcao for £2m, and it proved a bargain as he led them to a 2011 treble of league, cup and UEFA Europa League. He scored a then record 17 goals in the 2010-11 UEFA Europa League campaign and, following a move to Spain's Atletico Madrid, repeated the Europa League triumph 12 months later.

RADAMEL
FALCAO

73

Keeping clean sheets for Colombia all the way through the 2001 Copa America was Oscar Cordoba, who went on to make 73 appearances between 1993 and 2006.

3

All three of Paraguayan Paulo Da Silva's international goals have come against Chile – twice on 21 November 2007 in Santiago and, almost nine years later, on 1 September 2016.

TOURNAMENT TRIVIA
RUID AWAKENING

Peru ended a 31-year wait to beat Brazil with a 1-0 win in the first round of the 2016 Copa America Centenario. It put Ricardo Gareca's side in the second round and eliminated Dunga's Brazilians. The goal was contentious, however, as Raul Ruidiaz seemed to knock the ball into the goal with his hand from Andy Polo's cross. Ruidiaz insisted he had used his thigh and denied comparisons to Diego Maradona's "Hand Of God" goal at the 1986 FIFA World Cup, claiming his strike was "thanks to God". Peru's previous win over Brazil – 2016 was only the fourth ever – had been in April 1985, when Julio Cesar Uribe got the only goal in a friendly in Brasilia. Their other Copa America defeats of Brazil were in 1953 and 1975.

TOURNAMENT TRIVIA
COOL DUDAMEL

Venezuela suffered some bad defeats when missing out on the 1998 FIFA World Cup. They ended with no wins and 13 defeats in 16 games, scoring 13 and conceding 41 goals. The losses included 4-1 to Peru, 6-1 to Bolivia and 6-0 to Chile, for whom Ivan Zamorano scored five. But their goalkeeper Rafael Dudamel had a moment to savour against Argentina in October 1996, when he scored with a direct free-kick late in the game. Venezuela still lost 5-2. Dudamel became Venezuela coach in April 2016 and, two months later, led them to the second round of the Copa America Centenario.

NATIONAL LEGEND
HIGHS AND LOWS FOR LOLO

Teodoro "Lolo" Fernandez scored six goals in two games for Peru at the 1936 Summer Olympics, including five in a 7–3 defeat of Finland and another in a 4-2 victory over Austria. But Peru were outraged when the Austrians claimed that fans had been invading the pitch and were even more upset when officials ordered the match to be replayed. Peru withdrew from the tournament in protest, while Austria went on to claim silver. But Fernandez and his team-mates had a happier ending at the Copa America three years later, with Peru crowned champions and Fernandez finishing as top scorer with seven goals.

TEODORO
FERNANDEZ

AFRICA

The African confederation organized its inaugural Cup of Nations in 1957, only a year after it was founded. Now with more than 50 member associations, it can justly claim to be largest of the international confederations, with a rich football history to match.

Founded: 1956

Number of Federations: 56

Headquarters: Cairo, Egypt

Most Continental Championship Wins: Egypt, 7 (1957, 1959, 1986, 1998, 2006, 2008, 2010)

5

UNAF (Northern Africa)

WAFU-UFOA
(West Africa)

CECAFA
(East Africa)

UNIFFAC
(Central Africa)

COSAFA
(Southern Africa)

Africa is split into five regional federations based on location, with one non-regional member, Reunion.

6

Six African nations competed in the 2010 FIFA World Cup, more than any other edition of the tournament. They were hosts South Africa, Algeria, Cameroon, Ivory Coast, Ghana and Nigeria.

Egypt became the first African team to enter a FIFA World Cup in 1934. Africa had to wait until 1978 for a win though, from Tunisia.

2

Nigeria became the first African side to reach consecutive FIFA World Cup knockout stages – in 1994 and 1998.

SAMUEL
ETO'O

18

Samuel Eto'o has scored more goals than anyone else in the Africa Cup of Nations (18).

NORTH AFRICA

The most successful regional federation within Africa, the north of the continent has produced the most successful Africa Nations Cup side of all time, Egypt, along with the first team to have ever won a FIFA World Cup match, Tunisia.

Country: Algeria
Joined FIFA: 1964
Most Appearances: Lakhdar Belloumi, 100
Top Scorer: Abdelhafid Tasfaout, 34
Honours: 2 Africa Cup of Nations (1990, 2019)

Country: Egypt
Joined FIFA: 1923
Most Appearances: Ahmed Hassan, 184
Top Scorer: Hossam Hassan, 69
Honours: 7 Africa Cup of Nations (1957, 1959, 1986, 1998, 2006, 2008, 2010)

Country: Libya
Joined FIFA: 1964
Most Appearances: Tarik El Taib, 77
Top Scorer: Fawzi Al-Issawi, 40
Honours: -

Country: Morocco
Joined FIFA: 1960
Most Appearances: Noureddine Naybet, 115
Top Scorer: Ahmed Faras, 42
Honours: 1 Africa Cup of Nations (1976)

Country: Sudan
Joined FIFA: 1948
Most Appearances: Muhannad El Tahir, 79
Top Scorer: Haytham Tambal, 20
Honours: 1 Africa Cup of Nations (1970)

Country: Tunisia
Joined FIFA: 1960
Most Appearances: Sadok Sassi, 116
Top Scorer: Issam Jemaa, 36
Honours: 1 Africa Cup of Nations (2004)

TOURNAMENT TRIVIA
MOKHTAR RUNS AMOK

Egypt had to play only two matches to qualify for the 1934 FIFA World Cup, becoming the first African representatives at the tournament. Both games were against a Palestine side under the British mandate – and the Egyptians won both games handsomely, 7-1 in Cairo and 4-1 in Palestine. Captain and striker Mahmoud Mokhtar scored a hat-trick in the first leg, a brace in the second. Turkey were also meant to contest qualifiers against the two sides, but withdrew, leaving the path to the finals free for Egypt.

4

Four nations founded CAF, but South Africa were expelled before they could join the other three competing in the first Africa Cup of Nations: Egypt, Ethiopia and Sudan.

ANATAR YAHIA

TOURNAMENT TRIVIA
REDS IN A ROW

When **Antar Yahia** was sent off for a second bookable offence, three minutes into stoppage-time of Algeria's 1-0 defeat to the USA at the 2010 FIFA World Cup, it meant at least one player had been sent off on eight consecutive days of the 2010 tournament – a record run for any FIFA World Cup. It was also the latest red card shown in any World Cup game not featuring extra-time, until Switzerland's Michael Lang saw red in the 94th minute against Sweden in 2018.

SALAH THE FOOTBALLING PHAROAH

Egypt winger **Mohamed Salah** established himself as one of the world's outstanding players on his way to the 2018 FIFA World Cup. Salah scored a hat-trick against Zimbabwe in the 2014 World Cup qualifiers before his goals for both Egypt and Swiss club Basel earned an £11m transfer to Chelsea. Salah ended up at Liverpool in 2017 and was voted footballer of the year by both the Football Writers Association and Professional Footballers Assocation; he might have achieved Champions League glory but for a shoulder injury early in Liverpool's defeat against Real Madrid in the final. However, he was on the scoresheet when Liverpool successfully claimed the title against Tottenham Hotspur a year later.

MOHAMED SALAH

TOURNAMENT TRIVIA
HAIL HALLICHE

Algeria became the first African nation to score four goals in one game at a FIFA World Cup finals when they defeated South Korea 4-2 at Porto Alegre in their Group H contest in the Brazil 2014 tournament. The Algerians went on to finish second in the group, behind winners Belgium, and thus qualified for the knock-out stages for the first time. In the second round they faced one of the tournament favourites, Germany, and Algeria only departed after losing a thrilling match 2-1 after extra time. Centre-back Rafik Halliche made eight FIFA World Cup appearances by the end of in 2014 – a new Algerian record.

1-0

Morocco were the first North African country to reach the second round of a FIFA World Cup in 1986, though they were knocked out, 1-0, by eventual finalists West Germany.

44

Mohamed Salah broke Liverpool's scoring record for a debut season and was the Premier League's top scorer with 32 league goals and 44 in all competitions in 2017-2018.

NATIONAL LEGEND
HOMEGROWN HERO

Of the six African countries at the 2010 FIFA World Cup, Algeria's was the only squad with an African coach – **Rabah Saadane**, in his fifth separate stint in charge since 1981. He previously led his country to the 1986 FIFA World Cup in Mexico, where they were also eliminated in the first round. Along with Honduras, the Algeria team of 2010 were one of only two countries failing to score a single goal. However, they did concede just twice in their three games: 1-0 defeats to Slovakia and the USA, and a surprise goalless draw with England – Algeria's first-ever FIFA World Cup clean sheet.

TOURNAMENT TRIVIA
MOROCCAN ROLL

It was in Mexico in 1986 that Morocco were the first African team to top a FIFA World Cup group, finishing above England, Poland and Portugal. Crucial was their 3-1 victory over Portugal in their final group game, following goalless draws against the other two teams – including an England side who lost captain Bryan Robson to a dislocated shoulder and vice-captain Ray Wilkins to a red card. **Abderrazak Khairi** scored two of the goals against Portugal, while Lothar Matthaus's winning strike for Germany came with just three minutes remaining.

RABAH SAADANE

ABDERRAZAK KHAIRI

Unlucky Morocco suffered a double defeat in Russia at the 2018 World Cup. The Moroccan FA had lodged a bid with FIFA for hosting rights to the 2026 finals. Despite an imaginative proposal, FIFA's Congress preferred a co-host bid from the United States, Canada and Mexico. The Atlas Lions had no better luck in the finals, going out at the group stage after losing to Iran and Portugal and drawing 2-2 with Spain, thanks to goals from **Khalid Boutaib** and Youssef En-Nesyri.

KHALID
BOUTAIB

TOURNAMENT TRIVIA
SORE LOSERS

Libya could claim the record for highest-scoring victory by an African side, having racked up a 21-0 lead over Oman during the Arab Nations Cup in April 1966. But the Oman players walked off with 10 minutes remaining, in protest at Libya being awarded a penalty, and played no further part in the competition. Sudan's biggest official win came a year earlier, when they hammered a Muscat and Oman side 15-0.

2

Morocco's 2-1 defeat to Saudi Arabia in 1994 was one of the last two games to be played simultaneously at a FIFA World Cup, without falling on a final match-day of a group. Belgium were beating the Netherlands 1-0 at the same time, with every team in Group F having still one game to play. At later tournaments, every match has been played separately until the climactic two fixtures of any group.

TOURNAMENT TRIVIA
TUMULTUOUS TIMES FOR FOOTBALL IN EGYPT

Football in Egypt has been in a difficult place since the political upheavals which saw the overthrow of Presidents Hosni Mubarak in 2011 and Mohamed Morsi and 2013. Street protests and stadia shutdowns have marred the domestic league, though there have been signs of progress, as the country successfully stepped in to host the 2019 Africa Cup of Nations. The national team is the Africa Cup of Nations most successful team – seven wins, but they have reached only three World Cups: in 1934, 1990 and 2018.

RIYAD
MAHREZ

2016
In spring 2016, Riyad Mahrez became the first African to be voted England's Footballer of the Year by his fellow professionals after helping minnows Leicester City to a surprise first Premier League title.

STAR PLAYER
MAHREZ THE MARVEL

When first approached by Leicester in January 2014, Algerian winger **Riyad Mahrez** thought it was Leicester Tigers rugby club showing interest, but he still signed for just £380,000. His slight build had raised doubts about his ability to thrive in England. The first Algerian to win a Premier League winners medal recalled growing up as a sports-mad "street footballer", saying: "I was always with a ball – that's why I was so skinny, I would miss dinner."

ESSAM EL HADARY 1

TOURNAMENT TRIVIA
OFFICIAL INFLUENCE

The first African to referee a FIFA World Cup final was Morocco's Said Belqola, who controlled the 1998 climax in which hosts France beat Brazil 3-0. Perhaps his most notable moment was sending off France's Marcel Desailly in the 68th minute – brandishing only the third red card to be shown in a FIFA World Cup final. Belqola was 41 at the time. He died from cancer just under four years later.

36

Morocco's qualification for the 1970 FIFA World Cup ended a 36-year African exile from the finals. No African countries played at the 1966 FIFA World Cup in England, with 16 possible candidate countries all boycotting the event because FIFA wanted the top African team to face a side from Asia or Oceania in a qualification play-off.

45

Egypt goalkeeper **Essam El Hadary**, at 45 years and 161 days, became the oldest player in World Cup history when he played in a 2-1 defeat by Saudi Arabia in 2018.

TOURNAMENT TRIVIA
ABOUD AWAKENING

After the political upheaval in Libya in 2011, little was expected of the country's footballers at the 2012 Africa Cup of Nations. Yet they brought some joy to supporters with a surprise 2-1 victory over Senegal in their final first-round match – the first time Libya had ever won an Africa Cup of Nations match outside their own country. Their kit bore the new flag of the country's National Transitional Council. Among the star performers were Ihaab al Boussefi – scorer of both goals against Senegal – and goalkeeper and captain **Samir Aboud**, at 39 the oldest player at the tournament.

SAMIR ABOUD

NATIONAL LEGEND
SO FARAS, SO GOOD

Ahmed Faras not only heads Morocco's all-time scoring charts, with 42 goals between 1965 and 1979, he was also the captain who lifted the country's only Africa Cup of Nations trophy in 1976 – and was named the tournament's best player after scoring three goals in six games. He had previously come on twice as a sub when Morocco made their FIFA World Cup finals debut in 1970, the first African representatives since 1934.

1934

Abdelrahman Fawzi became the first African footballer to score at a FIFA World Cup, when he pulled a goal back for Egypt against Hungary in the first round of the 1934 tournament.

NATIONAL LEGEND
STRIKING RIVALS

A homegrown hero regained top spot in Tunisia's scoring ranks after Gabes-born **Issam Jemaa** overtook Francileudo Santos to total 36 goals in 80 appearances between 2005 and 2014. Jemaa moved from Esperance to play his club football in France for Lens, Caen, Auxerre and Brest and in the Gulf for Kuwait SC, Sl-Salliya (Qatar) and Dubai CSC. By contrast, Brazil-born Santos did not visit Tunisia until his late teens and accepted citizenship at the age of 24 in 2004.

ISSAM JEMAA

107

SUB SAHARAN AFRICA

From the Super Eagles to the Black Stars, Bafana Bafana to Les Elephants, Sub-Saharan football has delivered some of the biggest African stars of all time, and even hosted the first African FIFA World Cup in South Africa, in 2010.

Country: South Africa
Joined FIFA: 1992
Most Appearances: Aaron Mokoena, 107
Top Scorer: Benni McCarthy, 32
Honours: 1 Africa Cup of Nations (1996)

Country: Ghana
Joined FIFA: 1958
Most Appearances: Asamoah Gyan, 106
Top Scorer: Asamoah Gyan, 51
Honours: 4 Africa Cup of Nations (1963, 1965, 1978 and 1982)

Country: Cameroon
Joined FIFA: 1962
Most Appearances: Rigobert Song, 137
Top Scorer: Samuel Eto'o, 56
Honours: 5 Africa Cup of Nations (1984, 1988, 2000, 2002, 2017)

Country: Nigeria
Joined FIFA: 1960
Most Appearances: Vincent Enyeama/Joseph Yobo, 101
Top Scorer: Rashidi Yakini, 37
Honours: 3 Africa Cup of Nations (1980, 1994, 2013) 1 Olympic Games (1996)

Country: Gabon
Joined FIFA: 1966
Most Appearances: Didier Ovono,112
Top Scorer: Pierre-Emerick Aubameyang, 24
Honours: -

Country: Mali
Joined FIFA: 1964
Most Appearances: Seydou Keita, 102
Top Scorer: Seydou Keita, 25
Honours: -

Country: Senegal
Joined FIFA: 1964
Most Appearances: Henri Camera, 99
Top Scorer: Henri Camera, 29
Honours: -

Country: Liberia
Joined FIFA: 1964
Most Appearances: George Weah, 53
Top Scorer: George Weah, 20
Honours: -

Country: Zimbabwe
Joined FIFA: 1965
Most Appearances: Peter Ndlovu, 100
Top Scorer: Peter Ndlovu, 38
Honours: -

Country: Cote D'Ivoire
Joined FIFA: 1964
Most Appearances: Didier Zokora, 123
Top Scorer: Didier Drogba, 65
Honours: 2 Africa Cup of Nations (1992, 2015)

Country: Zambia
Joined FIFA: 1964
Most Appearances: Kennedy Mweene, 124
Top Scorer: Godfrey Chitalu, 79
Honours: 1 Africa Cup of Nations (2012)

Country: Togo
Joined FIFA: 1964
Most Appearances: Emmanuel Adebayor, 87
Top Scorer: Emmanuel Adebayor, 32
Honours: -

Country: Botswana
Joined FIFA: 1978
Most Appearances: Joel Mogorosi, 86
Top Scorer: Jerome Ramatlhakwane, 24
Honours: -

1985
The first African country to win an official FIFA tournament was Nigeria, when their "Golden Eaglets" beat Germany 2-0 in the final of the 1985 World Under-17 Championships.

JOHN OBI MIKEL

STAR PLAYER
CAPTAIN COOL
John Obi Mikel captained Nigeria in a crucial 2018 World Cup tie against Argentina, despite having just been told his father had been kidnapped back home. The midfielder arranged to pay a £21,000 ransom but told neither his coach Gernot Rohr nor any of his team-mates of his distress and the pressure on him because, "I couldn't let 180 million Nigerians down." Mikel's father was later released unharmed after a gunfight between kidnappers and police. Nigeria lost the game 2-1 and were eliminated.

STAR PLAYER
BROTHERS IN ARMS

The Boateng brothers made FIFA World Cup history in playing against each other at the 2010 finals in South Africa. Both were also selected for the "replay" in 2014. In 2010 Jerome played left-back for Germany while elder half-brother **Kevin-Prince**, who had switched nationalities a month earlier, was in the Ghana midfield. Germany won 1-0 in South Africa while the return in Brazil ended up 2-2. Kevin-Prince was the only brother to play a full 90 minutes, in South Africa. He was substituted during the game in Brazil while Jerome was replaced during both games. In the total 180 minutes they were on the pitch together for "only" 117 minutes.

4

Ghana went through four different managers during qualifiers for the 2006 FIFA World Cup, with Serbian coach Ratomir Dujkovic finally clinching the country a place at the finals for the very first time.

KEVIN-PRINCE
BOATENG

NELSON
MANDELA

NATIONAL LEGEND
MAD FOR MADIBA

Apart from the Dutch and Spanish sides competing in the 2010 FIFA World Cup final, one of the star attractions in Johannesburg's Soccer City stadium on 11 July 2010 was South Africa's legendary former president **Nelson Mandela**. The frail 91-year-old – known affectionately by his tribal name of "Madiba" – was driven on to the pitch before the game in a golf cart and given a rapturous reception by the crowd. It marked his one and only public appearance at the tournament. He had been a high-profile presence at the FIFA vote in 2004 which awarded South Africa hosting rights for 2010.

NATIONAL LEGEND
GOING FOR A SONG

Two players have been sent off at two separate FIFA World Cups: Cameroon's Rigobert Song, against Brazil in 1994 and Chile four years later, and France's Zinedine Zidane – red-carded against Saudi Arabia in 1998 and against Italy in the 2006 final. Song's red card against Brazil made him the youngest player to be dismissed at a FIFA World Cup – he was just 17 years and 358 days old. Song, born in Nkanglikock on 1 July 1976, is Cameroon's most-apped player, with 137 appearances – including winning displays in the 2000 and 2002 finals of the Africa Cup of Nations.

NATIONAL LEGEND
JOLLY ROGER

Cameroon striker **Roger Milla**, famous for dancing around corner flags after each goal, became the FIFA World Cup's oldest scorer against Russia in 1994 – aged 42 years and 39 days. He came on as substitute during that tournament with his surname handwritten, rather than printed, on the back of his shirt. Milla, born in Yaounde on 20 May 1952, had retired from professional football for a year before Cameroon's president, Paul Biya, persuaded him to join the 1990 FIFA World Cup squad. He finally ended his international career after the 1994 FIFA World Cup in the United States, finishing with 102 caps and 28 goals to his name.

ROGER
MILLA

116

Zambians believe the world record for goals in a calendar year should belong to their own Godfrey Chitalu and not to Lionel Messi. In 2012, Messi scored 91 goals for Argentina and Barcelona, but the Zambia FA insists that Chitalu had scored 116 goals, apparently unnoticed abroad, in 1972.

15

Fifteen-year-old Samuel Kuffour became the youngest footballer to win an Olympic medal when Ghana took bronze at the 1992 Olympics in Barcelona – 27 days before his 16th birthday.

NATIONAL LEGEND
THE FOURMOST

The only two African footballers to play at four FIFA World Cups – and the only three to be named in the squads for four – are all from Cameroon. Striker Samuel Eto'o became the latest in 2014, after playing in 1998, 2002 and 2010. He emulated defender Rigobert Song, who was in the Cameroon team in 1994, 1998, 2002 and 2010. Goalkeeper Jacques Songo'o was named in the country's squads for the four FIFA World Cups between 1990 and 2002, but he only actually played in the 1994 and 1998 versions.

1992
Zimbabwe's leading scorer Peter Ndlovu was the first African footballer to appear in the English Premier League when he made his Coventry City debut in August 1992.

STAR PLAYER
GABON ON SONG

Gabon's leading international goalscorer **Pierre-Emerick Aubameyang** ended Yaya Toure's four-year reign as CAF African Footballer of the Year in 2016. Toure had joined Cameroon's Samuel Eto'o as a four-time winner, but Aubameyang's 41 goals for club Borussia Dortmund and country relegated him to second. Born in Laval, France, Aubameyang launched his career in Italy with AC Milan, and was the first Bundesliga player to win the award. Later he joined Arsenal in 2018 for a club record £56m. Aubameyang, who played once for France under-21s, made his Gabon debut in 2009.

PIERRE-EMERICK **AUBAMEYANG**

3

Ghanian Asamoah Gyan became the first African to score at three separate FIFA World Cups in 2014 and his 11 matches took him level with Cameroon's Francois Omam-Biyik.

NATIONAL LEGEND
SUPER FRED

In 2007, Frederic Kanoute became the first non-African-born player to be named African Footballer of the Year. The striker was born in Lyon, France, and played for France U-21s. But the son of a French mother and Malian father opted to play for Mali in 2004, scoring 23 goals in 37 appearances before retiring from international football after the 2010 Africa Cup of Nations. As well as going down in history as one of Mali's greatest-ever players, he is also a hero to fans of Spanish side CF Sevilla, for whom he scored 143 goals, winning two UEFA Cups along the way. Only three men have scored more goals for the club.

NATIONAL LEGEND
PRESIDENT GEORGE

George Weah made history in December 2017 when he became the first star African footballer to go on and become president of his country. In Liberia's first democratic handover in decades, Weah succeeded Ellen Johnson Sirleaf, Africa's first elected female president. Weah, raised in a slum in the capital Monrovia, is the only former FIFA World Player of the Year whose country has never qualified for the World Cup finals. He starred in attack for Monaco, Paris Saint-Germain, Milan, Chelsea and Manchester City and dipped into his own earnings to help pay his national team's travel costs and kit.

GEORGE **WEAH**

14

Cameroonian Roger Milla's goals in the 1990 FIFA World Cup helped him win the African Footballer of the Year award for an unprecedented second time – 14 years after he had first received the trophy.

7

Benni McCarthy of South Africa and Egypt's Hossam Hassan both scored seven goals in the 1998 Africa Cup of Nations. No player has scored more than five in a single tournament since then.

NATIONAL LEGEND
FIRST ADE

Togo's all-time leading goalscorer – and 2008 African Footballer of the Year – **Emmanuel Adebayor** was captain during the country's only FIFA World Cup finals appearance, in Germany in 2006. They failed to win a game, but Adebayor's European club career has been more successful, with stints in France with Metz and Monaco, Spain with Real Madrid in England with Arsenal, Manchester City, Tottenham and Crystal Palace. His time with Spurs was disrupted by a family row in which he accused his mother of witchcraft against him.

EMMANUEL ADEBAYOR

NATIONAL LEGEND
SHOOTING STAR

Peter Ndlovu ended his international career with 38 goals in 100 games for Zimbabwe between 1991 and 2007 – before being appointed the country's assistant manager in 2011. The man nicknamed "the Bulawayo Bullet" had spearheaded in 2004 the first Zimbabwe side to reach an Africa Cup of Nations finals, following that up with repeat qualification two years later. His international team-mwates included brother Adam and flamboyant ex-Liverpool goalkeeper Bruce Grobbelaar. Adam Ndlovu tragically died in a car accident near Victoria Falls in Zimbabwe in December 2012. Peter was also in the car and although he suffered very serious head injuries and broken bones he managed to survive.

PETER NDLOVU

DISCIPLINARY-RELATED
HISTORY LESSON

Senegal made unwanted World Cup history at the 2018 finals as the first country ever to be eliminated by yellow cards. The Lions of Teranga and Japan finished their group on four points but the tiebreaker came down to a new "fair play" regulation. They drew their match 2-2 and finished with the same points, goal difference and goals scored. But Senegal "lost" 6-5 on bookings so Japan went into the second round, and Senegal went home.

DIDIER DROGBA

NATIONAL LEGEND
HOT DROG

Didier Drogba may have been raised in France but he was born in Ivory Coast and remains one of the African country's favourite sons for his actions both on and off the pitch. The Ivory Coast captain has a record 65 goals in 104 appearances for the Elephants. He has been credited with influence off the pitch, too, when he called for a ceasefire in the civil war-torn nation. He also pushed for an Africa Cup of Nations qualifier against Madagascar in June 2007 to be moved from the capital Abidjan to rebel army stronghold Bouake, in an effort to encourage reconciliation.

DISCIPLINARY-RELATED
KNOCKED OUT ON PENALTIES

Botswana goalkeeper and captain Modiri Marumo was sent off in the middle of a penalty shoot-out against Malawi in May 2003, after punching the opposing goalkeeper Philip Nyasulu in the face. Botswana defender Michael Mogaladi had to go in goal for the rest of the shoot-out, which Malawi won 4-1. "I over-reacted in an exchange of words between myself and my counterpart," admitted Marumo. "I hope my apology would be recognised and I pledge my commitment in serving the nation."

ASIA & OCEANIA

Asia will host the World Cup for the second time when the Gulf state of Qatar stages football's greatest showpiece in 2022. This will enhance the increasingly high status of the Asian game, allied to the remarkable investment in football emerging from China.

AFC

Confederation Founded:
1954

Number of Federations: 47

Headquarters: Bukit Jalil, Kuala Lumpur, Malaysia

Most Continental Ch'ship Wins: Japan, 4

OFC

Confederation Founded:
1966

Number of Federations: 11
(+3 non–FIFA members)

Headquarters: Auckland, New Zealand

Most Continental Ch'ship Wins: New Zealand, 5

88

The Indian national side qualified for the 1950 FIFA World Cup in Brazil but withdrew due to lack of funding.

2022's FIFA World Cup in **Qatar** will be the first time for 88 years – since 1934 – that the host nation will never have played at the tournament.

ALI
DAEI

10

For the 60th anniversary of its foundation in 2014, the AFC created a Hall of Fame for Asian players, inducting ten players to begin with, including **Ali Daei** (Iran), **Harry Kewell** (Australia) and Yasuhiko Okudera (Japan).

1964

In 1964, Israel won the Asian Cup. The nation were expelled from the federation though and later joined UEFA.

HARRY
KEWELL

The Asian Football Confederation was founded by 12 members, but has since grown to 47.

12

AUSTRALIA

Driven by new generations of players, many based with top European clubs, Australia have become regular FIFA World Cup qualifiers and in 2015 hosted and lifted the AFC Asian Cup for the first time.

Joined FIFA: 1922

Biggest Win:
31-0 vs. American Samoa, 2001

Highest FIFA Ranking: 14

Home Stadium:
Stadium Australia, Sydney

Honours:
4 OFC Nations Cups (1980, 1996, 2000, 2004), 1 Asian Cup (2015)

STAR PLAYER
A MILE AHEAD

Australia captain **Mile Jedinak** has scored his country's last three FIFA World Cup goals – all from the penalty spot. He found the net in their 3-2 defeat to the Netherlands in 2014, then four years later scored in a 2-1 defeat to France and a 1-1 draw with Denmark before Australia bowed out in the first round. Midfielder Jedinak had scored a hat-trick to secure Australia's place in Russia – including two penalties – when Honduras were beaten 3-1 in November 2017 play-off following a goalless first leg.

MILE JEDINAK

NATIONAL LEGEND
NATIVE HERO

Harry Williams holds a proud place in Australian football history as the first Aboriginal player to represent the country in internationals. He made his debut in 1970 and was part of the first Australian squad to compete at a FIFA World Cup finals, in West Germany in 1974. Despite a draw against Chile, Australia finished bottom of their group in 1974, losing to both East Germany and eventual champions West Germany.

HARRY WILLIAMS

TOURNAMENT TRIVIA
ARNOLD ON THE SPOT

Australia were otherthrown as AFC Asian Cup holders at the 2019 tournament, knocked out 1-0 in the quarter-finals by the hosts the United Arab Emirates. The Socceroos coach was Graham Arnold, who had scored 19 goals in 54 appearances for Australia as a striker before being Guus Hiddink's assistant between 2000 and 2006 and taking charge briefly in 2007. Australia's 2019 second-round victory over Uzbekistan, 4-2 on penalties, meant Arnold had been involved in all seven of the country's international penalty shoot-outs – including four as a player, as assistant manager for the 2006 FIFA World Cup qualifying play-off triumph over Uruguay and their 2007 AFC Asian Cup quarter-final loss to Japan.

5

Tim Cahill's total of five FIFA World Cup goals is only three fewer than all other Australians put together.

TIM CAHILL

CAHILL MAKES HISTORY

Tim Cahill scored Australia's first two World Cup goals, netting in the 84th and 89th minutes of a comeback 3-1 win over Japan in 2006. But he saved the most spectacular for last, a first-time volley in a 3-2 defeat to the Netherlands in 2014. Cahill also received his second yellow card of the competition later in that game and so missed Australia's final match. He scored twice in 2006, once in 2010 – but was also red-carded – and twice in 2014. He retired from international football in November 2018, having won 108 caps and scored 50 goals – more than half of them (26) with his head.

MOST APPEARANCES:

1 Mark Schwarzer, 109
2 Tim Cahill, 108
3 Lucas Neill, 96
4 Brett Emerton, 95
5 Alex Tobin, 87

29

Damian Mori's then-Australian record tally of 29 goals, in just 45 internationals, included no fewer than five hat-tricks: trebles against Fiji and Tahiti, four-goal hauls against the Cook Islands and Tonga, and five in Australia's 13-0 trouncing of the Solomon Islands in a 1998 FIFA World Cup qualifier.

TOP SCORERS:

1 Tim Cahill, 50
2 Damian Mori, 29
3 Archie Thompson, 28
4 John Aloisi, 27
5 Attila Abonyi, 25

SCORING RECORD
AUSTRALIA'S SHOOT-OUT RECORD

Australia are the only team to reach the FIFA World Cup finals via a penalty shoot-out – in the final qualifying play-off in November 2005. They had lost the first leg 1-0 to Uruguay in Montevideo. Mark Bresciano's goal levelled the aggregate score, which remained 1-1 after extra-time. Goalkeeper **Mark Schwarzer** made two crucial saves as Australia won the shoot-out 4-2, with John Aloisi scoring the winning spot-kick. Schwarzer passed Alex Tobin to become Australia's most-capped footballer with his 88th appearance, in January 2011, in the AFC Asian Cup final defeat to Japan. Tobin had been in defence when Schwarzer made his Australia debut against Canada in 1993.

3.69

Damian Mori didn't play at a FIFA World Cup but did claim a world record for scoring the fastest recorded goal ever – after just 3.69 seconds for his club side Adelaide City against Sydney United in 1996.

91

Tough-tackling Australia veteran Lucas Neill had to wait until his 91st international appearance before scoring his first goal for his country: the final strike in a 4-0 victory over Jordan in June 2013 that boosted their chances of reaching the 2014 FIFA World Cup.

1000

In March 2015, Mile Jedinak had scored Australia's 1,000th international goal, a stunning free-kick in a 2-2 friendly draw against world champions Germany.

MARK SCHWARZER

3

Graham Poll, in 2006, was not the first referee at a FIFA World Cup to show the same player three yellow cards. It happened in another game involving Australia, when their English-born midfielder Ray Richards was belatedly sent off against Chile at the 1974 FIFA World Cup.

NATIONAL LEGEND
BATTLER WILS

Peter Wilson was born in England but, after emigrating to Australia in 1969, the defender captained his adoptive country at their first FIFA World Cup in 1974. He became the first Australian to reach 50 caps, in 1976, before retiring from international football in 1979 with 65 appearances – a tally only overtaken in 1993, by Paul Wade. Another mainstay of the Australia side of that era was midfielder and later broadcaster Johnny Warren, after whom the annual award for the Australian A-League's best player is named.

PETER WILSON

JAPAN

Japan co-hosted the 2002 FIFA World Cup – where the team reached the second round for the first time. And AFC Asian Cup wins in 1992, 2000, 2004 and 2011 were celebrated keenly as proof of surging standards.

Joined FIFA: 1950

Biggest Win:
15-0 vs. Phillippines, 1967

Highest FIFA Ranking: 9

Home Stadium:
Rotation

Honours:
4 Asian Cups (1992, 2000, 2004, 2011)

50
Shinji Okazaki's 50 goals for his country include hat-tricks in consecutive matches, against Hong Kong and Togo in October 2009.

NATIONAL LEGEND
HONDA INSPIRES

Skilful midfielder **Keisuke Honda** is Japan's highest scorer at FIFA World Cups – four goals – and the only Japanese player to find the net at three finals. It started at South Africa in 2010, when he scored in Japan's victories over Cameroon and Denmark, and continued with a goal in the defeat against Costa Rica in Brazil four years later. Honda won two man-of-the-match awards at the 2010 FIFA World Cup and was named player of the tournament when Japan won the 2011 AFC Asian Cup. After Japan had exited the tournament in Russia, Honda retired from international football.

KEISUKE HONDA

STAR PLAYER
OKAZAKI'S A-OK

Shinji Okazaki became only the fifth man to reach 100 appearances for Japan, in a match against Syria in March 2016. Two months later, the striker ended the season with an English Premier League winner's medal, having scored five goals in Leicester City's 5,000-1 triumph (and one in the FA Cup). He was on the scoresheet during Japan's 3-1 victory over Denmark in Bloemfontein at the 2010 FIFA World Cup, along with Keisuke Honda and Yasuhito Endo – the first time an Asian side had scored three goals in one FIFA World Cup match since Portugal had beaten North Korea 5-3 in the 1966 quarter-finals.

SHINJI OKAZAKI

TOP SCORERS:

1 Kunishige Kamamoto, 75

2 Kazuyoshi Miura, 55

3 Shinji Okazaki, 50

4 Hiromi Hara, 37
= Keisuke Honda, 37

50
Japan's second most prolific international goalscorer Kazuyoshi Miura is also the world's oldest active professional high-level footballer. On 12 March 2017, aged 50 years and 14 days, Miura scored for Yokohama FC against Thespakusatsu Gunma in J.League Division 2.

TOURNAMENT TRIVIA
POLITICAL FOOTBALL

Japan were surprise bronze medallists in the football tournament at the 1968 Olympic Games in Mexico City. Star striker Kunishige Kamamoto finished top scorer overall with seven goals. He remains Japan's all-time leading scorer, with 80 goals in 84 matches (Japan consider Olympic Games matches full internationals). Since retirement, he has combined coaching with being elected to Japan's parliament and serving as vice-president of the country's football association.

At Russia 2018, Keisuke Honda came on after 72 minutes of the Group H game against Senegal and, six minutes later, scored the second equaliser in a 2-2 draw.

SCORING RECORD
FIFTEEN SECONDS OF FAME

Japan fell at the last hurdle in their attempt to win a fifth AFC Asian Cup title in 2019, losing 3-1 in the final to surprise champions Qatar. This was the first time Japan had reached the final but failed to win. Japan had warmed up for the tournament in style, beating Kyrgyzstan 4-0 in November 2018 in a game notable for their two goals in a mere 15 seconds to go three ahead. Substitute striker Yuya Osako hit a 72nd-minute strike, and fellow sub and midfielder Shoya Nakajima found the net almost immediately after the restart with his first touch after coming on.

TOURNAMENT TRIVIA
CLEAN BREAK

Japan reached the second round for the third time in the 2018 FIFA World Cup in Russia and almost enjoyed a first quarter-final appearance, despite having replaced their manager Valid Halilhodzic with former Japan international wmidfielder Akira Nishino just two months before the tournament. They led Belgium 2-0 in the second round, including a second goal of the tournament for Takashi Inui, but Belgium scored twice to equalize. Keisuke Honda then saw a long-range stoppage-time shot saved by Thibaut Courtois. Belgium counter-attacked from the resulting corner and Nacer Chadli scored to win the game.

YASUHITO ENDO

NATIONAL LEGEND
THE ENDO

Midfielder **Yasuhito Endo** scored the opening goal of Japan's defence of their AFC Asian Cup crown, as they began the 2015 tournament with a 4-0 win over debutants Palestine. However, after winning their three group matches, without conceding a goal, Japan lost next time out, a quarter-final against the United Arab Emirates, on penalties after a 1-1 draw. It was their worst showing at the AFC Asian Cup for 19 years. Endo had the consolation of becoming Japan's first international to reach 150 caps, but he left the international stage after the finals, having scored 15 times in 152 games.

No team scored more goals in one AFC Asian Cup tournament than Japan's 21 in six matches in Lebanon in 2000. Nine different players scored, with Akinori Nishizawa and Naohiro Takahara getting five apiece, including hat-tricks in the 8-1 first round win against Uzbekistan. One goal settled the final against Saudi Arabia and it came from Shigeyoshi Mochizuki.

2018
Japan's fans and players impressed many at the 2018 FIFA World Cup with their displays – and their manners. Japanese fans were filmed meticulously tidying up after themselves in the stands at full-time of their games, and the support staff took a similar approach to their dressing rooms.

Striker **Tadanari Lee** made his international debut in the first-round match against Jordan – and conjured perfect timing for his first Japan goal, with 11 minutes of extra-time left in the final against Australia.

TADANARI LEE

SOUTH KOREA

"Be the Reds!" was the rallying cry of South Korea's fervent fans as they co-hosted the 2002 FIFA World Cup – and saw their energetic team become the first Asian side to reach the semi-finals, ultimately finishing fourth.

Joined FIFA: 1948
Biggest Win:
vs. Nepal, 16-0, 2003
Highest FIFA Ranking: 17
Home Stadium: Seoul World Cup Stadium
Honours: 2 Asian Cups (1956, 1960)

NATIONAL LEGEND
HONG SETS FIFA WORLD CUP RECORD

Defender **Hong Myung-Bo**, on home soil, captained South Korea to fourth place in the 2002 FIFA World Cup and was voted third-best player of the tournament. As coach of the U-23 squad, Hong led South Korea to Olympic bronze at the 2012 Summer Games – beating Japan 2-0 in the medal play-off. Hong became South Korea's national team coach in June 2013, and was in charge at the 2014 FIFA World Cup, where one group game pitted him against Belgium and their coach Marc Wilmots – the pair having played against each other at the 1998 finals.

HONG
MYUNG-BO

22M
Son Heung-Min became Asia's most expensive footballer when English club Tottenham Hotspur bought him for £22m from Germany's Bayer Leverkusen in 2015.

200
Kim Byung-Ji set a new South Korean top-flight landmark of 200 clean sheets in June 2012, at the age of 42.

4
South Korea defender Hong Myung-Bo was the first Asian footballer to appear in four consecutive FIFA World Cup finals tournaments, from 1990 to 2002.

NATIONAL LEGEND
PARK LIFE

Park Ji-Sung can claim to be the most successful Asian footballer of all time. He became the first Asian player to lift the UEFA Champions League trophy when his club Manchester United beat Chelsea in 2008, despite missing the final. Park shares the Korean record for most FIFA World Cup goals – three – with Ahn Jung-Hwan, who got all of his in Germany in 2006. Park became the eighth South Korean to reach a century of caps when he captained the side in their 2011 AFC Asian Cup semi-final defeat to Japan, before announcing his international retirement to allow a younger generation to emerge.

PARK
JI-SUNG

TOP SCORERS:

1 Cha Bum-Kun, 58
2 Hwang Sun-Hong, 50
3 Park Lee-Chun, 36
4 Kim Jae-Han, 33
= Lee Dong-Gook, 33

STAR PLAYER
HERE COMES THE SON

South Korea's latest hero, **Son Heung-Min**, scored the consolation against Mexico and the second against Germany at the 2018 FIFA World Cup, minutes after Kim Young-Gwon's injury-time opener. Son tapped the ball into an empty net after German goalkeeper Manuel Neuer was stranded at the other end of the pitch. That lifted Son to 23 goals in 70 internationals and put him level with Park Ji-Sung and Ahn Jung-Hwan on three FIFA World Cup goals for South Korea. He was picked for the 2014 FIFA World Cup despite his former international footballer father Son Woong-Chun believing he needed more time to develop as a player.

SON HEUNG-MIN

3

Park Ji Sung became the first Asian footballer to score at three successive FIFA World Cups – beginning on home turf in 2002, when his goal broke the deadlock in a first-round game against Portugal, putting South Korea through to the knock-out stages for the first time ever.

NATIONAL LEGEND
CHA BOOM AND BUST

Even before South Korea made their FIFA World Cup breakthrough under Guus Hiddink, the country had a homegrown hero of world renown – thunderous striker **Cha Bum-Kun**, known for his fierce shots and suitable nickname "Cha Boom". He helped pave the way for more Asian players to make their name in Europe by signing for German club Eintracht Frankfurt in 1979 and later played for Bundesliga rivals Bayer Leverkusen. His achievements in Germany included two UEFA Cup triumphs – with Frankfurt in 1980 and with Leverkusen eight years later – while his performances helped make him a childhood idol for future German internationals such as Jurgen Klinsmann and Michael Ballack.

NATIONAL LEGEND
SPIDER CATCHER

Goalkeeper **Lee Woon-Jae** – nicknamed "Spider Hands" – made himself a national hero by making the crucial penalty save that took co-hosts South Korea into the semi-finals of the 2002 FIFA World Cup. He blocked Spain's fourth spot-kick, taken by winger Joaquin, in a quarter-final shoot-out. Lee, also played in the 1994, 2006 and 2010 FIFA World Cups, provided more penalty saves at the 2007 AFC Asian Cup – stopping three spot-kicks in shoot-outs on South Korea's way to third place. Lee's form restricted his frequent back-up, Kim Byung-Ji, to just 62 international appearances.

LEE WOON-JAE

TOURNAMENT TRIVIA
MILITARY GAMES

South Korea's players – captained by Tottenham Hotspur's Son Heung-Min – were granted lifelong immunity from the national requirement of two years' military service after winning the men's football tournament at the 2018 Asian Games in Indonesia, defending their title from 2014. Son was among three permitted over-23 players, but the star of the show was fellow striker Hwang Ui-Jo. He scored nine times in seven games to finish top scorer. South Korea beat Japan 2-1 after extra-time in the final thanks to strikes from left-winger Lee Seung-Woo and striker Hwang Hee-Chan.

MOST APPEARANCES:

1 **Hong Myung-Bo**, 136
2 **Cha Bun-Kun**, 134
3 **Lee Woon-Jae**, 133
4 **Lee Young-Pyo**, 127
5 **Kim Ho-Kon**, 124
= **Yoo Sang-Chui**, 124

CHA BUM-KUN

34

South Korea have played more FIFA World Cup games than any other Asian country, taking their tally to 34 with three first-round games in 2018.

ASIA : OTHER TEAMS

Iran won all 13 matches across their hat-trick of AFC Asian Cup triumphs in 1968, 1972 and 1976.

13

The lesser-known Asian footballing nations may well be the countries in which true football obsession has yet to take hold, but competition between, and achievements by, these teams are no less vibrant.

Country: Iraq
Joined FIFA: 1950
Most Appearances: Younis Mahmoud, 148
Top Scorer: Hussein Saeed, 78
Honours: 1 Asian Cup (2007)

Country: China
Joined FIFA: 1931
Most Appearances: Li Weifeng, 112
Top Scorer: Hao Haidong, 41
Honours: -

Country: Kuwait
Joined FIFA: 1952
Most Appearances: Bader Al-Mutawa, 165
Top Scorer: Bashar Abdullah, 75
Honours: 1 Asian Cup (1980)

Country: Saudi Arabia
Joined FIFA: 1956
Most Appearances: Mohamed Al-Deayea, 178
Top Scorer: Majed Abdullah, 71
Honours: 3 Asian Cups (1984, 1988, 1996)

Country: Iran
Joined FIFA: 1948
Most Appearances: Javad Nekounam, 151
Top Scorer: Ali Daei, 109
Honours: 3 Asian Cups (1968, 1972, 1976)

Country: Uzbekistan
Joined FIFA: 1994
Most Appearances: Server Djeparov, 126
Top Scorer: Maksim Shatskikh, 34
Honours: -

Country: Syria
Joined FIFA: 1937
Most Appearances: Mosab Balhous, 81
Top Scorer: Raja Rafe, 32
Honours: -

YOUNIS **MAHMOUD**

TOURNAMENT TRIVIA
IRAQ AND ROLL

One of the greatest – and most heart-warming – surprises of recent international football was Iraq's unexpected triumph at the 2007 AFC Asian Cup, barely a year after the end of the war that ravaged the country and forced them to play "home" games elsewhere. Despite disrupted preparations, they eliminated Vietnam and South Korea on the way to the 2007 final in which captain **Younis Mahmoud**'s goal proved decisive against Saudi Arabia. They were unable to retain their title four years later, losing to Australia in the quarter-finals.

TOURNAMENT TRIVIA
AHMED'S CONSOLATION

Qatar, the 2022 FIFA World Cup hosts, enjoyed their finest football triumph winning their first AFC Asian Cup in 2019. A team coached by Spaniard Felix Sanchez scored 19 goals and conceded only one – to Japan in their 3–1 final victory in Abu Dhabi - along the way. Their three goals came from Almoez Ali, Abdulaziz Hatem and Akram Hassan Afif. Ali scored four goals in 51 minutes in a 6-0 defeat of North Korea, and ended with a tournament record of nine goals. Uruguayan-born striker Sebastian Soria holds Qatar's record for most caps (123) and goals (40).

SCORING RECORD
SAUDIS LEAVE IT LATE

Saudi Arabia ended a run of 12 matches in the FIFA World Cup finals without a victory when they defeated Egypt 2-1 in their final group match in 2018. It was their first chance to celebrate a victory on the game's biggest stage since they defeated Belgium by 1-0 in June 1994. Egypt scored first, but the Saudis equalized with a penalty by midfielder Salman Al Faraj five minutes and 50 seconds in first half stoppage time – the latest goal in the first half of a finals tie since 1966. Their winner was also late – winger **Salem Muhamed Al-Dawsari** striking five minutes into second-half stoppage time.

SALAM MUHAMED
AL-DAWSARI

130,000
The highest attendance for an Asian team in a home FIFA World Cup qualifier was the 130,000 who watched Iran draw 1-1 with Australia in the Azadi Stadium, Tehran, on 22 November 1997.

CUP RECORDS
AFC FIGUREHEADS

Iran dominate AFC Asian Cup records although they reached "only" the 2019 semi-final in the United Arab Emirates. Iran have the most games played (131), wins (41), draws (19) and goals scored (131). Palestine, with one in two tournaments have the fewest goals scored, while China have conceded the most (65), Myanmar and Singapore have the fewest (four) in one appearance. Japan have won a record four championships; Iran and Saudi Arabia have three apiece.

The 2015 AFC Asian Cup set a remarkable international tournament record for consecutive matches without a draw. All 24 matches in the group stage and then the first two quarter-finals turned up positive results after 90 minutes.

TOURNAMENT TRIVIA
CHINA YET TO REALISE POTENTIAL

China have qualified just once for the FIFA World Cup, in 2002, but they suffered in the finals, failing to score in defeats by Costa Rica (2-0), Brazil (4-0) and Turkey (3-0). That squad included record caps-holder Li Weifeng (112 appearances) and leading scorer Hao Haidong (37 goals). They were one of a record three teams (along with Japan and South Korea) to complete the first round of the 2015 AFC Asian Cup with three wins out of three and no goals conceded, the first time China had achieved maximum points in an opening stage. Under French coach Alain Perrin they lost 2-0 to eventual champions Australia in the quarter-finals.

OMAR
KHARBIN

NATIONAL LEGEND
PRIDE OF SYRIA

In 2017, **Omar Kharbin** became the first Syrian to be named AFC Player of the Year. The free-scoring winger helped his Saudi Arabian club Al-Hilal to their first domestic league title in six years, and to be AFC Champions League runners-up to Japan's Urawa Red Diamonds. Kharbin, who made his debut as a 15-year-old for Al-Wahda in his home city of Damascus, also equalised for Syria in a 2019 AFC Asian Cup first-round defeat by defending champions Australia. Qatari defender Abdelkarim Hassan, a 2019 AFC Asian Cup winner, claimed the 2018 award.

NATIONAL LEGEND
HAPPY DAEI

Iran striker **Ali Daei** ended his career having scored 109 times for Iran in 149 internationals between 1993 and 2006 – though none of his goals came during FIFA World Cup appearances in 1998 and 2006. He is also the all-time leading scorer in the AFC Asian Cup, with 14 goals, despite failing ever to win the tournament. His time as national coach was less auspicious – he lasted only a year from March 2008 to March 2009 before being fired, as Iran struggled in qualifiers for the 2010 FIFA World Cup.

ALI
DAEI

4

Four teams carry the name of China. The China national team receives the most attention, but Hong Kong (a former British colony) and Macau (a former Portuguese colony) both retain their autonomous status for football – as Hong Kong China and Macau China respectively. Taiwan competes in the FIFA World Cup and other competitions as Chinese Taipei.

1938

The first Asian country to play in a FIFA World Cup finals was Indonesia, who played in France in 1938 as the Dutch East Indies. The tournament was a straight knockout and, on 5 June in Reims, Hungary beat them 6-0.

TOURNAMENT TRIVIA
BHUTAN DO THE BEATING

Bhutan enjoyed an unprecedented winning streak in March 2015. The world's then-lowest-ranked nation had won only two official internationals in 34 years before they beat Sri Lanka twice in a two-legged 2018 FIFA World Cup qualifier. Tshering Dorji scored the only goal of the first leg and the nation's only professional footballer – **Chencho Gyeltshan** – struck both in a 2-1 victory a week later. The Himalayan nation reached the second round of the AFC qualification for the first time, but lost all eight matches with a goal difference of -52.

4-0

On the same day that Brazil and Germany contested the FIFA World Cup final on 30 June 2002, the two lowest-ranked FIFA countries were also taking each other on. Asian side Bhutan ran out 4-0 winners over CONCACAF's Montserrat.

CHENCHO
GYELTSHAN

NATIONAL LEGEND
ONE OF BARCA'S BEST

The first Asian footballer ever to play for a European club was also, for almost a century, the all-time leading scorer for Spanish giants Barcelona, before being finally overtaken by Lionel Messi in March 2014. Paulino Alcantara, from the Philippines, scored 369 goals in 357 matches for the Catalan club between 1912 and 1927. He made his debut aged just 15, and remains Barcelona's youngest-ever first-team player. Alcantara was born in the Philippines, but had a Spanish father, and appeared in internationals for Catalonia, Spain and the Philippines, for whom he featured in a record 15-2 trouncing of Japan in 1917.

TOURNAMENT TRIVIA
FIRST ROUND FIRSTS

In January 2019, India finally ended a 55-year wait for victory in the AFC Asian Cup finals when they defeated Thailand 4-1 in what was also their biggest ever win in the competition. Two goals from Sunil Chhetri took his overall tally for his country to a national record 67. Those proved to be their only points of the tournament, however. Thailand responded by firing their Serbian coach Milovan Rajevac and replacing him with Sirisak Yodyardthai. They recovered to beat Bahrain and draw with hosts UAE and reach the knock-out stages for the first time in 47 years, before falling 2-1 to China in the second round.

Iran's Ali Daei became the first footballer to score a century of international goals, when his four in a 7-0 defeat of Laos on 17 November 2004 took him to 102.

MAKSIM
SHATSKIKH

NATIONAL LEGEND
UAE KO ZAGALLO

Brazilian great Mario Zagallo, who won the FIFA World Cup as both player and manager, coached the United Arab Emirates when they qualified for their one and only FIFA World Cup finals in 1990. But despite his success in the Asian qualifiers, he was sacked on the eve of the FIFA World Cup itself. Zagallo was replaced by Polish coach Bernard Blaut, whose UAE team lost all three matches at Italia 90. Other big names to have managed the UAE over the years include Brazil's Carlos Alberto Parreira (another FIFA World Cup winner with Brazil), England's Don Revie and Roy Hodgson, Ukraine's Valery Lobanovsky and Portugal's Carlos Queiroz.

NATIONAL LEGEND
MAXIMUM MAKSIM

Uzbekistan's record marksman **Maksim Shatskikh** retired from international football after winning his 61st cap in a friendly against Oman in 2014. He had equalled previous top scorer Mirjalol Qosimov's 31-goal tally in a 7-3 defeat of Singapore in June 2008 and also holds the Uzbek single-game record with five goals against Taiwan in 2007. At Ukraine's Dynamo Kiev, Shatskikh joined ex-Alania Vladikvkaz striker Qosimov as the only Uzbeks to score in UEFA club competition. Qosimov was twice national coach, leading them to the 2015 AFC Asian Cup quarter-finals. The nation's most-capped player remains forward Serjer Deparov, who retired in 2017 on 128 caps.

1934
Palestine, then under British rule, were the first Asian team to enter the FIFA World Cup qualifiers. They lost 7-1 away to Egypt on 16 March 1934.

NATIONAL LEGEND
WORTH HIS KUWAIT IN GOLD

Bader Al-Mutawa is both Kuwait's most-capped player and leading goalscorer. He moved to 156 appearances and 51 goals for his country in September 2015, having made his debut 14 years earlier. He also finished runner-up as 2006 AFC Asian Footballer of the Year – having mistakenly been named third initially. Unfortunately for Al-Mutawa, his national team career was interrupted in 2015 when Kuwait was suspended from international football by FIFA – a decision which also cost Kuwait staging rights for the 2019 AFC Asian Cup – it was switched to the UAE.

STAR PLAYER
SAMI TO THE FORE

Sami Al-Jaber is one of Saudi Arabia's greatest players. Not only is he second-leading scorer with 44 goals, but he became only the second Asian player to appear at four FIFA World Cups when he started against Tunisia in Munich in 2006. He marked the occasion with his third FIFA World Cup goal, after previously netting in the 1994 and 1998 tournaments. Al-Jaber was also a key man for Saudi Arabia as the team won their third AFC Asian Cup title in 1996, beating the hosts UAE on penalties in the final.

SAMI
AL-JABER

BADER
AL-MUTAWA

OCEANIA

Football in Oceania can claim some of the most eye-catching football statistics – though not necessarily in a way many there would welcome, especially the long-suffering goalkeepers from minnow islands on the end of cricket-style scorelines.

Country: New Zealand
Joined FIFA: 1948
Most Appearances: Ivan Vicelich, 88
Top Scorer: Vaughan Coveny, 28
Honours: 5 OFC Nations Cups (1973, 1998, 2002, 2008 and 2016)

Country: Fiji
Joined FIFA: 1964
Most Appearances: Esala Masi, 52
Top Scorer: Esala Masi, 33
Honours: -

Country: Tahiti
Joined FIFA: 1989
Most Appearances: Angelo Tchen, 34
Top Scorer: Teaonui Tehau, 16
Honours: 1 OFC Nations Cup (2012)

STAR PLAYER
THE WOOD LIFE

Chris Wood scored four goals at the 2016 OFC Nations Cup, only one behind the tournament's top scorer Raymond Gunemba of Papua New Guinea – as New Zealand lifted the trophy for a record fifth time. Wood scored his first international goal in October 2010 in a 1-1 draw with Honduras – though received an instant yellow card for his celebration, which involved revealing underpants bearing his nickname "Woodzee". On 14 November 2014, for a friendly against China, he became New Zealand's second-youngest captain, aged 22 years and 343 days.

CHRIS WOOD

2

Ricki Herbert is one of only two New Zealand-born men to be national coach, along with Barrie Truman who was in charge between 1970 and 1976.

NATIONAL LEGEND
RETURNING RICKI

Ricki Herbert is the only New Zealander to reach two FIFA World Cup finals. A left-back at the 1982 tournament in Spain, he then coached the country to their second World Cup appearance, in 2010. This second qualifcation came after a play-off defeat of Asian Football Confederation representatives Bahrain. Herbert resigned in November 2013, and briefly was in charge of The Maldives. The man currently in charge – he replaced Anthony Hudson who resigned after the All Whites failed to qualify for the 2018 FIFA World Cup finals – is Swiss coach Fritz Schmid.

RICKI HERBERT

TOURNAMENT TRIVIA
TEHAU ABOUT THAT

Pacific Island underdogs Tahiti finally broke the stranglehold Australia and New Zealand had over the OFC Nations Cup by winning the tournament when it was held for the ninth time in 2012, following four previous triumphs for Australia and four for New Zealand. Tahiti scored 20 goals in their five games at the event in the Solomon Islands – 15 of which came from the Tehau family: brothers Lorenzo (five), Alvin and Jonathan Tehau (four each) and their cousin Teaonui (two). Steevy Chong Hue scored the only goal of the final, against New Caledonia, to give the team the trophy and a place at the 2013 FIFA Confederations Cup.

34

Commins Menapi is the Solomon Islands' record scorer, with 34 in 37 games between 2000 and 2009

COMMINS
MENAPI

31-0
American Samoa set an unwanted international record, losing 31-0 to Australia in April 2001 – two days after Australia had crushed Tonga 22-0.

24

Tahiti conceded a whopping 24 goals in three games of the FIFA Confederations Cup 2013. Ten came against Spain in one match.

ETIENNE
MERMER

TOURNAMENT TRIVIA
BAD LUCK OF THE DRAW

Despite featuring at only their second-ever FIFA World Cup – and their first since 1982 – New Zealand did not lose a game in South Africa in 2010. They drew all three first-round matches, against Slovakia, Italy and Paraguay. The three points were not enough to secure a top-two finish in Group F, but third-placed New Zealand did finish above defending world champions Italy. The only other three teams to have gone out despite going unbeaten in their three first-round group games were Scotland (1974), Cameroon (1982) and Belgium (1998).

TOURNAMENT TRIVIA
PAIA FIRE IN VAIN

No team from Oceania other than Australia or New Zealand has ever qualified for the men's football tournament at the Summer Olympic Games – but Fiji came close to reaching the 2012 event, only losing 1-0 to New Zealand in the final of the qualifying competition. The top scorers were the Solomon Islands, but they didn't make it out of their opening group. They recorded a best first-round goal difference of +12 – thanks to a 16-1 destruction of American Samoa, including seven goals by Ian Paia. However, defeats by Fiji and Vanuatu left them third in the four-team section.

NATIONAL LEGEND
RIGHT VAN MEN

Vanuatu's best performance at an OFC Nations Cup was their fourth place in 2007, but three years earlier they pulled off one of the tournament's biggest surprises, beating New Zealand 4-2 in a first-round clash. Recent star players included most-capped **Etienne Mermer**, who played 29 times as a striker and took over as national manager in 2017, and leading scorer Richard Iwai, who struck 19 goals for his nation and later took over as U23s coach. Vanuatu's biggest victory saw them defeat Kiribati 18-0 in July 2003, although one of Mermer's first games in charge was a December 2017 10-0 away win in Tuvalu.

17

Chris Wood made his New Zeland debut aged 17, against Tanzania, in June 2009 – the same year he became the fifth and youngest New Zealander to play in England's Premier League, for West Bromwich Albion.

125

CONCACAF

The passion of football in Central and North America and the Caribbean will be illustrated when the United States, Canada and Mexico stage the first three-way hosting of the FIFA World Cup in 2026. Their "United 2026" bid was backed by FIFA congress in Russia in June 2018.

Founded: 1961

Number of Federations: 41

Headquarters: Miami, United States

Most Continental Championship Wins: Mexico, 11

2026 FIFA WORLD CUP™

The Member Associations of

CANADA, MEXICO, USA

have been selected by the FIFA Congress to host the 2026 FIFA World Cup™

3

Come 2026, Mexico will have hosted or co-hosted the FIFA World Cup three times, more than any other nation.

4

There are four CONCACAF zones: North America, Central America, Caribbean and South America.

The best performance from a CONCACAF team in the FIFA World Cup was in 1930, where the USA came 3rd.

2000

Between them, Mexico and USA have won all but one CONCACAF Gold Cup. The other was won in 2000 by Canada.

The Mexican national team is the only CONCACAF team to win an official FIFA tournament by winning the 1999 FIFA Confederations Cup.

MEXICO

Mexico may well be the powerhouse of the CONCACAF region - they have missed out on the finals of the tournament just five times (in 1934, 1938, 1974, 1982 and 1990) - but they have always struggled to impose themselves on the international stage.

Joined FIFA: 1927

Biggest Win: 13-0 vs. Bahamas, 1987

Highest FIFA Ranking: 4

Home Stadium: Estadio Azteca, Mexico City

Honours: 11 CONFACAF Championships (1965, 1971, 1977, 1993, 1996, 1998, 2003, 2009, 2011, 2015, 2019)

HUGO **SANCHEZ**

NATIONAL LEGEND
VICTOR HUGO

Javier Hernandez may have overtaken Jared Borghetti to hold the record as Mexico's all-time leading goalscorer, but perhaps the country's most inspirational striker remains **Hugo Sanchez**, famed for his acrobatic bicycle-kick finishes and somersaulting celebrations. During spells in Spain with Atletico Madrid and Real Madrid he finished as La Liga's top scorer five years out of six between 1985 and 1990. He was less successful as Mexico coach from 2006 to 2008, the best result being third in the 2007 Copa America.

16

Only four countries – Argentina, Brazil, Germany and Italy – have more FIFA World Cup finals appearances than Mexico's 16.

NATIONAL LEGEND
INSPIRATIONAL IGNACIO

Ignacio Trelles, who turned 102 in July 2018, holds the record for most games in charge of Mexico – overseeing 50 wins in 106 games during three spells between 1958 and 1976. These included Mexico's first victory at a FIFA World Cup, beating Czechoslovakia 3-1 in 1962, although they departed Chile in the first round and again in England four years later. Bora Milutinovic was manager for 104 matches in two stints between 1983 and 1986 and from 1995 to 1997, including Mexico's run to the quarter-finals as stand-in hosts in 1986 after FIFA's original choice Colombia pulled out. Gerardo Martino took over as Mexico's latest coach in January 2019, their third Argentinian coach.

JARED **BORGHETTI**

TOP SCORERS:

1 Javier Hernandez, 51

2 Jared Borghetti, 46

3 Cuahtemoc Blanco, 39

4 Carlos Hermosillo, 35
= Luis Hernandez, 35

MAKING HIS MARQUEZ

Centre-back Rafael Marquez holds many of Mexico's records in the FIFA World Cup. His 19 matches in the finals are seven more than Javier Hernandez. He – along with Cuauhtemoc Blanco and Hernandez – are the only Mexican players to score in three World Cup finals. Also, at the age of 39 years and 139 days, Marquez is – by six days – the second oldest outfielder to start a FIFA World Cup knock-out match; he was beaten by England winger Stanley Matthews, against Uruguay in 1954.

MOST APPEARANCES:

1 Claudio Suarez, 177
2 Andreas Guardado, 158
3 Rafael Marquez, 146
= Pavel Pardo, 146
= Gerardo Torrado, 146

JAVIER HERNANDEZ

STAR PLAYER
LITTLE PEA FROM A POD

Javier Hernandez's goal against Costa Rica on 24 March 2017 saw him join Jared Borghetti as Mexico's leading scorer – both men with 46 goals from 89 games. Further goals have followed – as has Hernandez's 100-cap milestone – and he reached 50 goals with a strike against South Korea in the 2018 FIFA World Cup. In June 2010, playing against South Africa in the opening match, he became the third generation of his family to play at a FIFA World Cup.

3

Hugo Sanchez played for Mexico at three FIFA World Cups - 1978, 1986 and 1994 - and would surely have done so had they qualified in 1982 and 1990.

SUAREZ IS NUMBER TWO ALL-TIME

Only Egypt's Ahmed Hassan (184) played more internationals than Mexico defender **Claudio Suarez**, who made 177 appearances between 1992 and 2006. Suarez – nicknamed "The Emperor" – played in all of Mexico's four games at the 1994 and the 1998 FIFA World Cups, but had to miss the 2002 finals after suffering a broken leg. He was a member of the squad for the 2006 tournament in Germany, but did not play and retired after the finals.

CLAUDIO SUAREZ

42

Mexico's Manuel Rosas scored the first penalty ever awarded in the FIFA World Cup finals when he converted a 42nd-minute spot-kick in his country's match against Argentina in 1930.

5

In 2014 commanding centre-back Rafael Marquez became the first player to captain his country at four consecutive FIFA World Cups – a record he extended to five in Mexico's second-round tie against Brazil in 2018. He, with compatriot Antonio Carbajal and Germany's Lothar Matthaus, are the only men to play at five FIFA World Cup finals.

TOURNAMENT TRIVIA
SECOND ROUNDS OUT

Mexico have yet to go beyond the quarter-finals of the FIFA World Cup and their two last-eight visits, in 1970 and 1986, were only achieved when they hosted the tournament. Mexico's place at the 2018 finals in Russia owed plenty to winger **Hirving Lozano**, who top-scored with five goals in their qualifying campaign, including the only goal in a win over Panama in September 2017 that booked their place in Russia. He then got Mexico's challenge off to the ideal start with the only goal of their opening game, defeating defending champions Germany and winning himself the man of the match prize.

22

Mexico's shock 7-0 trouncing by Chile in the quarter-finals of the 2016 Copa America Centenario was their heaviest defeat in an official competition - and brought to an end a 22-match unbeaten run, a Mexican international record.

HIRVING LOZANO

UNITED STATES

Some of football's biggest names – from Pele to David Beckham – have graced league football in the United States which remains one of only 17 nations to have hosted the FIFA World Cup.

Joined FIFA: 1913

Biggest Win: 8-0 vs. Barbados, 2008

Highest FIFA Ranking: 4

Home Stadium: (Rotation)

Honours: 6 CONCACAF Championships (1991, 2002, 2005, 2007, 2013, 2017)

NATIONAL LEGEND
LANDON HOPE AND GLORY

The US's joint all-time leading scorer **Landon Donovan** was the star of their 2010 FIFA World Cup campaign, scoring three goals in four matches, including a stoppage-time winner against Algeria to help his team top Group C. His four games at the tournament meant he featured in 13 FIFA World Cup matches for the USA, two ahead of Earnie Stewart, Cobi Jones and DaMarcus Beasley. His goal in the second-round loss to Ghana also made him the USA's all-time top scorer in the finals, with five – one more than 1930 hat-trick hero Bert Patenaude and Clint Dempsey, who scored twice in 2014.

LANDON DONOVAN

3

Landon Donovan was the first man to score more than one hat-trick for the US, with four goals against Cuba in July 2003 and trebles versus Ecuador in March 2007 and Scotland in May 2012.

TIM HOWARD

NATIONAL LEGENDS
GLOVE STORIES

Five goalkeepers head the rankings for most international wins for the US men's team – led by ex-Manchester United and Everton stopper **Tim Howard** on 62, followed by Kasey Keller (53), Tony Meola (37), Brad Guzan (30) and Brad Friedel (27). Yet the order shifts when it comes to clean sheets, with Keller on top with 47, followed by Howard's 42, Meola's 32, Friedel's 24 and Guzan's 18. Keller claimed the most silverware with the US side, winning the CONCACAF Gold Cup three times, compared to two apiece for Howard and Meola.

TOP SCORERS:

1 **Landon Donovan,** 57
= **Clint Dempsey,** 57
3 **Jozy Altidore,** 42
4 **Eric Wynalda,** 34
5 **Brian McBride,** 30

148
No one has coached the USA men's team more often than Bruce Arena, who stepped down in October 2017, following the United States' shock failure to qualify for the 2018 FIFA World Cup. Arena was coach for a total of 148 matches.

19

Jozy Altidore became the United States' youngest scorer of an international hat-trick in a 3-0 victory over Trinidad and Tobago on 1 April 2009, aged 19 years and 146 days.

STAR PLAYER
MAGIC CHRISTIAN

Philadelphia native **Christian Pulisic** moved to Germany as a 16-year-old in 2015 to sign for Borussia Dortmund. He was joined there a year later by his cousin Will, a goalkeeper who has played for the USA's U-17s. In March 2017 Christian Pulisic scored the USA's fastest second-half goal, taking just 12 seconds after the restart to find the net in a 6-0 victory over Honduras. He became his country's youngest captain, aged 20 years and 63 days, against Italy in November 2018 and two months later was revealed to be the most expensive US footballer when it was announced he would be joining English club Chelsea in the summer for $73million or £58million.

17

Christian Pulisic became the United States' youngest international goalscorer when he netted against Bolivia, aged 17 years and 253 days, in May 2016.

2

The United States became the first CONCACAF nation to have two players each reaching a half-century of goals. Clint Dempsey equalled Landon Donovan's national record after scoring his 57th goal for his country in a 2-0 win over Costa Rica in July 2017.

CHRISTIAN PULISIC

MOST APPEARANCES:

1 **Cobi Jones**, 164
2 **Landon Donovan**, 157
3 **Michael Bradley**, 150
4 **Clint Dempsey**, 141
5 **Jeff Agoos**, 134

CLINT DEMPSEY

TOURNAMENT TRIVIA
ENGLAND STUNNED BY GAETJENS

The US's 1-0 win over England on 29 June 1950 ranks among the biggest surprises in FIFA World Cup history. England, along with hosts Brazil, were joint favourites to win the trophy. The US had lost their last seven matches, scoring just two goals. Joe Gaetjens scored the only goal, in the 37th minute, diving to head Walter Bahr's cross past goalkeeper Bert Williams. England dominated the game, but US keeper Frank Borghi made save after save. Defeats by Chile and Spain eliminated the US at the group stage, but their victory over England remains the greatest result in the country's football history.

SCORING RECORD
ALTIDORE OPENS THE FLOOD GATES

After **Jozy Altidore**'s hat-trick against Trinidad and Tobago in April 2009, he endured an 18-month barren spell between November 2011 and June 2013, when he scored the opener in a 4-3 win over Germany in a Washington DC friendly marking the 100th anniversary of the national team. Altidore then scored against Jamaica, Panama and Honduras to equal a national record of scoring four games in a row, joining William Lubb, Eric Wynalda, Eddie Johnson, Brian McBride and Landon Donovan. His scoring spree came in a 2012-13 season in which he also set a US record for goals in a European club league, with 31 for Dutch club AZ Alkmaar.

JOZY ALTIDORE

STAR PLAYER
WEAH ON THE WAY

In March 2018, striker **Tim Weah** became the first man born in the 21st century to appear in a full international for the United States when an 86th-minute substitute in a 1-0 friendly victory over Paraguay. Weah – the son of former World Footballer of the Year and now Liberian president George Weah – was born in New York City on 22 February 2000, but moved to join French club Paris Saint-Germain in 2014. One of Weah's U-17 team-mates, Werder Bremen forward Josh Sargent, became in November 2017, became the first man to be selected for US squads at U-17, U-20 and senior level in the same calendar year.

TIM WEAH

CONCACAF: OTHER TEAMS

Mexico and the United States are the powerhouses of the CONCACAF region, but with recent standout performances from Costa Rica in FIFA World Cup competition, and Panama making the 2018 tournament, the CONCACAF region is starting to boast more talent.

Country: Costa Rica
Joined FIFA: 1927
Most Appearances: Walter Centeno, 137
Top Scorer: Rolando Fonseca, 47
Honours: -

Country: Honduras
Joined FIFA: 1946
Most Appearances: Maynor Figueroa, 157
Top Scorer: Carlos Pavon, 57
Honours: -

Country: Canada
Joined FIFA: 1912
Most Appearances: Julian de Guzman, 89
Top Scorer: Dwayne De Rosario, 22
Honours: 1 CONCACAF Gold Cup, 2000

Country: El Salvador
Joined FIFA: 1938
Most Appearances: Alfredo Pacheco, 82
Top Scorer: Raul Diaz Arce, 39
Honours: -

Country: Trinidad & Tobago
Joined FIFA: 1964
Most Appearances: Angus Eve, 117
Top Scorer: Stern John, 70
Honours: -

Country: Panama
Joined FIFA: 1938
Most Appearances: Gabriel Gómez, 147
Top Scorer: Luis Tejada/Blas Pérez, 43
Honours: -

NATIONAL LEGEND
PAN-TASTIC TORRES

Panama made their FIFA World Cup finals debut in 2018 in Russia, captained by mighty centre-back **Roman Torres**, whose goal three minutes from time sealed a 2-1 win over Costa Rica and secured their place at the expense of the USA, who lost by the same scoreline to Trinidad and Tobago that night. Panama's president Juan Carlos Valera declared a national holiday to celebrate. Panama lost all three games in Russia – 3-0 to Tunisia, 6-1 to England and 2-1 to Tunisia – but their fans celebrated exuberantly in Nizhny Novgorod when substitute Felipe Baloy scored their first ever FIFA World Cup goal, against England.

ROMAN TORRES

TOURNAMENT TRIVIA
ALL FOR EL SALVADOR

El Salvador can claim to be the first Central American country – other than Mexico or the United States – to have qualified for the FIFA World Cup twice, doing so in 1970 and 1982. Recent years have brought more struggles, however, although left-back Alfredo Pacheco became his country's pride and most-capped player with 86 appearances between 2002 and 2013. His life ended tragically, however, with a life ban for match-fixing in 2013 followed by his fatal shooting at a petrol station two years later at the age of 33.

STERN JOHN

70

Only 13 men have netted more than the 70 international goals – in 115 matches – scored by Trinidad and Tobago's **Stern John** between his debut in 1995 and his final game in 2011.

STAR PLAYER
KEYLOR IS THE KEY

Costa Rica made their FIFA World Cup finals debut in 1990 and goalkeeper Luis Gabelo Conejo shared the best goalkeeper award with Argentina's Sergio Goycochea as his displays helped his team reach the knock-out stages. "Los Ticos" did even better in 2014 and while goalscorers Joel Campbell and Bryan Ruiz impressed, again a goalkeeper was crucial: **Keylor Navas** was named man of the match four times in five games. At the other end of the pitch, the first man to score twice for Costa Rica at FIFA World Cups was charismatic striker Paulo Wanchope, who found the net both times for his country when they lost the 2006 tournament's opening match 4-2 to hosts Germany. His record tally of 45 for Costa Rica was later passed by 47-goal striker Rolando Fonseca.

KEYLOR
NAVAS

NATIONAL LEGEND
DWAYNE'S REIGN

Canada's all-time leading goalscorer with 22, **Dwayne De Rosario** ended his footballing career in fitting style, playing in a January 2015 international friendly against Iceland – and he scored his team's goal in a 1-1 draw. De Rosario's 18-year playing career took in five different Major League Soccer clubs – including two stints with Toronto FC. He was part of the Canada side which lifted their first CONCACAF Gold Cup in 2000, although team-mate Carlo Carazzin finished tournament top scorer with four goals. De Rosario could also claim to be a footballing rarity in being vegetarian and was even vegan for 10 years until taking up fish in 2004.

DWAYNE
DE ROSARIO

99
Weighing 99kg, Panama's Roman Torres was the heaviest player at the 2018 FIFA World Cup, and he announced his international retirement after the tournament, having scored ten goals in 114 appearances.

NATIONAL LEGEND
CELSO LIKE HIS FATHER

Costa Rica playmaker Celso Borges was delighted, in 2014, to emulate his father by reaching the knock-out stages of the FIFA World Cup. He actually went one better as he scored the first penalty of Los Ticos' 5-3 shoot-out defeat of Greece in the second round. His Brazilian-born father, Alexandre Borges Guimares, played at the 1990 FIFA World Cup and set up the late winner scored by Hernan Medford against Sweden to take the FIFA World Cup finals debutants beyond the first round. The man affectionately known as "Guima" was Costa Rica's coach at both the 2002 and 2006 FIFA World Cup finals.

3 Canada, Haiti, Jamaica, Panama and Trinidad & Tobago all played three matches in their only World Cup finals appearances. Jamaica won once and Trinidad drew once; all their other games were lost.

9 The number of players from Costa Rica with 100 caps. In CONCACAF, only the United States – with 17 – and Mexico – 14 – have more.

2 In 2014 Costa Rica became only the second CONCACAF side, after Mexico in 1986, to go out of a FIFA World Cup without losing a game in regulation-time.

TOURNAMENT TRIVIA
BROTHERS IN ARMS

One of three brothers, Stoke City defensive midfielder **Wilson Palacios** was perhaps the most famous and acclaimed player in the first Honduras side to reach a FIFA World Cup in 28 years. Like the 1982 side, though, Reinaldo Rueda's men went three games without a win. An older brother, Milton Palacios, played 14 times as a defender for Honduras between 2003 and 2006. Both Jerry and Wilson made it into the 2014 FIFA World Cup squad, but it was not a happy time, especially for Wilson, who was sent off in the opener against France, and Honduras lost all three matches, but did at least score in the defeat against Ecuador.

WILSON
PALACIOS

FIFA WORLD CUP

France triumphed at the 2018 FIFA World Cup for the second time when Les Bleus climaxed a thrilling tournament in Russia by defeating surprise outsiders Croatia 4-2 in the final at Luzhniki stadium in Moscow.

First Held:
1930

Current Champions:
France

Most Wins:
Brazil, 5

Next Edition:
Qatar, 2022

210 teams entered qualification for the 2018 World Cup. The first in 1930 was the only one not to feature qualification.

The **2018 FIFA World Cup** saw stadia at 98 per cent capacity, the Fan Fests drew 7.7m visitors, Russia recorded more than 1m tourists and the tournament attracted more than three billion television viewers and record numbers to FIFA's digital channels.

180

169

There were 169 goals at the FIFA World Cup in 2018, an average of 2.64 a game.

KYLIAN
MBAPPE

Kylian Mbappe was named as Best Young Player at the 2018 FIFA World Cup finals after his explosive performances for France. Mbappe, 19, had cost Paris Saint-Germain €180m from Monaco the previous year and he justified the fee in Russia.

Estadio Azteca in Mexico is the only stadium to have hosted the World Cup final twice. Brazil's Maracana has hosted the deciding game twice, but in 1950, the tournament was held in a round-robin format with no set final.

FIFA WORLD CUP QUALIFIERS

To get to the greatest show on Earth, first countries must fight it out in regional confederations.

NATIONAL QUALIFICATION RECORD
GERMANY IN A HURRY

2014 world champions Germany were the only European team to complete their 2018 qualifying campaign with a 100 percent record, winning all 10 group stage matches. Coach Joachim Low's team scored 43 goals and conceded only four. Remarkably Germany's goals were shared among 22 players (including one own goal). Their top marksmen, Thomas Muller and Sandro Wagner, scored a modest five goals apiece. In between qualification, they won the Confederations Cup in 2017.

OFF THE MARK
Norjmoogiin Tsedenbal of Mongolia scored the first goal of the 2022 FIFA World Cup qualification campaign in a 2-0 defeat of Brunei Darussalam on 6 June 2019.

ROBERT LEWANDOWSKI

BIGGEST EVER QUALIFYING WINS:

1 **Australia 31-0 American Samoa,** 11 April 2001

2 **Australia 22-0 Tonga,** 9 April 2001

3 **Maldives 0-17 Iran,** 2 June 1997

4 **Australia 13-0 Solomon Islands,** 11 June 1997

= **New Zealand 13-0 Fiji,** 16 August 1981

= **Fiji 13-0 American Samoa,** 7 April 2001

SCORING RECORD
LEWANDOWSKI IN POLE POSITION

Poland's **Robert Lewandowski** was the 16-goal joint-leading marksman in the qualifying campaign for the 2018 finals, level with Mohammad Al-Sahlawi from Saudi Arabia and Ahmed Khalil from the United Arab Emirates. The trio scored one more than Portugal captain Cristiano Ronaldo, FIFA's Best Player in both 2016 and 2017. Both Lewandowski and Ronaldo – now the all-time leading goalscorer in European qualification history with 30 – beat the 14-goal European record set by Yugoslavia's Predrag Mijatovic in the 1998 preliminaries.

32

Just 32 countries entered qualification for the 1934 FIFA World Cup. Sweden and Estonia played the first match on 11 June 1933.

39

With 39 goals Guatemala's Carlos Ruiz is the all-time top scorer in FIFA World Cup qualifiers, despite never reaching the finals.

41

At 41, Zambia's Kalusha Bwalya is the oldest player to have scored a match-winning goal in a FIFA World Cup qualifying match.

17.7 SECONDS

Abdel Hamid Bassioumy of Egypt scored the fastest-ever qualification hat-trick in their 8-2 win over Namibia on 13 July 2001.

NATIONAL LEGEND
THIERRY'S TRICKERY

France qualified for the 2010 FIFA World Cup finals thanks to one of the most controversial international goals of recent history. The second leg of their play-off against the Republic of Ireland in November 2009 was 14 minutes into extra-time when striker **Thierry Henry** clearly controlled the ball with his hand, before crossing to William Gallas who gave his side a decisive 2-1 aggregate lead. After Swedish referee Martin Hansson allowed the goal to stand, the Football Association of Ireland first called for the game to be replayed, then asked to be allowed into the finals as a 33rd country – but both requests proved in vain.

THIERRY HENRY

NATIONAL QUALIFICATION RECORD
ORANJE AND AZZURRI OFF COLOUR

Among the notable European absentees from the party in Russia were 2006 champions Italy, and the Netherlands, runners-up in 2010 and third in Brazil in 2014. The Oranje were eliminated after finishing third in Group A, behind Sweden on goal difference. Italy lost 1-0 on aggregate to Sweden in the playoffs. The Swedes won 1-0 at home then withstood everything the Azzurri could throw at them at the Stadio Giuseppe Meazza in Milan. In 1934, Italy were the only hosts ever to go through the qualifying competition, but this was to be only their third-ever absence from the finals: they did not enter in 1930; and failed to qualify in 1958.

NATIONAL QUALIFICATION RECORD
WELCOME NEWCOMERS

Panama and Iceland qualified for their first World Cup finals in Russia. The Icelanders followed up their historic quarter-finals run at UEFA Euro 2016 by becoming the smallest nation (population 335,000) to qualify for the FIFA World Cup finals. Panama left it late to make their own little bit of history. A goal two minutes from time by defender Roman Torres earned a 2-1 win over Costa Rica in their last game to clinch an all-important third place in the final CONCACAF group.

ALL-TIME QUALIFICATIONS BY REGIONAL CONFEDERATION:

1 Europe – 245

2 South America – 85

3 Africa – 44

4 North/Central America & Caribbean – 42

5 Asia – 37

NATIONAL QUALIFICATION RECORD
THE "FOOTBALL WAR"

War broke out between El Salvador and Honduras after El Salvador beat Honduras 3-2 in a play-off on 26 June 1969 to qualify for the 1970 finals. Tension had been running high between the neighbours over a border dispute and there had been rioting at the match. On 14 July, the Salvador army invaded Honduras. El Salvador lost all three matches at the 1970 World Cup, and left without scoring a single goal.

FIFA WORLD CUP TEAM RECORDS

From the most decorated nations in world football to those that have only played a single game, and every team in between.

138

TOURNAMENT TRIVIA
CHAMPIONS CURSE

Germany, at the 2018 FIFA World Cup finals, became the fourth holders since 2000 to be eliminated at the group stage. France were eliminated in the group stages in 2002, Italy went out in the first round in 2010 in South Africa and Spain followed their unfortunate example in Brazil four years later. In 2018, the Germans never recovered from an opening 1-0 defeat by Mexico. They beat Sweden 2-1, only with a stoppage-time goal from **Toni Kroos**, before losing 2-0 to South Korea.

TONI **KROOS**

TOURNAMENT TRIVIA
ONE TIME WONDERS

Indonesia, then known as the Dutch East Indies, made one appearance in the finals, in the days when the tournament was a strictly knockout affair. On 5 June 1938, they lost 6-0 to Hungary in the first round, and have never qualified for the tournament since. This is the fewest number of World Cup games ever played by a country, though El Salvador have the worst ever World Cup record; in six matches across two tournaments, they've scored one goal and conceded 22.

7 Brazil's record of seven wins in the 2002 FIFA World Cup – a 100% record – is the most by any country at any tournament ever.

NATIONAL LEGEND
BRAZIL COLOUR UP

Brazil's yellow shirts are famous around the world, but they wore white shirts at the first four FIFA World Cup finals. Their 2-1 loss to Uruguay in the 1950 tournament's final match – when a draw would have given Brazil the Cup – was such a shock that they switched to yellow. The Brazilian confederation insisted no further colour change would follow the shock of the 7-1 semi-final defeat by Germany and 3-0 third-place play-off loss to Holland in 2014.

SOUTH AFRICA
South Africa are the only host country to fail to progress from the first round of a World Cup they've hosted.

MOST APPEARANCES IN THE FIFA WORLD CUP FINAL:

1 Germany/West Germany – 8

2 Brazil – 7

3 Italy – 6

4 Argentina – 5

5 France – 3
  = Netherlands – 3

MOST APPEARANCES IN FINALS TOURNAMENTS:

1. Brazil – 21
2. Germany/West Germany – 19
3. Italy – 18
4. Argentina – 17
5. Mexico – 16

FRANCE

France hold the record for the worst performance from a defending champion: they scored no goals and managed a single draw in 2002.

NATIONAL RECORD
SAFE EUROPEAN HOME

Germany's 1-0 victory over Argentina in the 2014 FIFA World Cup final meant they became the first European nation to win the FIFA World Cup in any of the eight tournaments staged in North, Central or South America, going back to 1930. Spain, winners of the 2010 FIFA World Cup in South Africa, were the first European victors to achieve it outside their home continent, and only since 2010 has a team other than Brazil won the trophy in a foreign continent; Brazil achieved it in 1958 (Sweden), 1970 (Mexico), 1994 (USA) and 2002 (Japan/South Korea).

LUKA **MODRIC**

KIT TRIVIA
EVER RED

England's victory in 1966 remains the only time the FIFA World Cup final has been won by a team wearing red. Spain, who usually wear red, changed into blue for their 2010 victory over the Netherlands to avoid a colour-clash. **Luka Modric** and his Croatia teammates did wear their unique red-and-white checks in the 2018 final but lost to France. Wearing red also proved unlucky for losing finalists Czechoslovakia in 1934 then Hungary in both 1938 and 1954.

VICENTE **DEL BOSQUE**

NATIONAL LEGEND
TODAY EUROPE, TOMORROW THE WORLD

Spain's 2010 trophy-lifting coach **Vicente del Bosque** became only the second manager to have won both the FIFA World Cup and the UEFA Champions League or its previous incarnation, the European Champions' Cup. Marcello Lippi won the UEFA prize with Juventus in 1996, 10 years before his Italy team became world champions. Del Bosque won the UEFA Champions League twice with Real Madrid, in 2000 and 2002, though he was sacked in summer 2003 for "only" winning the Spanish league title the previous season.

0
Switzerland hold the record for least number of goals conceded in one tournament (2006), despite losing in the second round on penalties to Ukraine.

18
Brazil (1930-58) and West Germany (1934-58, 1986-98) share the record for most consecutive games scoring a goal at the FIFA World Cup

FIFA WORLD CUP GOALSCORING

The goals are what everyone remembers from the FIFA World Cup. Over the years, some of the world's greatest strikers have showcased their talents on the world stage.

11

Hakan Sukur of Turkey holds the record for the fastest-ever FIFA World Cup goal, scored after 11 seconds against South Korea in 2002.

7-5

The highest-scoring game in the FIFA World Cup finals was the quarter-final between Austria and Switzerland on 26 June 1954, which ended 7-5 to Austria.

9

Brazil have scored more goals than any other nation in opening matches of the FIFA World Cup: 9

2,500

Tunisia's Fakhreddine Ben Youssef scored the 2,500th FIFA World Cup finals goal against Panama in 2018.

TOURNAMENT TRIVIA
FINAL FLURRY

France's 4-2 victory over Croatia in the 2018 World Cup Final was the highest 90-minute aggregate in the showdown since Brazil defeated hosts Sweden by 5-2 in 1958 in Stockholm. England and West Germany tallied six goals in the hosts' 4-2 victory in 1966, but the score was 2-2 after 90 minutes. The overall goals total at the 2018 tournament was 169, two short of the 171 from both 1998 and 2014, which is the record for the 32-team, 64-match finals.

TOURNAMENT TRIVIA
PENALTY PROGRESS

The 2018 FIFA World Cup finals in Russia equalled the number of shoot-outs in the knock-out stage, with four matches decided from the penalty spot, matching the number in 1990, 2006 and 2014. Croatia became only the second team, after Argentina in 1990, to win consecutive shootouts, against Denmark and Russia. They were also the first team to be taken to extra-time in all three knock-out ties on their way to the final, meaning that they played 90 minutes more than final opponents France.

TOURNAMENT TRIVIA
GENEROUS OPPONENTS

Chile were the first team to benefit from an opponent's own goal at the FIFA World Cup. Mexico's Manuel Rosas put the ball into his own net during the Chileans' 3-0 win at the inaugural 1930 finals in Uruguay. France, courtesy of two in both 2014 and 2018 are out on their own as recipients of the most own goals with six; Germany and Italy have four apiece. In 2018 **Mario Mandzukic** of Croatia scored the first own goal in a FIFA World Cup final, while the other France own goal came from Australia's Aziz Behich in the groups.

MARIO
MANDZUKIC

LEADING ALL-TIME FIFA WORLD CUP GOALSCORERS:

1 **Miroslav Klose, Germany – 16** (2002, 2006, 2010, 2014)
2 **Ronaldo, Brazil – 15** (1998, 2002, 2006)
3 **Gerd Muller, West Germany – 14** (1970, 1974)
4 **Just Fontaine, France – 13** (1958)
5 **Pele, Brazil – 12** (1958, 1962, 1966, 1970)

PELE

MESSI'S ASSISTS
Lionel Messi is the only player to have recorded an assist in each of the last four FIFA World Cups.

MIROSLAV KLOSE

NATIONAL LEGEND
PELE SO UNLUCKY

Pele would surely have been the all-time FIFA World Cup top scorer but for injuries. He was sidelined early in the 1962 finals, and again four years later. He scored six goals in Brazil's 1958 triumph, including two in the 5-2 final victory over Sweden. He also netted Brazil's 100th FIFA World Cup goal as they beat Italy 4-1 in the 1970 final. Despite his bad luck with injuries, Pele is the only player to have won three FIFA World Cup titles: 20 players have won two.

NATIONAL LEGEND
KLOSE ENCOUNTERS

Eight players have scored at FIFA World Cups 12 years apart: the most notable was **Miroslav Klose**. The Polish-born centre-forward opened with a hat-trick when Germany beat Saudi Arabia 8-0 in Japan in 2002 and scored a 16th goal in the 7-1 destruction of hosts Brazil in the 2014 semi-finals. That established Klose as the finals' all-time record marksman with one more goal than Brazil's Ronaldo. The other seven men to have scored in FIFA World Cups 12 years apart are: Pele (Brazil), Uwe Seeler (West Germany), Diego Maradona (Argentina), Michael Laudrup (Denmark), Henrik Larsson (Sweden), Sami Al-Jaber (S Arabia) and Cuauhtemoc Blanco (Mexico).

SCORING RECORD
NO GUARANTEE FOR TOP SCORERS

Topping the FIFA World Cup finals scoring chart is a great honour for all strikers, but few have been leading scorer and won the tournament. Argentina's Guillermo Stabile started the luckless trend in 1930, topping the scoring charts but finishing up on the losing side in the final. The list of top scorers who have played in the winning side is small: Garrincha and Vava (joint top scorers in 1962), Mario Kempes (top scorer in 1978), Paolo Rossi (1982) and Ronaldo (2002). Gerd Muller, top scorer in 1970, gained his reward as West Germany's trophy winner four years later.

MOST GOALS IN ONE FIFA WORLD CUP:

1 **Hungary – 27** (1954)
2 **West Germany – 25** (1954)
3 **France – 23** (1958)
4 **Brazil – 22** (1950)
5 **Brazil – 19** (1970)

FIFA WORLD CUP APPEARANCES

Since the dawn of the FIFA World Cup, many players have left their mark on the competition. But some have left bigger legacies than others…

NATIONAL LEGEND
LEADING CAPTAINS

Three players have each captained their teams in two FIFA World Cup finals – **Diego Maradona** of Argentina, Dunga of Brazil and West Germany's Karl-Heinz Rummenigge. Maradona lifted the trophy in 1986, but was a loser four years later. Dunga was the winning skipper in 1994, but was on the losing side in 1998. Rummenigge was a loser on both occasions, in 1982 and 1986. Maradona has made the most appearances as captain at the FIFA World Cup finals, leading out Argentina 16 times between 1986 and 1994.

TOURNAMENT TRIVIA
THE "DOUBLE" CHAMPIONS

Didier Deschamps joined Franz Beckenbauer and Mario Zagallo in the history books at the 2018 FIFA World Cup finals. Until France's victory in Russia under Deschamps, their 1998 winning captain, Zagallo and Beckenbauer had been the only men to win the World Cup as both player and manager. Zagallo won the World Cup in 1958 and 1962 on the wing; he took over at short notice from Joao Saldanha as Brazil manager and secured his third triumph at the 1970 final. Beckenbauer played in 1970 too for West Germany whom he captained to victory on home soil in 1974. Beckenbauer was appointed national coach in 1984, and won the FIFA World Cup in 1990.

NATIONAL LEGEND
PROSINECKI'S SCORING RECORD

Robert Prosinecki is the only player to have scored for different countries in FIFA World Cup finals tournaments. He netted for Yugoslavia in their 4-1 win over the United Arab Emirates in the 1990 tournament. Eight years later, following the break-up of the old Yugoslavia, he scored for Croatia in their 3-0 group-game win over Jamaica, and then netted the first goal in his side's 2-1 third-place play-off victory over the Netherlands.

MOST APPEARANCES IN FIFA WORLD CUP FINALS:

1 Lothar Matthaus (West Germany/Germany) – 25
2 Miroslav Klose (Germany) – 24
3 Paulo Maldini (Italy) – 23
4 Diego Maradona (Argentina) – 21
= Uwe Seeler (West Germany) – 21
= Wladyslaw Zmuda (Poland) – 21

ANDREAS GRANQVIST

FABIAN DELPH

EXTRA TIME HISTORY

Russie's Aleksandr Erokhin became the first ever fourth substitution at a FIFA World Cup in 2018, a rule amendment by FIFA's law-making International Board that teams could make a fourth substitution, but only in extra-time.

TOURNAMENT TRIVIA
OH BABIES

Sweden's **Andreas Granqvist** and England's **Fabian Delph** took different approaches to fatherhood during the 2018 FIFA World Cup. Manchester City midfielder Delph flew home to welcome his new daughter before flying back to Russia to rejoin the England squad. Granqvist stayed at the finals while his wife Sofia gave birth to a daughter. She had insisted her husband stay with the team because "it's these World Cup moments that he dreamed about as a little boy."

The three fastest substitutions in the history of the FIFA World Cup have been made in the fourth minute: Steve Hodge (England, 1986), Giuseppe Bergomi (Italy, 1998) and Peter Crouch (England, 2006).

Northern Ireland's Norman Whiteside is the youngest player in FIFA World Cup finals history, being just 17 years and 41 days when he started against Yugoslavia in 1982.

Manchester City sent more players than any other club to the 2018 FIFA World Cup. Their 16 included one who collected a winner's medal, defender Benjamin Mendy.

The most players sent off in one FIFA World Cup finals game is four during a match between Portugal and the Netherlands, refereed by Russian referee Valentin Ivanov in 2006.

FEDERATION HISTORY
GERMANY UNITED

Germany and West Germany are counted together in World Cup records because the Deutscher Fussball-Bund, founded in 1900, Germany's the original governing body, was in charge of the national game before World War II, during the East–West split and post-reunification. German sides have won the World Cup four times and appeared in the final a record eight times. In 2014, match-deciding substitutes Andre Schurrle and Mario Gotze were the first players born in Germany since reunification to win the World Cup, while team-mate Toni Kroos was the only 2014 squad-member to have been born in what was East Germany. Kroos was also the first player from the former East Germany to win the World Cup.

RAPHAEL VARANE

NATIONAL LEGEND
VARANE AT THE DOUBLE

Raphael Varane became the 11th player to clinch the double of success in the UEFA Champions League and FIFA World Cup when he anchored France's defence at the 2018 finals in Russia. Varane, born in Lille and a youth protege at Lens, joined Real Madrid in 2011, two years before making his senior debut for France. By the time he lined up at the 2018 FIFA World Cup, he had won 15 major club honours with Madrid. At the World Cup he played every minute in all seven of France's games including the final victory over Croatia.

FASTEST SENDINGS-OFF IN FIFA WORLD CUP FINALS:

1 Jose Batista (Uruguay) vs Scotland, 1986 – 1 min
2 Carlos Sanchez (Colombia) vs Japan, 2018 – 4 min
3 Giorgio Ferrini (Italy) vs Chile, 1962 – 8 min
4 Zeze Procopio (Brazil) v Czechoslovakia, 1938 – 14 min
5 Mohammed Al Khlaiwi (Saudi Arabia) v France 1998 – 19 min
= Miguel Bossio (Uruguay) v Denmark, 1986 – 19 min

FIFA WORLD CUP GOALKEEPING

The FIFA World Cup has produced a fair few legends between the sticks. From the old dependables to the crazy keepers, many have written their names in the history books.

TONY **MEOLA**

RIGHT WAY FOR RICARDO

Spain's Ricardo Zamora became the first man to save a penalty in a FIFA World Cup finals match, stopping Valdemar de Brito's spot-kick for Brazil in 1934. Spain went on to win 3-1.

WILLY **CABALLERO**

NATIONAL LEGEND
TONY AWARD

United States goalkeeper **Tony Meola** left the national team after the 1994 FIFA World Cup because he wanted to switch sports and take up American football instead. He failed to make it in gridiron and returned to soccer, but did not play for his country again until 1999. He retired for a second time after reaching a century of international appearances and still holds the record for being the youngest FIFA World Cup captain, having worn the armband for the US's 5-1 defeat to Czechoslovakia in 1990, aged 21 years 316 days.

RECENT HISTORY
KEEPERS CAUGHT OUT

FIFA World Cup 2018 proved a testing tournament for goalkeepers. Mistakes by **Willy Caballero** cost goals in Argentina's opening 1-1 draw against Iceland and the next game, a 3-0 defeat by Croatia. Uruguay's Fernando Muslera began well with three clean sheets but then misjudged a goal-bound shot from Antoine Griezmann in their quarter-final defeat by France. Even Germany's goalkeeper-captain Manuel Neuer had a tough time on returning to duty after a long injury lay-off. In the last group game, as Germany chased an equaliser against South Korea, Neuer was caught in the opposition half by a high-speed counter-attack which provided the Koreans' second goal.

NATIONAL LEGEND
KING HUGO THE FOURTH

Hugo Lloris became the fourth goalkeeper to captain his country to FIFA World Cup glory when France became champions for the second time in Russia in 2018. Lloris joined Italians Gianpiero Combi (1934) and Dino Zoff (1982) as well as Spain's Iker Casillas (2010). A mistake by Lloris on a back-pass in the final cost France their second goal, but they went on to beat Croatia 4-2. The final was Loris's 104th appearance in 10 years for France. The former Nice and Lyon keeper had been appointed national team captain in 2012.

HUGO
LLORIS

MANUEL
NEUER

1 There was just a single shot from a goalkeeper in the 2014 FIFA World Cup: Switzerland's Diego Benaglio was the only goalkeeper who swung at the target.

6 Spain goalkeeper David De Gea had a terrible time at the 2018 FIFA World Cup, conceding six goals despite facing just seven shots.

16 Tim Howard famously made an incredible 16 saves United States' second round clash with Belgium in 2014.

OLIVER'S ARMS
Germany's Oliver Kahn is the only goalkeeper to have been voted FIFA's Player of the Tournament, winning the award at the 2002 FIFA World Cup – despite taking a share of the blame for Brazil's winning goals in the final.

NATIONAL LEGEND
BATTERING RAMON

Argentina's 6-0 win over Peru at the 1978 FIFA World Cup aroused suspicion because the hosts needed to win by four goals to reach the final at the expense of arch-rivals Brazil – and Peruvian goalkeeper Ramon Quiroga had been born in Argentina. He insisted though, that his saves prevented the defeat from being even more embarrassingly emphatic. Earlier in the same tournament, Quiroga had been booked for a foul on Grzegorz Lato after running into the Polish half of the field.

TOURNAMENT TRIVIA
END TO END STUFF

When Miroslav Klose raced on to a long ball from German team-mate **Manuel Neuer** to score against England in their 2010 FIFA World Cup second round tie, it made Neuer the first goalkeeper to directly set up a finals goal for 44 years. The last before then had been the Soviet Union's Anzor Kavazashvili, providing an assist for Valery Porkuyan's late winner against Chile in the 1966 group stage.

NATIONAL LEGEND
ITALY'S ELDER STATESMEN

Dino Zoff became both the oldest player and oldest captain to win the FIFA World Cup when Italy lifted the trophy in Spain in 1982. He was 40 years 133 days old. A predecessor as goalkeeper and captain of both Italy and Juventus, Gianpiero Combi, had led Italy to World Cup glory in 1934. Zoff also holds the record (1142 minutes) for the longest stretch without conceding in international football, set between 1972 and 1974.

DINO
ZOFF

FIFA WORLD CUP MANAGERS

GARETH **SOUTHGATE**

Behind every great team is a tactical mastermind, and the FIFA World Cup has introduced the world to some of the greatest minds football has ever seen.

NATIONAL LEGEND
WAISTCOAT WONDER

England manager **Gareth Southgate** became an unlikely style icon at the 2018 World Cup by eschewing a suit or tracksuit and wearing a waistcoat during matches. Southgate was the first man to have represented England in semi-finals as both a player (UEFA Euro 1996) and a manager (Russia 2018). After missing the decisive penalty that sent England out of UEFA Euro 1996, it was some redemption that Southgate became the first England manager to win a penalty shoot-out at a FIFA World Cup.

ZLATKO **DALIC**

NATIONAL LEGEND
BETTER LATE THAN NEVER

Zlatko Dalic proved at the 2018 FIFA World Cup that a pedigree of club success is not essential to succeed in the national team sphere. Dalic had been working in club football in Saudi Arabia and the United Arab Emirates before being selected to replace Ante Cacic when Croatia struggled in qualifying. Under Dalic they finished second in the group behind Iceland and reached Russia by defeating Greece in the playoffs. Dalic then varied his tactics masterfully to achieve three wins in the group stage plus two nerve-jangling victories on penalties and one in extra-time to take Croatia to their first final.

27

Juan Jose Tramutola is the youngest ever FIFA World Cup finals coach, leading Argentina to the 1930 final at the age of 27 years 267 days.

TOURNAMENT TRIVIA
DIVIDED LOYALTIES

No coach has won the FIFA World Cup in charge of a foreign team, but several have faced their homeland. These include Jurgen Klinsmann, who played for Germany when they won the Cup in 1990 and then managed them to third place in 2006. Klinsmann, who was German boss from 2004 to 2006, having already made his home in California, was appointed United States coach in 2011. In the 2014 FIFA World Cup, "Klinsi" and the US lost 1-0 in a group match to Germany, now led by his former assistant, Joachim Low, whom he had appointed in 2004.

NATIONAL LEGEND
CRASHING BORA

Only one tournament behind record-holder Carlos Alberto Parreira, **Bora Milutinovic** has coached at five different FIFA World Cups – with a different country each time, two of them being the hosts. As well as Mexico in 1986 and the United States in 1994, he led Costa Rica in 1990, Nigeria in 1998 and China in 2002. He reached the knockout stages with every country except China – who failed to score a single goal.

BORA
MILUTINOVIC

TOURNAMENT TRIVIA
PUFF DADDIES

The coaches of the two sides appearing at the 1978 FIFA World Cup final were such prolific smokers that an oversized ashtray was produced for Argentina's Cesar Luis Menotti and the Netherlands's Ernst Happel so they could share it on the touchline. Cesar Luis Menotti, the triumphant coach that day, also managed Barcelona and Atletico Madrid in an illustrious managerial career.

71

The oldest manager in a finals was German Otto Rehhagel, aged 71 years 307 days when he led Greece in South Africa in 2010.

25

West Germany's Helmut Schon was coach for more FIFA World Cup matches than any other man – 25, across the 1966, 1970, 1974 and 1978 tournaments.

6

Carlos Alberto Parreira holds the record for most FIFA World Cups attended as a coach. Parreira won with Brazil in 1994 and fell at the quarter-finals with them in 2006, but also led Kuwait (1982), the United Arab Emirates (1990), Saudi Arabia (1998) and hosts South Africa (2010).

1

There's only ever been one FIFA World Cup-winning manager who's won the trophy twice: Vittorio Pozzo of Italy, in 1934 and 1938.

LUIZ FELIPE
SCOLARI

NATIONAL LEGEND
DREAM TO NIGHTMARE

Luiz Felipe Scolari quit as Brazil coach after the 2014 FIFA World Cup brought the worst defeat in their history, by 7-1 against Germany in the semi-finals, and then a 3-0 defeat to the Netherlands in the third-place play-off. However, he had won the FIFA World Cup with Brazil in 2002 and went on, with Portugal in 2006, to set an individual record of 11 successive wins at the finals.

LAST TEN
FIFA WORLD CUP WINNERS:

2018: Didier Deschamps, France

2014: Joachim Low, Germany

2010: Vicente Del Bosque, Spain

2006: Marcelo Lippi, Italy

2002: Luiz Felipe Scolari, Brazil

1998: Aime Jacquet, France

1994: Carlos Alberto Parreira, Brazil

1990: Franz Beckenbauer, Germany

1986: Carlos Bilardo, Argentina

1982: Enzo Bearzot, Italy

FIFA WORLD CUP ATTENDANCES

From the modest hundreds of 1930 to the hundreds of thousands who watch these days, FIFA World Cups are all about the fans. Every four years, millions pack into the stadiums to watch the greatest show on Earth.

ATTENDANCE RECORD
RUSHING TO RUSSIA

FIFA claimed a near-perfect attendance rate at the 2018 World Cup finals after concern over empty seats at low-profile matches in some of the early group stage matches. Colin Smith, the world federation's chief competitions officer, reported an average 98 per cent capacity in the 12 stadia in the 11 Russian cities. The largest slice of the 2.4m tickets were bought by Russian fans (872,000), with the United States recording the greatest number of foreign sales (88,825). English ticket sales, normally amongst the highest in visiting nations, was a disappointing 10th overall – around 33,000 sales.

7,000,000
More than 7m fans visited Fan Fest sites over the 31 days of the 2018 finals in Russia – an increase of 2m on the totals in Brazil in 2014.

ATTENDANCE RECORD
MORBID MARACANA

The largest attendance for a FIFA World Cup match was at Rio de Janeiro's Maracana for the last clash of the 1950 tournament – though no one is quite sure how many were there. The final tally was officially given as 173,850, though some estimates suggest as many as 210,000 witnessed the host country's traumatic defeat. Tensions were so high at the final whistle; FIFA president Jules Rimet described the crowd's overwhelming silence as "morbid, almost too difficult to bear". Uruguay's triumphant players barricaded themselves inside their dressing room for several hours before they judged it safe enough to emerge.

NATIONAL STADIUM
LUZHNIKI'S NEW LIFE

Moscow's Luzhniki Stadium, which staged seven matches at the 2018 FIFA World Cup, including the Opening Match and final, is one of sport's historic venues. Originally the Lenin Stadium, it was opened in 1956 as a multi-sport venue with a 100,000 capacity. Major events included the 1980 Olympic Games and it also hosted the finals of the UEFA Champions League in 2008 and the UEFA Cup in 1999. Recent redevelopment meant a 78,011 capacity in a football-specific stadium for the World Cup.

3,587,538
The highest attendance of a FIFA World Cup came in 1994, in USA, where over 3.5 million people attended matches.

363,000
Only 363,000 people attended the 1934 FIFA World Cup in Italy. At 21,352, it's the lowest average attendance for any tournament.

ATTENDANCE RECORD
CAPACITY PLANNING

The Lusail World Cup stadium in Qatar, which will host the 2022 FIFA World Cup final, could record the biggest attendance for the competition climax since 1994. The planned capacity for Lusail is 86,250, which would exceed the final attendances recorded at Saint-Denis (1998), Yokohama (2002), Berlin (2006), Johannesburg (2010), Rio de Janeiro's Maracana (2014) and Moscow (2018) – but not the 94,194 who attended in Pasadena in 1994. Initially Qatar's Supreme Committee for Delivery & Legacy proposed 12 new stadia, but this was later scaled back to eight. A number of these stadia will be reduced in size or even dismantled altogether after the finals.

300
The 300 people who were recorded as watching Romania beat Peru 3-1 in 1930 formed the FIFA World Cup finals' smallest attendance, at the Estadio Pocitos in Montevideo. A day earlier, ten times as many people are thought to have been there for France's 4-1 win over Mexico.

TOP TEN
FIFA WORLD CUP ATTENDANCES:

1 173,850 – **Estadio do Maracana,**
Rio De Janeiro, Brazil, 1950

2 114,600 – **Estadio Azteca,**
Mexico City, Mexico, 1986

3 107,412 – **Estadio Azteca,**
Mexico City, Mexico, 1970

4 98,000 – **Wembley Stadium,**
London, England, 1966

5 94,194 – **Rose Bowl,**
Padadena, USA, 1994

6 93,000 – **Estadio Centenario,**
Montevideo, Uruguay, 1930

7 90,000 – **Estadio Santiago Bernabeu,**
Madrid, 1982

8 84,490 – **Soccer City,**
Johannesburg, South Africa 2010

9 80,000 – **Stade De France,**
Paris, France, 1998

10 78,011 – **Luzhniki,**
Moscow, Russia, 2018

ATTENDANCE RECORD
ABSENT FRIENDS

Only 2,823 spectators turned up at the Rasunda Stadium in Stockholm to see Wales play Hungary in a first-round play-off match during the 1958 FIFA World Cup. More than 15,000 had attended the first game between the two sides, but boycotted the replay in tribute to executed Hungarian uprising leader Imre Nagy. It's not the lowest ever attendance at a FIFA World Cup match though: that goes to Romania vs Peruat Estadio Pocitos in Montevideo, Uruguay, in 1930. Just 300 fans showed their faces.

40,000
FIFA regulation states that the minimum capacity of any stadium hosting a World Cup match has to 40,000. Stadiums hosting quarter-finals must have a minimum of 60,000 and those hosting the opening ceremony or final must have a capacity of at least 80,000.

TOURNAMENT TRIVIA
GENDER EQUALITY

Only two stadiums have hosted the finals of the FIFA World Cup for both men and women. The Rose Bowl, in Pasadena, California, was the venue for the men's final in 1994 – when Brazil beat Italy – and the women's showdown between the victorious US and China five years later, which was watched by 90,185 people. But Sweden's Rasunda Stadium, near Stockholm, just about got there first – though it endured a long wait between the men's final in 1958 and the women's in 1995. Both sets of American spectators got their money's worth, watching games that went into extra-time and which were settled on penalties.

FIFA WORLD CUP STADIUMS AND HOSTS

From the hosts with the most to the stadiums where so many classic tournament moments have occurred, the FIFA World Cup has visited almost every corner of the Earth.

GIANNI **INFANTINO**

FIFA

FUTURE TOURNAMENT
FUTURE PERFECT

The future of the FIFA World Cup depends more and more on neighbouring countries banding together to play host. **Gianni Infantino**, elected as FIFA president in 2016, has declared himself in favour of co-hosting as a means both to encourage more countries to share organization of the finals and to guard against the building of "white elephant" stadia. The United States, Mexico and Canada will host 2026 and a co-hosting bid for 2030 is planned by Uruguay, Argentina and Paraguay.

FUTURE TOURNAMENTS
THREE WAY WINNERS

The FIFA World Cup finals in 2026 will make history twice over. Firstly, it will feature 48 teams – playing 80 matches – after the world federation decided to open up the finals to more national teams than the current 32 which competed in Russia in 2018. Secondly, staging the finals will be shared between three countries after the United States, Canada and Mexico were awarded host rights by FIFA Congress in Moscow in June 2018. Canada and Mexico will host 10 matches each with the US the other 60, including all ties from the quarter-finals onward.

HOST HISTORY
ARCHITECTS' PREROGATIVE

Distinctive and creative elements were added to the stadiums built especially for the 2010 FIFA World Cup in South Africa, including the giraffe-shaped towers at Nelspruit's Mbombela stadium, the 350-metre-long arch with its mobile viewing platform soaring above Durban's main arena, and the white "petals" shrouding the Nelson Mandela Bay stadium in Port Elizabeth. 2002's Sapporo Dome turned heads for being an indoor arena with a retractable pitch: it was the first ever stadium to host a FIFA World Cup match "indoors".

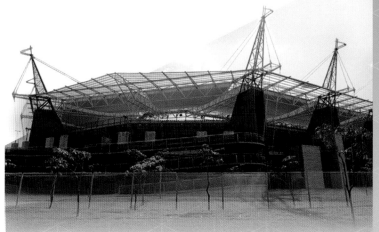

MOSCOW

HOST HISTORY
RATIONAL IN RUSSIA

Organizers of the 2018 FIFA World Cup in Russia tried to return to the "clusters" system of adjacent venues to ease travel, accommodation and logistical problems around the 11 host cities, thus reducing costs for fans. Two stadia were used in Moscow – Luzhniki and Spartak. The system was compromised, however, by the use of Ekaterinburg in the far eastern region of European Russia. The "clusters" concept had been abandoned by the French hosts for 1998. Michel Platini, president of the local organizing committee, preferred a rotation schedule so the top teams' matches could be spread all around the country.

HOST HISTORY
BERLIN CALL

Despite later becoming the capital of a united Germany, then-divided Berlin only hosted three group games at the 1974 FIFA World Cup in West Germany – the host country's surprise loss to East Germany took place in Hamburg. An unexploded World War II bomb was discovered beneath the seats at Berlin's Olympiastadion in 2002, by workers preparing the ground for the 2006 tournament. Germany, along with Brazil, had applied to host the tournament in 1942, before it was cancelled due to the outbreak of World War II.

23
With 19 games at Estadio Azteca and 4 at Estadio Olimpico Universitario, Mexico City has hosted more FIFA World Cup games than any other city on Earth.

5
Morocco have failed on five attempts to lure the FIFA World Cup to their country, with failed bids in 1994, 1998, 2006, 2010 and 2026. This is a record high.

6
Six stadiums have staged both the final of a FIFA World Cup and the summer Olympics athletics: Berlin's Olympiastadion, Paris's Stade Colombes, London's Wembley, Rome's Stadio Olimpico and Munich's Olympiastadion.

14
In 1982, Spain spread the FIFA World Cup across 14 venues, still a record for single country hosting the finals.

HOST HISTORY
MEXICAN SAVE

Mexico was not the original choice to host the 1986 FIFA World Cup, but stepped in when Colombia withdrew in 1982 due to venue problems. Mexico held on to the staging rights despite suffering from an earthquake in September 1985 that left approximately 10,000 people dead, but which left the stadiums unscathed. The Azteca Stadium went on to become the first venue to host two FIFA World Cup final matches – and Mexico the first country to stage two FIFA World Cups.

FIFA WORLD CUP PENALTIES

A quick-draw battle of nerves from 12 yards, the penalty shoot-out is either one of the most anticipated moments of a FIFA World Cup, or one of the most dreaded: it often depends on your history…

18
Spain have been awarded the most tournament penalties during regulation time. Of the 18 given, they've converted 15.

TOURNAMENT TRIVIA
WOE FOR ASAMOAH

Ghana striker Asamoah Gyan is the only player to have missed two penalties during match-time at FIFA World Cups. He hit the post with a spot-kick against the Czech Republic during a group game at the 2006 tournament, then struck a shot against the bar with the final kick of extra-time in Ghana's 2010 quarter-final versus Uruguay. Had he scored then, Gyan would have given Ghana a 2-1 win – following Luis Suarez's goal-stopping handball on the goal-line – and a first African place in a FIFA World Cup semi-final. Despite such a traumatic miss, Gyan score Ghana's first penalty in the shoot-out. His team still lost, though, 4-2 on penalties.

SCORING RECORD
GERMAN EFFICIENCY

Germany, or West Germany, have won all four of their FIFA World Cup penalty shoot-outs, more than any other team. The run began with a semi-final victory over France in 1982, when goalkeeper Harald Schumacher was the match-winner. West Germany also reached the 1990 final thanks to their shoot-out expertise, this time proving superior to England. In that 2006 quarter-final, Germany's goalkeeper Jens Lehmann consulted a note predicting the direction the Argentine players were likely to shoot towards. The only German national team to lose a major tournament penalty shoot-out were the West Germans, who contested the 1976 UEFA European Championships final against Czechoslovakia.

8
England and Italy share the record for most players to miss in FIFA World Cup shoot-outs. Notable "missers" include Franco Baresi, Boberto Baggio, Stuart Pearce, Steven Gerrard, and Frank Lampard, the latter of which never scored a World Cup goal.

YUSSUF POULSEN

TOURNAMENT TRIVIA
DOUBLE TROUBLE

Denmark's **Yussuf Poulsen**, at the 2018 FIFA World Cup, became the first player to concede two penalties in a single tournament since Serbia's Milan Dudic in 2006. In the teams' opening game, Poulsen fouled Christian Cueva, but the Peruvian fired his spot- kick over the bar and Poulsen made amends by scoring Denmark's winner, then received a yellow card in additional time. In the next game, he not only gave away a penalty against Australia but also collected another yellow card that ruled him out of the final group game, against France. Mile Jedinak scored the equalizer in 1-1 draw.

LAST FIVE FIFA WORLD CUP PENALTY SHOOT-OUTS:

1 Croatia 4-3 Russia, Quarter-final, 2018 (2-2 AET)
2 England 4-3 Colombia, Second-round, 2018 (2-2 AET)
3 Croatia 3-2 Denmark, Second-round, 2018 (1-1 AET)
4 Russia 4-3 Spain, Second-round, 2018 (1-1 AET)
5 Argentina 4-2 Netherlands, Semi-final, 2014 (0-0 AET)

DANIJEL
SUBASIC

RECENT HISTORY
DANIJEL THE LION

At the 2018 FIFA World Cup in Russia, **Danijel Subasic** of Croatia became the second goalkeeper to save four penalties in shoot-outs in one tournament. The Monaco man saved three against Denmark in a second-round shoot-out and then another in Croatia's quarter-final victory over hosts Russia. Before Subasic the only other goalkeeper to have saved four kicks in shootouts in the same tournament had been Sergio Goycoechea of Argentina in the 1990 finals. Goycoechea saved two against Yugoslavia in the quarter-final and another two against Italy in the last four to book Argentina's final place.

29

A record 29 penalties were awarded at the 2018 FIFA World Cup in Russia. The sharp rise, from 13 in 2014, was down to the introduction of Video Assistant Referees (VAR).

3-0

The biggest ever margin in a FIFA World Cup shoot-out came in 2006, as Ukraine defeated Switzerland 3-0 in the second round of the competition.

TOURNAMENT TRIVIA
FRENCH KICKS

The first penalty shoot-out at a FIFA World Cup finals came in the 1982 semi-final in Seville between West Germany and France, when French takers Didier Six and **Maxime Bossis** were the unfortunate players to miss. The same two countries met in the semi- finals four years later – and West Germany again won, though in normal time, 2-0. The record for most shoot-outs is shared by the 1990 and 2006 tournaments, with four apiece. Both semi-finals in 1990 went to penalties, while the 2006 final was the second to be settled that manner – Italy beating France 5-3 after David Trezeguet struck the crossbar.

MAXIME
BOSSIS

TOURNAMENT TRIVIA
BAGGIO OF DISHONOUR

Pity poor **Roberto Baggio**: the Italian maestro stepped up in three FIFA World Cup penalty shoot-outs, more than any other player – and has been a loser in every one. Most painfully, it was his shot over the bar that gifted Brazil the trophy at the end of the 1994 Final. But he had also ended on the losing side against Argentina in a 1990 semi-final and would do so again, against France in a 1998 quarter-final. At least, in 1990 and 1998, his own attempts were successful.

ROBERTO
BAGGIO

UEFA EUROPEAN CHAMPIONSHIP

The UEFA European Championship finals have gone from being a four-team curiosity, snubbed by major nations, to perhaps the third-biggest sporting event on earth, behind only the FIFA World Cup and the Summer Olympic Games.

First Held: 1960

Current Champions: Portugal

Most Wins: Germany, Spain, 3

Next Edition: 2020, Various

1968

The 1968 finals in Italy were used as the backdrop to a famous English-language film – **The Italian Job**, starring Michael Caine – about a British gang who use the cover of the finals to stage a daring gold robbery in Turin.

108

The expanded, 24-team UEFA European Championship may have boasted **more goals** than any previous Euros – 108 in all. But these came at a rate of just 2.12 per game – the lowest since the 1996 UEFA European Championship's 2.06.

9

Michel Platini scored more goals than any player in a single European Championship finals in 1984.

MICHEL
PLATINI

3

France have **hosted the tournament three times**, more than any other nation.

OLIVER
BIERHOFF

Germany's **Oliver Bierhoff** scored the first golden goal in the history of the tournament when he hit the winner against the Czech Republic in the Euro 96 final at Wembley on 30 June.

155

UEFA NATIONS LEAGUE

The Nations League was devised by UEFA as a competition to replace increasingly unpopular friendly matches. Mooted first in 2011, it was finally unveiled in 2017. Europe's 55 national teams were ranked according to a coefficient and distributed among across four divisions. Promotion and relegation would decide the divisions' make-up for the event's second edition in the autumn of 2020.

JOACHIM
LOW

NATIONAL LEGEND
LOW'S HIGH EXPECTATIONS

Germany coach **Joachim Low** emerged as an early advocate for the Nations League after his team were drawn in the top group of League A against France and Netherlands. Low said: "I like these kind of games against big nations with very good players. It's interesting for us, for our players and of course for our fans. It's better than the friendly games we have sometimes. I'm really happy."

Low was not so happy, however, after Germany lost a 2-0 lead in their last game against the Dutch and were relegated after a 2-2 draw. The Netherlands went on to the finals.

16

The Nations League consists of 16 groups in total, spread across four divisions, with each containing either three or four teams.

STAR PLAYER
PICK THAT ONE OUT

Jordan Pickford was England's penalty shoot-out hero in the third-place victory over Switzerland. The Everton goalkeeper not only saved from Josip Drmic in the shootout but converted his own spot-kick as the Three Lions won 6-5 on penalties. This was England's second shootout success in a year after victory over Colombia in the second round of the 2018 World Cup. England thus finished third in a senior tournament for the first time since Euro 1968. They had reached the finals when late goals from Jesse Lingard and Harry Kane earned a 2-1 win over Croatia, which sent them top of Group A4 and relegated the World Cup runners-up.

JORDAN
PICKFORD

UEFA NATIONS LEAGUE A

	PLAYED	WON	DRAWS	LOST	FOR	AGAINST	POINTS
GROUP 1							
Netherlands	4	2	1	1	8	4	7
France	4	2	1	1	4	4	7
Germany	4	0	2	2	3	7	2
GROUP 2							
Switzerland	4	3	0	1	14	5	9
Belgium	4	3	0	1	9	6	9
Iceland	4	0	0	4	1	13	0
GROUP 3							
Portugal	4	2	2	0	5	3	8
Italy	4	1	2	1	2	2	5
Poland	4	0	2	2	4	6	2
GROUP 4							
England	4	2	1	1	6	5	7
Spain	4	2	0	2	12	7	6
Croatia	4	1	1	2	4	10	4

SEMI-FINALS

Portugal 3–1 Switzerland
Netherlands 3–1 England (AET)

THIRD PLACE PLAY-OFF

England 0–0 Switzerland
(6-5 on pens, aet)

FINAL

Portugal 1–0 Netherlands

GONÇALO GUEDES

TOURNAMENT TRIVIA

PORTUGUESE PREMIERE

Hosts Portugal won the inaugural UEFA Nations League in June 2019 to make eventual amends for defeat in front of their own fans in the European Championship final in 2004. Back then, a teenaged Cristiano Ronaldo was among the tearful runners-up. Some 15 years later he was captain and three-goal leading scorer as his Portuguese team defeated Netherlands 1-0 in the final in Porto. **Gonçalo Guedes** scored the goal.

53

Cristiano Ronaldo's 53rd career hat-trick fired Portugal into the Nations League final with a 3-1 win over Switzerland. It was his seventh treble for his country.

CRISTIANO RONALDO

UEFA EUROPEAN CHAMPIONSHIP TEAM RECORDS

In nearly 60 years, the UEFA European Championship has grown to become arguably the most important international football tournament after the FIFA World Cup.

JORDI
ALBA

TOURNAMENT RECORD
FRANCE BOAST PERFECT RECORD

France, on home soil in 1984, are the only side to win all their matches since the finals expanded beyond four teams. They won them without any shoot-outs, too, beating Denmark 1-0, Belgium 5-0 and Yugoslavia 3-2 in their group, Portugal 3-2 after extra-time in the semi-finals and Spain 2-0 in the final. Michel Platini was the star of the tournament for the French, netting nine goals; Platini went on to pick up his second Ballon D'Or that year.

6-1

In Yugoslavia's last ever Euros as a unified nation, they recorded the worst defeat ever at the tournament, as Netherlands thrashed them 6-1.

17

Just 17 teams entered the first four-team tournament, won by the Soviet Union in 1960 – yet 53 took part in qualifying for the right to join hosts France in a newly expanded 24-team event in 2016.

TOURNAMENT TRIVIA
FANCY SEEING YOU AGAIN

When Spain beat Italy 4-0 in the 2012 final it was the fourth time UEFA European Championship opponents had faced each other twice in the same tournament. Each time, it followed a first-round encounter. The Netherlands lost to the Soviet Union, then beat them in the final in 1988; Germany beat the Czech Republic twice at Euro 96, including the final; and Greece did the same to Portugal in 2004. Spain and Italy drew in Euro 2012's Group C, with Cesc Fabregas replying to Antonio Di Natale's opener for Italy. Their second showdown was rather less even.

TOSS FAVOURS THE HOSTS
Italy reached the 1968 final on home soil thanks to the toss of a coin: the only game in finals history decided in such fashion. Italy drew 0-0 against the Soviet Union after extra-time in Naples on 5 June 1968.

TOURNAMENT TRIVIA
SAME OLD SPAIN

Spain not only cruised their way to the largest winning margin of any UEFA European Championship final by trouncing Italy 4-0 in the climax to 2012 – they also became the first country to successfully defend the title. David Silva, **Jordi Alba** – with his first international goal – and substitutes Fernando Torres and Juan Mata got the goals in Kiev's Olympic Stadium on 1 July. Spain thus landed their third major trophy in a row, having won Euro 2008 and the 2010 FIFA World Cup.

BERTI VOGTS

GERMANY IN THE ASCENDANCY

Germany (formerly West Germany) and Spain have each won the UEFA European Championship three times, though the Germans have played and won most matches (49 and 26, respectively), as well as scoring and conceding more goals (72 and 48) than any other nation. Defender **Berti Vogts** is the only man to win the tournament as a player (1972) and coach (1996), both with the Germans. Portugal's 2016 triumph, in their 35th UEFA European Championship finals match, means England have now played most tournament games (31) without ever managing to lift the trophy.

TOP UEFA EUROPEAN CHAMPIONSHIP WINNERS:

1 3 – West Germany/ Germany
= 3 – Spain

2 2 – France

3 1 – Soviet Union
= 1 – Italy
= 1 – Czechoslovakia
= 1 – Netherlands
= 1 – Denmark
= 1 – Greece
= 1 – Portugal

3

Czechoslovakia's 3-1 semi-final win over the Netherlands in Zagreb, on 16 June 1976, featured a record three red cards.

14

France scored 14 goals in their own Euros in 1984: more than any other nation a tournament ever.

TRAIANOS DELLAS

SCORING RECORD
DELLAS TIMES IT RIGHT FOR GREECE

Greece scored the only "silver goal" victory in Euro history in a 2004 semi-final. (The silver goal rule meant that a team leading after the first period of extra-time won the match.) **Traianos Dellas** headed Greece's winner seconds before the end of the first period of extra-time against the Czech Republic in Porto on 1 July. Both golden goals and silver goals were abandoned for UEFA Euro 2008, and drawn knockout ties reverted to being decided over the full 30 minutes of extra-time, and penalties if necessary.

🏆 TOURNAMENT TRIVIA
DENMARK'S UNEXPECTED TRIUMPH

Denmark were unlikely winners of UEFA Euro 1992. They had not even expected to take part after finishing behind Yugoslavia in their qualifying group, but they were invited to complete the final eight when Yugoslavia were barred for security fears following the country's collapse. Goalkeeper **Peter Schmeichel** was their hero – in the semi-final shoot-out win over the Netherlands and again in the final against Germany, when goals by John Jensen and Kim Vilfort earned Denmark a 2-0 win.

PETER SCHMEICHEL

UEFA EUROPEAN CHAMPIONSHIP PLAYER RECORDS

The UEFA European Championship has played host to some of the continent's greatest ever footballers for nearly sixty years.

SCORING RECORD
KIRICHENKO NETS QUICKEST GOAL

The fastest goal in the history of the finals was scored by Russia forward **Dmitri Kirichenko**. He netted after just 67 seconds to give his side the lead against Greece on 20 June 2004. Russia won 2-1, but Greece still qualified for the quarter-finals – and went on to become shock winners. The fastest goal in the final was Spain midfielder Jesus Pereda's sixth-minute strike in 1964, when Spain beat the Soviet Union 2-1. The latest opening goal was Eder's 109th-minute winner for Portugal against France in the 2016 final.

DMITRI KIRICHENKO

38

The oldest scorer in finals history is Austria's Ivica Vastic. He was 38 years and 257 days old when he equalized in the 1-1 draw with Poland at UEFA Euro 2008.

TOURNAMENT RECORD
GOLDEN ONE-TOUCH

Spain striker Fernando Torres claimed the Golden Boot, despite scoring the same number of goals – three – as Italy's Mario Balotelli, Russia's Alan Dzagoev, Germany's Mario Gomez, Croatia's Mario Mandzukic and Portugal's Cristiano Ronaldo. The decision came down to number of assists – with Torres and Gomez level on one apiece – then amount of time played. The 92 fewer minutes spent on the pitch by Torres, compared to Gomez, meant his contributions were deemed better value for the prize.

6

Antoine Griezmann bagged six Euros goals in France in 2016: the most since fellow Frenchman Michel Platini scored 9 in 1984: also hosted in France.

ALAN SHEARER

NATIONAL LEGEND
SHEARER TALLY BOOSTS ENGLAND

Alan Shearer is the only Englishman to top the finals scoring chart. Shearer led the scorers with five goals as England lost on penalties to Germany in the Euro 96 semi-final at Wembley. He netted against Switzerland, Scotland and the Netherlands (two) in the group and gave England a third-minute lead against the Germans. He added two more goals at Euro 2000 and now is behind only Michel Platini and Cristiano Ronaldo in the all-time list.

10

The most red cards were shown at Euro 2000, when the ten dismissals included Romania's Gheorghe Hagi, Portugal's Nuno Gomes, Italy's Gianluca Zambrotta and the Czech Republic's Radoslav Latal who, having been sent off at Euro 96, is the only man to be dismissed in two tournaments.

SCORING RECORD
VONLANTHEN BEATS ROONEY RECORD

The youngest scorer in finals history was Switzerland midfielder **Johan Vonlanthen**. He was 18 years 141 days when he netted in their 3-1 defeat by France on 21 June 2004. He beat the record set by England forward Wayne Rooney four days earlier. Rooney was 18 years 229 days when he scored the first goal in England's 3-0 win over the Swiss. Vonlanthen retired from football at the age of 26 in May 2012 due to a knee injury.

JOHAN **VONLANTHEN**

SCORING RECORD
PONEDELNIK'S MONDAY MORNING FEELING

Striker Viktor Ponedelnik headed the Soviet Union's extra-time winner to beat Yugoslavia 2-1 in the first final on 10 July 1960 – and sparked some famous headlines in the Soviet media. The game in Paris kicked off at 10pm Moscow time on Sunday, so it was Monday morning when Ponedelnik – whose name means "Monday" in Russian – scored. He said: "When I scored, all the journalists wrote the headline 'Ponedelnik zabivayet v Ponedelnik' – 'Monday scores on Monday'." This goal, in the 113th minute, remains the latest ever in a European Championship/Nations Cup final.

ILYIN MAKES HISTORY
Anatoly Ilyin of the Soviet Union scored the first goal in UEFA European Championship history when he netted after four minutes against Hungary on 29 September 1958.

1

Only one man has been sent off in a UEFA European Championship final: France defender Yvon Le Roux, who received a second yellow card with five minutes remaining of his team's 2-0 triumph over Spain in 1984.

NATIONAL LEGEND
BIERHOFF NETS FIRST GOLDEN GOAL

Germany's **Oliver Bierhoff** scored the first golden goal in the history of the tournament when he hit the winner against the Czech Republic in the Euro 96 final at Wembley on 30 June. (The golden goal rule meant the first team to score in extra-time won the match.) Bierhoff netted in the fifth minute of extra-time. His shot from 20 yards deflected off defender Michal Hornak and slipped through goalkeeper Petr Kouba's fingers.

OLIVER **BIERHOFF**

TOP SCORERS IN FINALS HISTORY:

1 9 – **Michel Platini**, France

9 – **Cristiano Ronaldo**, Portugal

2 7 – **Alan Shearer**, England

3 6 – **Nuno Gomes**, Portugal

6 – **Antoine Griezmann**, France

6 – **Thierry Henry**, France

6 – **Zlatan Ibrahimovic**, Sweden

6 – **Patrick Kluivert**, Netherlands

6 – **Wayne Rooney**, England

6 – **Ruud van Nistelrooy**, Netherlands

UEFA EUROPEAN CHAMPIONSHIP OTHER RECORDS

BIRKIR MAR SAEVARSSON

The European Championship has provided tons of trivia over the years, from the goal droughts to the host countries and everything in between.

RECENT HISTORY
GOALS AREN'T EVERYTHING

The expanded, 24-team UEFA European Championship may have boasted more goals than any previous Euros – 108 in all. But these came at a rate of just 2.12 per game – the lowest since the 1996 UEFA European Championship's 2.06. Euro 2016's three own goals was another competition record – the unlucky players putting into their own nets were the Republic of Ireland's Ciaran Clark, Northern Ireland's Gareth McAuley and Iceland's **Birkir Mar Saevarsson**.

Only three red cards were shown during Euro 2016: the same tally as at each of the 2008 and 2012 UEFA European Championships. In contrast, twice as many players were sent off at the 2004 tournament.

XABI ALONSO

LAST TEN UEFA EUROPEAN CHAMPIONSHIP FINAL REFEREES:

2016 – **Mark Clattenburg** (England)

2012 – **Pedro Proenca** (Portugal)

2008 – **Roberto Rosetti** (Italy)

2004 – **Markus Merk** (Germany)

2000 – **Anders Frisk** (Sweden)

1996 – **Pierluigi Palretto** (Italy)

1992 – **Bruno Galler** (Switzerland)

1988 – **Michel Vautrot** (France)

1984 – **Vojtech Christob** (Czechoslovakia)

1980 – **Nicolae Rainea** (Romania)

TOURNAMENT RECORD
RECORD EURO GOAL DROUGHT

Between **Xabi Alonso**'s added-time penalty in Spain's 2-0 quarter-final defeat of France and Mario Balotelli's 20th-minute semi-final strike for Italy in their 2-1 victory against Germany, Euro 2012's goalless spell lasted 260 minutes – a UEFA European Championship record. In the goalless interim, Italy drew 0-0 with England before beating them on penalties, and Spain drew 0-0 with Portugal before beating them on penalties.

3-0

When Greece were drawn against Albania in the first round of the 1964 tournament, the Greeks immediately withdrew, handing Albania a 3-0 walkover win. The countries had technically been at war since 1940.

NATIONAL LEGEND
LOW CONQUERS ALMOST ALL

Germany coach **Joachim Low** holds the record for most UEFA European Championship matches and victories in charge. His side's shoot-out victory over Italy in a Euro 2016 quarter-final took him to 12 victories, before their 2-0 defeat to France in the semi-finals put him on 17 games across the 2008, 2012 and 2016 competitions. Despite this, Low has never won the competition; he has however won the FIFA World Cup and FIFA Confederations Cup.

JOACHIM **LOW**

REFEREE TRIVIA
TAKE CLATT

In 2012, Pedro Proenca from Portugal achieved the double feat of refereeing the UEFA Champions League final between Chelsea and Bayern Munich and that summer's UEFA European Championship final between Spain and Italy. English referee **Mark Clattenburg** went one better in 2016: he did his homeland's FA Cup final between Manchester United and Crystal Palace and the UEFA Champions League final between Real Madrid and Atletico Madrid in May and the UEFA European Championship final between France and Portugal in July.

MARK **CLATTENBURG**

2016

The 2016 UEFA European Championship final between hosts France and eventual champions Portugal was the sixth to go to extra-time but the first to be goalless after 90 minutes, before Eder's 109th minute winner.

HOST HISTORY
HOSTS WITH THE ALMOST

In 2000, Belgium and the Netherlands began the trend for dual hosting the UEFA European Championship finals – it was the first time the tournament was staged in more than one country. The opening game was Belgium's 2-1 win over Sweden in Brussels on 10 June, with the final in Rotterdam. Austria and Switzerland co-hosted Euro 2008, starting in Basel and climaxing in Vienna, before Poland and Ukraine teamed up in 2012. Warsaw staged the opening match and Kiev was the host city for the final.

HOST HISTORY
SHARE AND SHARE ALIKE

Ten venues across France were used for the 2016 UEFA European Championship. This equalled the record set by Portugal in 2004, and was two more than the eight stadia which were used in the three shared tournaments (four in each country): Belgium and the Netherlands in 2000; Austria and Switzerland in 2008; and Poland and Ukraine in 2012. It will be all change for the finals in 2020, however, as, for the first time, the first round group stage and first two knock-out rounds will be played across 13 cities in 13 different countries. England has the honour of hosting both semi-finals and the final, with all three to be played at London's Wembley Stadium.

76,833

The Euro 2016 final between France and Portugal could not claim the event's biggest crowd. Instead, that honour went to the French hosts' 5-2 victory over Iceland in the quarter-finals, watched in the Stade de France by 76,833 spectators.

1992

Players wore their names as well as their numbers on the back of their shirts for the first time at Euro 92. They had previously been identified only by numbers.

COPA AMERICA

The world's oldest surviving international championship finds its rich history repeating itself, even in a modern football world otherwise unrecognizable since the days when Uruguay won the inaugural South American Championship in 1916.

Founded: 1916

Current Champions: Brazil

Most Wins: Uruguay, 15 titles

Next Edition: Argentina/Colombia, 2020

6

The 2019 Copa America was hosted across six venues in Brazil in five cities.

In 1984, CONMEBOL adopted the policy of rotating the right to host the Copa América amongst the ten member confederations.

3

The Copa America has been hosted across the whole continent three times (1975, 1979, 1983).

In 1916, the current Copa América trophy was purchased from "Casa Escasany", a jewelry shop in Buenos Aires, at the cost of 3,000 Swiss francs.

Across more than 100 years of the Copa America, there have been only three editions in which neither Argentina nor Brazil has finished in the top four (1939, 2001, 2011).

COPA AMERICA 2019 REVIEW

The 2019 edition of the Copa America featured no shortage of magical moments, captivating contests and controversial incidents as hosts Brazil ultimately came out on top.

SUFFERING SUAREZ

Luis Suarez is Uruguay's all-time top scorer but he was the only player to miss his penalty as the record South American champions crashed out in the quarter-finals in 2019. Suarez saw his first kick in the shootout saved by goalkeeper Pedro Gallese and the Celeste lost 5-4 on spot-kicks to Peru after a 0-0 draw. They also had three goals disallowed, with Giorgian de Arrascaeta, Edinson Cavani and Suarez all being denied by the video assistance system. Uruguay thus joined Paraguay and Colombia in being eliminated from the 2019 Copa America after losing a penalty shoot-out.

LUIS **SUAREZ**

TOURNAMENT TRIVIA
PRICE OF SUCCESS

Poor attendances were a disappointment for Copa organisers in 2019. Even Brazil's 3-0 win over Bolivia in the opening game was watched by only 46,000 fans in the 66,000-capacity Estadio do Morumbi in Sao Paulo. CONMEBOL president Alejandro Dominguez denied that the high ticket prices had been a factor but, at $230 each, tickets to the final cost only a little less than the host country's national monthly minimum wage.

NATIONAL LEGEND
GARECA'S HOME COMFORT

Ricardo Gareca's leadership of Peru to the final enhanced his steadily growing reputation as a coach. Argentinian Gareca had been a goal-scoring centre-forward with Boca Juniors and also scored for his national team. Gareca believes in the quality of South American football, despite the steady star exodus to European clubs. After Peru's knockout wins over Uruguay and then-holders Chile he said: "We don't need to automatically imitate Europe or other continents as a way to improve. We know who we are, we should work on our own style, our own culture."

DANI **ALVES**

Dani Alves was voted the official best player of the tournament after captaining Brazil to victory and claiming the 40th winner's medal of his career.

RICARDO **GARECA**

FINAL PLACEMENT:

1 Brazil

2 Peru

3 Argentina

4 Chile

TOP SCORERS:

1. Everton, 3
= Paolo Guerrero, 3
2. 13 players, 2

14

LIONEL MESSI

Lionel Messi was sent off for the second time in his career during Argentina's third place play-off victory over Chile. His first red card had been 14 years earlier against Hungary.

🏆 TOURNAMENT TRIVIA
SHARING THE FUN

The 2020 Copa America – the fourth edition of the tournament in six years – will be hosted jointly at opposite ends of the continent by Colombia and Argentina. Colombia will host a "northern" section featuring Brazil, Ecuador, Peru and Venezuela while Argentina will welcome Bolivia, Chile, Paraguay and Uruguay. Guest nations will be Australia and Qatar, hosts of the next World Cup.

🖥 TERRIFIC TECH
VAR LEAVES ITS MARK

Copa America organisers were happy with the introduction of VAR for the first time at the tournament in Brazil. But some fans and players were not so satisfied with the use of video assistance. VAR stoppages averaged two minutes 26 seconds. This was almost double the time taken per incident at the 2018 World Cup in Russia, the first time the technology had been implemented on a major international stage. Venezuela had no doubts, however. VAR ruled out four "goals" scored against them including two in a goalless draw with hosts Brazil. "Long live VAR," said coach Rafael Dudamel after the game.

🏆 TOURNAMENT TRIVIA
BRAZIL PLAYING CATCH-UP

Brazil, despite a record five World Cups, still have a long way to go before becoming kings of their own continent. They have won the Copa America nine times, fewer than both Uruguay and Argentina. They also had to wait 12 years between their eighth and ninth triumphs, and even then needed home advantage to triumph in 2019. Success was achieved thanks to a 3-1 win against Peru in Maracana, despite the absence of injured superstar Neymar and the expulsion of **Gabriel Jesus**. The Manchester City centre-forward set up Everton's opening goal, then scored Brazil's second, before being sent off after collecting two yellow cards. Brazil, even with 10 men, extended their lead through a penalty from substitute Richarlison.

GABRIEL JESUS

🏆 TOURNAMENT TRIVIA
PAYING GUESTS

"Foreign" nations have been invited to ramp up the numbers at the Copa America by CONMEBOL ever since 1993. One reason is a push to promote the continent's football worldwide, while the other is additional commercial and broadcasting revenue. Hence regular invitations always go first to media-focused Mexico and the United States plus, this latest time, Japan and Qatar. Japan crashed 4-0 initially to Chile, then drew with Uruguay and Ecuador before flying home after the group stage. Asian champions Qatar drew 2-2 with Paraguay then suffered narrow defeats by Colombia and Argentina. They will be back in 2020.

COPA AMERICA TEAM RECORDS

The South Americans decided to organize their own international competitions, which led to the creation, in 1916, of the South American Championship. Four countries contested that opening tournament, hosts Argentina, Brazil, Chile and Uruguay, who were the inaugural winners.

NATIONAL LEGEND
HOW IT STARTED

The first South American "Championship of Nations", as it was then known, was held in Argentina from 2–17 July 1916, during the country's independence centenary commemorations. The tournament was won by Uruguay, who drew with Argentina in the last match of the tournament. It was an inauspicious beginning. The 16 July encounter had to be abandoned at 0-0 when fans invaded the pitch and set the wooden stands on fire. The match was continued at a different stadium the following day and still ended goalless ... but Uruguay ended up topping the mini-league table and were hailed the first champions.

ISABELINO
GRADIN

3

19-year-old Uruguayan **Isabelino Gradin** was the inaugural tournament's top scorer with three goals. The event also saw the foundation of the South American federation CONMEBOL, which took place a week into the competition on 9 July 1916.

150

The longest match in the history of the Copa America was the 1919 final between Brazil and Uruguay. It lasted 150 minutes, 90 minutes of regular time plus two extra-time periods of 30 minutes each.

COPA AMERICA TITLES :

1 Uruguay, 15 (1916, 1917, 1920, 1923, 1924, 1926, 1935, 1942, 1956, 1959, 1967, 1983, 1987, 1995, 2011)

2 Argentina, 14 (1921, 1925, 1927, 1929, 1937, 1941, 1945, 1946, 1947, 1955, 1957, 1959, 1991, 1993)

3 Brazil, 9 (1919, 1922, 1949, 1989, 1997, 1999, 2004, 2007, 2019)

4 Peru, 2 (1939, 1975)
= **Paraguay, 2** (1939, 1979)
= **Chile, 2** (2015, 2016)

PAULO
DYBALA

TOURNAMENT TRIVIA
RECORD BREAKERS

Argentina, despite finishing only third in the 2019 Copa America, maintained their proud record of having achieved the most victories in the history of the tournament: 122. The Argentinians have also scored the most goals with 462, the last of which was claimed by **Paulo Dybala** in the 2-1 victory over Chile in the third place play-off in Brazil. Less happily, Argentina also share with Uruguay the record of five defeats in penalty shootouts. Lionel Messi & Co lost to Chile on penalties in the finals of the both the 2015 Copa and the 2016 Copa Centenario.

TOURNAMENT TRIVIA
SUB-STANDARD

During the 1953 Copa America, Peru were awarded a walkover win when Paraguay tried to make one more substitution than they were allowed. Would-be substitute Milner Ayala was so incensed, he kicked English referee Richard Maddison and was banned from football for three years. Yet Paraguay remained in the tournament and went on to beat Brazil in the final – minus, of course, the disgraced Ayala. The entire tournament was staged at the Estadio Nacional de Lima.

TOURNAMENT TRIVIA
HISTORY MEN

The Copa America is the world's oldest surviving continental national team football tournament, having been launched in 1916 when four nations entered: Argentina, Brazil, Chile and Uruguay. Bolivia, Colombia, Ecuador, Paraguay, Peru and Venezuela had all joined by 1967. In 1910, an unofficial South American championship was won by Argentina, who beat Uruguay 4–1 in the decider – though the final match had been delayed a day after rioting fans burnt down a stand at the Gimnasia stadium in Buenos Aires.

31

In 1942, Ecuador and their goalkeeper Napoleon Medina conceded more goals in one tournament than any other team, when they let in 31 goals across six games – and six defeats.

VICTOR **ARISTAZABAL**

TOURNAMENT TRIVIA
WELCOME VISITORS

Nine guest nations have appeared in the Copa America. **Mexico**, from central America, have not only been the most popular with 10 appearances but nearly achieved what would have been embarrassing victories in 1993 and 2001. Each time they reached the final before losing 2–1 to Argentina and 1–0 to Colombia respectively. Four guests have appeared only once: Honduras (2001), Haiti and Panama (both 2016) plus Qatar (2019).

HOSTING RIGHTS BY COUNTRY:

1 **Argentina, 9** (1916, 1921, 1925, 1929, 1937, 1946, 1959, 1987, 2011)

2 **Chile, 7** (1920, 1926, 1941, 1945, 1955, 1991, 2015)

= **Uruguay, 7** (1917, 1923, 1924, 1942, 1956, 1967, 1995)

3 **Peru, 6** (1927, 1935, 1939, 1953, 1957, 2004)

4 **Brazil, 5** (1919, 1922, 1949, 1989, 2019)

In 2001, Colombia, who went on to win the trophy for the first and only time in their history, became the only country to go through an entire Copa America campaign without conceding a single goal. They scored 11 themselves, more than half of them from six-goal tournament top scorer **Victor Aristazabal**.

0

Paraguay reached the 2011 final despite not winning a single game in normal play. Instead, they drew all three matches in the first-round group stage, then needed penalties to win their quarter-final against Brazil and semi-final versus Venezuela after both games ended goalless.

TOURNAMENT TRIVIA
MORE FROM MORENO

Argentina were not only responsible for the Copa America's biggest win, but also the tournament's highest-scoring game, when they put 12 past Ecuador in 1942 – to no reply. Jose Manuel Moreno's five strikes in that game included the 500th goal in the competition's history. Moreno, born in Buenos Aires on 3 August 1916, ended that tournament as joint top scorer with team-mate Herminio Masantonio – hitting seven goals. Both men ended their international careers with 19 goals for their country, though Moreno did so in 34 appearances – compared to Masantonio's 21. Masantonio scored four in the Ecuador thrashing.

COPA AMERICA PLAYER RECORDS

For more than a century, the Copa America has showcased the very best of South America's football talent on the pitch. Unsurprisingly, its goalscoring and appearance records read as a who's who of the continent's most enduring sporting superstars.

NATIONAL LEGEND
LIKE GRANDFATHER, LIKE FATHER, LIKE SON

Diego Forlan's two goals in the 2011 Copa America final helped Uruguay to a 3-0 victory over Paraguay and their record 15th South American championship. They also ensured he followed in family footsteps in lifting the trophy – his father **Pablo** was part of the Uruguay side who won in 1967, when his grandfather Juan Carlos Corazzo was the triumphant coach. Corazzo had previously managed Uruguay's winning team in 1959. The brace against Paraguay put the youngest Forlan level with Hector Scarone as Uruguay's all-time leading scorer, with 31 goals. Yet it was Forlan's strike partner Luis Suarez who was voted best player of the 2011 tournament.

PABLO
FORLAN

NATIONAL LEGEND
FROG PRINCE

Chilean goalkeeper Sergio Livingstone holds the record for most Copa America appearances, with 34 games, from 1941 to 1953. Livingstone, nicknamed "The Frog", was voted player of the tournament in 1941 – becoming the first goalkeeper to win the award – and might have played even more Copa America matches had he not missed out on the 1946 competition. Livingstone, born in Santiago on 26 March 1920, spent almost his entire career in his home country – save for a season with Argentina's Racing Club in 1943–44. Overall, he made 52 appearances for Chile between 1941 and 1954, before retiring and becoming a popular TV journalist and commentator.

NATIONAL LEGEND
MAGIC ALEX

Ecuador's Alex Aguinaga, a midfielder born in Ibarra on 9 July 1969, played a total of 109 times for his country – 25 of them in the Copa America, a competition that yielded four of his 23 international goals. His Copa America career certainly began well: Ecuador went undefeated for his first four appearances, at the 1987 and 1989 events, but his luck had ran out by the time his Ecuador career was coming to an end: he lost his final seven Copa America matches.

OVERALL TOP SCORERS:

1 **Norberto Mendez** (Argentina), 17
= **Zizinho** (Brazil), 17
3 **Teodoro Fernandez** (Peru), 15
= **Severino Varela** (Uruguay), 15
5 **Paolo Guerrero** (Peru), 14

NORBERTO
MENDEZ

1917
The first Copa America own goal was scored by Chile's Luis Garcia, giving Argentina a 1-0 win in 1917, in the second edition of the tournament.

8

When Alex Aguinaga lined up for Ecuador against Uruguay in his country's opening game at the 2004 event, he became only the second man to take part in eight different Copa Americas – joining legendary Uruguayan goalscorer Angel Romano.

MOST GAMES PLAYED:

1 **Sergio Livingstone** (Chile), 34

2 **Zizinho** (Brazil), 33

3 **Leonel Alvarez** (Colombia), 27

= **Carlos Valderrama** (Colombia), 27

= **Lionel Messi** (Argentina), 27

NATIONAL LEGEND
START TO FINISH

Colombia playmaker Carlos Valderrama and defensive midfielder **Leonel Alvarez** played in all 27 of their country's Copa America matches between 1987 and 1995, winning ten, drawing ten and losing seven – including third- place finishes in 1987, 1993 and 1995. Valderrama's two Copa America goals came in his first and final appearances in the competition – in a 2–0 victory over Bolivia in 1987 and a 4–1 thrashing of the United States eight years later.

17

Brazilian forward Zizinho jointly holds the all-time goalscoring record for the Copa America, along with Argentina's Norberto Mendez. Both men struck 17 goals, Zizinho across six tournaments and Mendez three.

4–0

The first-ever Copa America goal, in 1916, was scored by Jose Piendibene – setting Uruguay on the way to a 4–0 triumph over Chile.

LEONEL ALVAREZ

NATIONAL LEGEND
REPEATING THE FEAT

Gabriel Batistuta is the only Argentinian to win the award twice as leading marksman at the Copa America. He made his Albiceleste debut only days before the 1991 event in which his six goals – including a crucial strike in the concluding match (it was a mini group as opposed to a final) victory over Colombia – earned a transfer from Boca Juniors to Fiorentina. Nicknamed "Batigol" in Italy, he was joint top scorer in 1995, with four goals, along with Mexico's Luis Garcia.

GABRIEL BATISTUTA

5

Four players have scored five goals in one Copa America game: Hector Scarone was the first in Uruguay's 6–0 win over Bolivia in 1926

NATIONAL LEGEND
PELE'S INSPIRATION

Brazilian forward **Zizinho** jointly holds the all-time goalscoring record for the Copa America, along with Argentina's Norberto Mendez. Mendez was top scorer once and runner-up twice and won championship medals on all three occasions, while Zizinho's goals helped Brazil take the title only once, in 1949. Zizinho, Pele's footballing idol, would emerge from the 1950 FIFA World Cup as Brazil's top scorer and was also voted the tournament's best player – but was forever traumatized by the hosts' surprise defeat to Uruguay that cost Brazil the title.

ZIZINHO

171

COPA AMERICA OTHER RECORDS

CAPTAIN CONSISTENT

Uruguay's 1930 World Cup-winning captain **Jose Nasazzi** is the only footballer to be voted player of the tournament at two different Copa America tournaments. Even more impressively, he achieved the feat 12 years apart – first taking the prize in 1923, then again in 1935. He was a Cup winner in 1923, 1924, 1926 and 1935. Nasazzi also captained Uruguay to victory in the 1924 and 1928 Olympic Games and in the 1930 World Cup.

Format changes, guest teams and a highly competitive field have meant that the Copa America rarely looks the same from one edition to the next. Despite that, a number of records have stood the test of time.

JOSE
NASAZZI

38

Uruguay have a unique record in remaining unbeaten in 38 Copa America games on home turf, all played in the country's capital Montevideo – comprising 31 wins, seven draws.

TROPHY-WINNING COACHES:

1 **Guillermo Stabile,** 6 (Argentina 1941, 1945, 1946, 1947, 1955, 1957)

2 **Alfio Basile,** 2 (Argentina 1991, 1993)

= **Juan Carlos Corazzo,** 2 (Uruguay 1959, 1967)

= **Ernesto Figoli,** 2 (Uruguay 1920, 1926)

3 (34 coaches on 1 title each)

NATIONAL LEGEND
KEEP COMING BACK

Hernan Dario Gomez coached Panama at the 2016 Copa American Centenario, making him only the third man to manage at six different Copa America tournaments. He was joined three years later by Oscar Washington Tabarez, who took charge of Uruguay at a sixth Copa America in 2019, having been in charge in 1989, 2007, 2011, 2015 and 2016. Dario Gomez previously led his native Colombia in 1995, 1997 and 2011, and Ecuador in 2001 and 2004.

HERNAN DARIO
GOMEZ

44

Guillermo Stabile solely holds the record for managing most Copa America matches (44), followed by Chile's Luis Tirado (35), Paraguay's Manuel Fleitas Solich (33), and Uruguay's Oscar Tabarez (30).

GUILLERMO STABILE

NATIONAL LEGEND
MULTI-TASKING

Argentina's **Guillermo Stabile** coached Argentina from 1939 to 1960, having been appointed at the age of just 34. He lasted for 123 games in charge, winning 83 of them – and still managed to coach three clubs on the side at different times throughout his reign. He remained as Red Star Paris manager during his first year in the Argentina role, then led Argentine club Huracan for the next nine years – before leading domestic rivals Racing Club from 1949 to 1960. Stabile's Argentina missed out on Copa America success in 1949, but that year brought the first of three Argentina league championships in a row for Stabile's Racing Club.

SCORING RECORD
GOALS AT A PREMIUM

In terms of goals per game, the 2011 Copa America was the second tightest of all time – with only 54 strikes hitting the back of the net in 26 matches, an average of 2.08 per game. The 1922 tournament, in Brazil, saw fewer – 22 goals in 11 games, an average of two. Both competitions were a far cry from the prolific 1927 event in Peru, where 37 goals across six games averaged out at 6.17. The 91 goals in 2016 came at an average of 2.84 per match.

6

Argentina's Guillermo Stabile not only holds the record for most Copa America triumphs as coach – he trounces all opposition. He led his country to the title on no fewer than six occasions – in 1941, 1945, 1946, 1947, 1955 and 1957. No other coach has lifted the trophy more than twice

Six guests were invited to the centenary tournament in 2016: Costa Rica, Haiti, Jamaica, Mexico, Panama and the United States.

TOURNAMENT TRIVIA
AWAY WINNERS

Only four men have coached a country other than their native one to Copa America glory. The first was Englishman Jack Greenwell, with Peru in 1939. Brazilian Danilo Alvim was the second to do it, with Bolivia in 1963 – against Brazil. History repeated itself in 2015 and 2016, when Argentina-born Jorge Sampaoli and then Juan Antonio Pizzi took Chile to Copa glory, both times beating Argentina in final penalty shoot-outs.

TOURNAMENT TRIVIA
SEEING RED

Brazil may have the worst FIFA World Cup disciplinary record, but neighbours Uruguay assume that unenviable position in the Copa America. Uruguayan players have been sent off 32 times – the latest being **Matias Vecino** against Mexico in 2016 – followed by Argentina on 25 dismissals, Peru (24), Brazil and Venezuela (21 each), Chile (19), Paraguay (15), Bolivia and Ecuador (13 apiece), Colombia (11), Mexico (ten), the United States (three), Costa Rica (two), and Honduras, Jamaica, Japan and Panama (one each).

MATIAS VECINO

INVITED GUESTS:

1. **Mexico,** 10
2. **Costa Rica,** 5
3. **United States,** 4
4. **Jamaica,** 2
   = **Japan,** 2
6. **Qatar,** 1
   = **Honduras** 1
   = **Haiti** 1
   = **Panama** 1

21

It took 21 years, but Uruguay's Juan Emilio Piriz became the first Copa America player sent off, against Chile in 1937.

AFRICA CUP OF NATIONS

The African governing football confederation
– Confederation Africaine de Football (or
CAF) – is three years younger than UEFA,
yet its cross-continental tournament, the
Africa Cup of Nations, kicked off before
the first European Championship
in 1957.

Founded: 1957

Current Champions:
Algeria

Most Wins:
Egypt, 7 titles

Next Edition:
Cameroon, 2021

6

Six different nations won titles from 1970 to 1980: Sudan, Congo, Zaire, Morocco, Ghana, and Nigeria.

As of 2013, the Africa Cup of Nations was switched to being held in odd-numbered years so as not to clash with the FIFA World Cup.

11

The UNAF (North Africa) regional federation has won more titles than any other in Africa.

24

24 teams competed in the 2019 tournament, an increase from 16 in 2017.

The original Africa Cup of Nations trophy, was the Abdelaziz Abdallah Salem Trophy, named after the first CAF president, Egyptian Abdelaziz Abdallah Salem.

AFRICA CUP OF NATIONS 2019 REVIEW

A new, expanded format and a new time in June and July ensured this was an Africa Cup of Nations like none before it. After some shock results and a host of late drama, Algeria's Desert Foxes triumphed to claim their second continental title.

AWARDS:

BEST PLAYER:
Ismael Bennacer (Algeria)

BEST GOALKEEPER:
Rais M'Bolhi (Algeria)

BEST YOUNG PLAYER:
Ismael Bennacer (Algeria)

FAIR PLAY: Senegal

STAR PLAYERS
RIVALRY RENEWED

The 2019 Africa Cup of Nations final was billed as a duel between **Riyad Mahrez** and **Sadio Mane** after the pair's battle to claim the English Premier League title ended with Mahrez's Manchester City finishing top of the table above Mane's Liverpool by a single point. Algeria's 1–0 victory meant Mahrez added the continental trophy to the domestic triple of league, FA Cup and League Cup he won with his club. Liverpool forward Mane had to settle for a runners-up medal weeks after lifting the UEFA Champions League in Madrid as Liverpool beat Tottenham Hotspur 2–0. Both players were kept quiet in the ACN final but had made their mark on the tournament – Mahrez's free-kick strike five minutes into stoppage-time gave his side a 2–1 triumph over Nigeria in the semi-finals, and both players ended the competition with three goals apiece.

RIYAD **MAHREZ**

SADIO **MANE**

6

Six stadia staged matches at the 2019 Africa Cup of Nations, whittled down from original plans for eight to play host.

TOURNAMENT TRIVIA
ALGERIA HYSTERIA

The decisive goal owed a little to luck but Algeria were not worried as they won the Africa Cup of Nations for only the second time in 2019 – some 29 years since their first success. Striker Baghdad Bounedjah was the hero. His long-range effort after only two minutes took a deflection off Senegal defender Salif Sane before looping over goalkeeper Alfred Gomis. It was Bounedjah's second goal of the tournament – his first was Algeria's opener, in a 2–0 Group C victory over Kenya. AC Milan and former Arsenal midfielder Ismael Bennacer was named both the tournament's best player and best young player. Algeria manager and former international midfielder **Djamel Belmadi,** who had taken over in August 2018, said: "Without the players I am nothing. They are the main ones. I suppose the staff played its part in guiding the players but they applied the instructions incredibly well." Wild celebrations erupted not only across Algeria, but also in Paris and central London, where expatriate Algerians set off fireworks in Trafalgar Square.

DJAMEL **BELMADI**

TOP SCORERS:

1 Odion Ighalo
(Nigeria), 5

2 Riyadh Mahrez
(Algeria), 3

= Adam Ounas
(Algeria), 3

= Cedric Bakambu
(DR Congo), 3

= Sadio Mane
(Senegal), 3

ODION IGHALO

STAR PLAYER
WELL DONE, ODION

Nigeria striker **Odion Ighalo** was not only the top scorer in qualifying for the 2019 Africa Cup of Nations, with seven goals, but also claimed the Golden Boot at the tournament itself. Ighalo found the net five times, including a brace as defending champions Cameroon were beaten 3-2 in the second round, and the third-minute winner against Tunisia in the third-place play-off. Ighalo suffered a hamstring injury in his last appearance in Egypt before announcing he would not play for Nigeria again – only to swiftly reverse his international retirement.

TOURNAMENT TRIVIA
MAD FOR IT

The 2019 Africa Cup of Nations was the first to be staged in the middle of the year rather than at the start – and also the first to feature 24 teams rather than 16. There were three nations making their tournament debut: Burundi, Madagascar and Mauritania. Burundi and Mauritania both finished winless and bottom of their first-round groups, but Madagascar proved the surprise package of the summer. They reached the quarter-finals, after stand-out displays including a second-round 4-2 penalty shoot-out besting of DR Congo following a dramatic 2-2 draw. Stars included striker Carolus Andriamatsinoro, who scored in a 2-2 draw with Guinea and in a 2-0 surprise win over Nigeria on the way to topping Group B. Madagascar's dream run ended in the quarter-finals, as they were beaten 3-0 by Tunisia.

TOURNAMENT TRIVIA
PHARAOHS NOT ENOUGH

Fans of host nation Egypt were shocked by their second-round elimination by South Africa, thanks to a late winner by Thembinkosi Lorch – especially after African Footballer of the Year Mohamed Salah had scored twice to help them top Group A. He and Pharaohs captain Ahmed Elmohamady were both on the scoresheet in 2-0 victories over DR Congo and Uganda, but their second-round exit saw their Mexican coach Javier Aguirre fired within hours. He was one of seven managers who lost their jobs in defeat. Morocco head coach Herve Renard – a two-time African Cup of Nations winner – stepped down on 21 July after a second-round defeat on penalties by 10-man Benin, after Ajax playmaker Hakim Ziyech had missed an added-time spot-kick. Morocco departed the tournament despite winning all three of their first-round matches without conceding a goal. Defending champions Cameroon dismissed former Netherlands international Clarence Seedorf and his assistant Patrick Kluivert after they too departed at the second stage.

TOURNAMENT TRIVIA
WILLIAM, IT WAS REALLY SOMETHING

Unfortunate defender William Troost-Ekong went from hero to villain for Nigeria. The Dutch-born Udinese centre-back bundled the ball into the net with just a minute remaining of Nigeria's quarter-final against South Africa, securing a 2-1 win in the Cairo International Stadium – but four days later he scored a 40th-minute own goal in the same ground, inadvertently opening the scoring in their 2-1 loss to eventual champions Algeria.

TOURNAMENT TRIVIA
TEAM VALUES

Senegal lost to Algeria in the final but had most players in the official team of the tournament. Their five nominees included defenders Lamine Gassama and Youssouf Sabaly, midfielder Idrissa Gueye and forward Sadio Mane as well as inspirational Napoli centre-back Kalidou Koulibaly who was ruled out of the final through suspension. Algeria were represented by goalkeeper Rais M'Bohli, midfielders Adlene Guedioura and **Ismael Bennacer** and playmaker Riyad Mahrez. Tunisia defender Yassine Meriah and Golden Boot winner Odion Ighalo of Nigeria completed the 11 players selected.

ISMAEL BENNACER

AFRICA CUP OF NATIONS TEAM RECORDS

Only three nations competed in the inaugural 1957 Africa Cup of Nations, while 51 vied for the 15 qualification spots at the 2017 event, and the 24 places in 2019. Egypt were late replacements as hosts, so participated in qualifying. The three countries not to play were Chad, Eritrea and Somalia.

9

Ghana have now reached nine finals in all – a tally Egypt matched in 2017. Egypt are also the most prolific hosts, having held the tournament five times, including in 2019.

TOURNAMENT TRIVIA
GIMME GUINEA GIMME

Guinea equalled the record for biggest ever win at an Africa Cup of Nations when they beat Botswana 6-1 in a first-round match in 2012 – though both teams failed to make it out of Group D. Guinea were also only the third team to score six times in one match at a finals, following Egypt's 6-3 win over Nigeria in 1963 and Ivory Coast's 6-1 defeat of Ethiopia seven years later. The only other game to match the record-winning margin saw Guinea not as the victors but the victims, going down 5-0 to Ivory Coast in 2008.

TOURNAMENT TRIUMPHS:

1. **7 – Egypt** (1957, 1959, 1986, 1998, 2006, 2008, 2010)
2. **5 – Cameroon** (1984, 1988, 2000, 2002, 2017)
3. **4 – Ghana** (1963, 1965, 1978, 1982)
4. **3 – Nigeria** (1980, 1994, 2013)
5. **2 – Ivory Coast** (1992, 2015)
   = **Zaire/DR Congo, 2** (1968, 1974)
   = **Algeria, 2** (1990, 2019)

TOURNAMENT TRIVIA
FROM TRAGEDY TO TRIUMPH

Zambia's unexpected glory at the 2012 Africa Cup of Nations was fitting and poignant as the setting for their glory was just a few hundred metres from the scene of earlier calamity. The 2012 players spent the day before the final against Ivory Coast laying flowers in the sea in tribute to the 30 people killed when a plane crashed off the coast of Gabonese city Libreville on 27 April 1993. Victims that day included 18 Zambian internationals flying to Senegal for a FIFA World Cup qualifier. Coach Herve Renard dedicated the 2012 victory to the dead, after Zambia beat Ivory Coast on penalties following a goalless draw after extra-time.

2

The 2012 event was only the second to be shared between two host nation – Equatorial Guinea and Gabon – after Ghana and Nigeria shared duties in 2000.

TOURNAMENT TRIVIA
REIGNING PHARAOHS

Egypt dominate the Africa Cup of Nations records. They won the first tournament, in 1957, having been helped by a bye to the final when semi-final opponents South Africa were disqualified, and have emerged as champions another six times since – more than any other country. Their victories in 2006, 2008 and 2010 make them the only country to have lifted the trophy three times in a row. They have also appeared in a record 24 tournaments, one more than Ivory Coast and two more than Ghana.

4

Ghana's "Black Stars" became the first country to reach the final of four consecutive Africa Cup of Nations, lifting the trophy in 1963 and 1965 and finishing runners-up in 1968 and 1970.

TOURNAMENT TRIVIA
FOUR SHAME

Hosts Angola were responsible for perhaps the most dramatic collapse in Africa Cup of Nations history, when they threw away a four-goal lead in the opening match of the 2010 tournament. Even more embarrassingly, they were leading 4-0 against Mali with just 11 minutes left, in the capital Luanda's Estadio 11 de Novembro. Mali's final two goals, by Barcelona's Seydou Keita and Boulogne's Mustapha Yatabare, were scored deep into stoppage-time. Mali failed to make it through the first round, while Angola went out in the quarter-finals.

FISTON ABDUL RAZAK

TOURNAMENT TRIVIA
THE WAITING IS THE HARDEST PART

Some 12 of the 54 full members of the African football confederation have yet to appear in the finals of the Cup of Nations. The latest newcomers to join the party were Burundi, Madagascar and Mauritania in 2019 – with Madagascar especially causing a stir by reaching the quarter-finals. Mauritania made it there thanks to a 2-1 victory over Botswana in November 2018, with both their goals scored by forward Ismael Diakite – while Burundi were spearheaded by striker **Fiston Abdul Razak** who struck four times that month in their 5-2 defeat of South Sudan. Still waiting to make their first finals are Central African Republic, Chad, Comoros, Djibouti, Eritrea, Gambia, Lesotho, Sao Tome e Principe, Seychelles, Somalia, Swaziland and South Sudan. The latter made their qualifying debut only in 2015.

24

The Ivory Coast have won two of the highest-scoring penalty shoot-outs in full international history – they defeated Ghana 11-10 over 24 penalties in the 1992 Africa Cup of Nations final, and Cameroon 12-11, over the same number of kicks, in the quarter-finals of the 2006 Africa Cup of Nations.

3

In 2012, both Ivory Coast and Zambia were competing in their third Africa Cup of Nations final, Ivory Coast having won in 1992 and lost in 2006, while Zambia had finished runners-up in 1974 and 1994.

AFRICA CUP OF NATIONS PLAYER RECORDS

Ghana striker Asamoah Gyan became the third man to appear at eight different Africa Cup of Nations tournaments when he captained the side in 2019, following Cameroon's Rigobert Song and Egypt's Ahmed Hassan.

The global prominence of the Africa Cup of Nations has also grown, especially when the spotlight fell on major African stars taking time off from European club duties every other January. Now, more than ever, the tournament is a showcase for many of the most talented and successful players in the sport.

TOURNAMENT TRIVIA
SIBLING HARMONY

Both teams in the final of the 2015 Africa Cup of Nations called upon a pair of brothers. Runners-up Ghana included Jordan and Andre Ayew, while Ivory Coast's champions were spearheaded by captain **Yaya Toure** and his centre-back brother Kolo. All four brothers took penalties in the 2015 final and scored, unlike in 2012, when the Ivory Coast were beaten in another penalty shoot-out, this time against Zambia. Yaya had been substituted in extra time, but Kolo missed in the 8-7 loss. Zambia's triumphant captain in 2012, player of the tournament Christian Katongo, had among his team-mates brother Felix – he came off the bench – and they both scored in that shoot-out.

YAYA TOURE

1957
The first Africa Cup of Nations goal was a penalty scored by Egypt's Raafat Ateya in the 21st minute of their 2-1 semi-final win over Sudan in 1957.

SAMUEL ETO'O

ALL-TIME TOP SCORERS :

1 **Samuel Eto'o** (Cameroon), 18
2 **Laurent Pokou** (Ivory Coast), 14
3 **Rashidi Yekini** (Nigeria), 13
4 **Hassan El-Shazly** (Egypt), 12
5 **Andre Ayew** (Ghana), 11
   = **Didier Drogba** (Ivory Coast), 11
   = **Hossam Hassan** (Egypt), 11
   = **Patrick Mboma** (Cameroon), 11

NATIONAL LEGEND
SAM THE MAN

Cameroon's Samuel Eto'o, who made his full international debut – away to Costa Rica on 9 March 1997 – one day short of his 16th birthday, is the Africa Cup of Nations' all-time leading goalscorer. He was part of Cameroon's victorious teams in 2000 and 2002, but had to wait until 2008 to pass Laurent Pokou's 14-goal Africa Cup of Nations record. That year's competition took his overall tally to 16 goals – only for the former Real Madrid and Barcelona striker, now with Italy's Internazionale, to add another two in 2010. In 2005, Eto'o became the first player to be named African Footballer of the Year three years running.

STAR PLAYER
MANE SHOWS HOW MUCH HE MATTERS

The Africa Cup of Nations' cost to European clubs was illustrated perfectly after Senegal's **Sadio Mane** left Liverpool to play at the finals in Gabon in January 2017. Mane had first played in England with Senegal at the London 2012 Olympic Games and returned two years later to play in the Premier League with Southampton. In 2016 Liverpool bought him for £30m, making him, at the time, the most expensive ever African player. Mane won the 2019 UEFA Champions League final with Liverpool in June 2019 but said he would happily trade that for victory in the Africa Cup of Nations final in Egypt the following month, only to end the game forlorn as Senegal were beaten 1-0 by Algeria. This was thezir second runners-up finish after losing the 2002 final on penalties to Cameroon.

SADIO **MANE**

SINGLE TOURNAMENT TOP SCORERS:

1 **Ndaye Mulamba** (Zaire), 9 – 1974

2 **Laurent Pokou** (Ivory Coast), 8 – 1970

3 **Hossam Hassan** (Egypt), 8 – 1998

= **Benni McCarthy** (South Africa), 8 – 1998

4 **Hassan El Shazly** (Egypt), 6 – 1963

= **Laurent Pokou** (Ivory Coast), 6 – 1968

NATIONAL LEGEND
NO HASSLE FOR HASSAN

Egypt's **Ahmed Hassan** not only became the first footballer to play in the final of four different Africa Cup of Nations in 2010 – he also became the first to collect his fourth winners' medal. Earlier in the same tournament, his appearance in the quarter-final against Cameroon gave him his 170th cap – an Egyptian record. Hassan marked the game with three goals – one in his own net and two past Cameroon goalkeeper Carlos Kameni – although one appeared not to cross the line.

AHMED **HASSAN**

LAURENT **POKOU**

5

Ivory Coast striker Laurent Pokou scored a record five goals in one Africa Cup of Nations match, as his side trounced Ethiopia 6-1 in the first round of the 1968 tournament. He finished top scorer at that tournament, and the following one – though ended both without a winners' medal.

NATIONAL LEGEND
YO, YOBO

Nigeria's **Joseph Yobo** was brought on as a late substitute to the fans' acclaim in the closing minutes of the Green Eagles' victory over Burkina Faso in the 2013 Africa Cup of Nations final in Johannesburg, South Africa. As captain, the one-time Marseille and Everton defender then had the honour of lifting the trophy. Yobo retired from international football in 2014, have made a record 101 appearances in his 13-year career.

JOSEPH **YOBO**

9

No player has scored more goals in one Africa Cup of Nations than Zaire's Ndaye Mulamba's nine during the 1974 tournament.

AFRICA CUP OF NATIONS OTHER RECORDS

STEPHEN KESHI

More different countries have won the ACON than any other continental championship, with glory being shared among 14 separate nations – including Africa's largest three countries Sudan, Algeria and Congo DR.

TOURNAMENT TRIVIA
ATAK ATTACKS

South Sudan won an international for the first time on 5 September 2015, when midfielder Atak Lual got the only goal of a 2017 Africa Cup of Nations qualifier against Equatorial Guinea. The game was played at South Sudan's national stadium in Juba. South Sudan had initially gained independence as a country in 2011, receiving CAF admission in February 2012 and FIFA status three months later. They drew their first official international, 2–2 against Uganda on 10 July 2012, but their winless run continued with one more draw and ten defeats before that success against Equatorial Guinea.

1.96
The 2019 tournament in Egypt was the second-lowest-scoring Cup of Nations ever, with an average of a mere 1.96 goals per game.

NATIONAL LEGEND
RENARD REDEEMED

In 2015, Frenchman **Herve Renard** became the first coach to win the Africa Cup of Nations with two different countries. This time he was in charge of Ivory Coast as they defeated Ghana on penalties. Three years earlier, Renard's Zambia had defeated the Ivorians, also on spot-kicks, in what was his second spell as national coach. He had resigned in 2010 to become Angola's coach, and his return was not universally welcomed in Zambia. All was forgiven when his team won their first Africa Cup of Nations. Renard's celebrations included carrying on to the pitch injured defender Joseph Musonda, who had limped off after ten minutes of the final.

LAST FIVE AFRICA CUP OF NATIONS-WINNING COACHES:

1. 2019 – Djamel Belmadi (Algeria)
2. 2017 – Hugo Broos (Cameroon)
3. 2015 – Herve Renard (Ivory Coast)
4. 2013 – Stephen Keshi (Nigeria)
5. 2012 – Herve Renard (Zambia)

HERVE RENARD

TOURNAMENT TRIVIA
TOGO'S TRAGIC FATE

Togo were the victims of tragedy shortly before the 2010 Africa Cup of Nations kicked off – followed by expulsion from the event. The team's bus was fired on by Angolan militants three days before their first scheduled match, killing three people: the team's assistant coach, press officer and bus driver. The team returned home to Togo for three days of national mourning, and were then thrown out of the competition by the CAF as punishment for missing their opening game against Ghana. Togo were later expelled from the 2012 and 2014 competitions, but this sanction was overturned on appeal in May 2010.

5

Mauritania made unwanted Africa Cup of Nations history by having five players sent off during a qualifier away to Cape Verde in June 2003, forcing the match to be abandoned. The hosts were leading 3-0 at the time and that stood as the final result.

15

The last of the Africa Cup of Nations' 15 hat-tricks was scored back in 2008, by **Soufiane Alloudi** in the opening half-hour of Morocco's 5-1 first-round win over Namibia.

MOHAMED **NAGY**

SOUFIANE **ALLOUDI**

TOURNAMENT TRIVIA
UNFINISHED BUSINESS

Beware – if you go to see Nigeria play Tunisia, you may not get the full 90 minutes. Nigeria were awarded third place at the 1978 Africa Cup of Nations after Tunisia walked off after 42 minutes of their play-off, with the score at 1-1. They were protesting about refereeing decisions, but thus granted Nigeria a 2-0 victory by default. Oddly enough, it had been Nigeria walking off when the two teams met in the second leg of a qualifier for the 1962 tournament. Their action came when Tunisia equalized after 65 minutes. The punishment was a 2-0 win in Tunisia's favour – putting them 3-2 ahead on aggregate.

NATIONAL LEGEND
GEDO BLASTER

Egypt's hero in 2010 was **Mohamed Nagy**, better known by his nickname "Gedo" – Egyptian Arabic for "Grandpa". He scored the only goal of the final, against Ghana, his fifth of the tournament, giving him the Golden Boot. Yet he did all this without starting a single game. He had to settle for coming on as a substitute in all six of Egypt's matches, playing a total of 135 minutes in all. Gedo – born in Damanhur on 3 October 1984 – made his international debut only two months earlier, and had played only two friendlies for Egypt before the tournament proper.

TOURNAMENT TRIVIA
MISSING THE POINT

The absences of Cameroon, Nigeria and reigning champions Egypt from the 2012 African Cup of Nations were surprising – though each could at least comfort themselves on not missing out in quite such embarrassing circumstances as South Africa. They appeared happy to play out a goalless draw with Sierra Leone in their final qualifier, believing that would be enough to go through – and greeted the final whistle with celebrations on the pitch. But they were mistaken in thinking goal difference would be used to separate teams level on points in their group, with Niger qualifying instead thanks to a better head-to-head record.

2

Only Egypt's Hassan El-Shazly has hit two ACON hat-tricks: his first came in a 6-3 victory over Nigeria in 1963; he repeated the feat, six years later, in a 3-1 victory over Ivory Coast.

OTHER FIFA TOURNAMENTS

More than three billion people are involved in football in one way or another. This passion and ambition explains why the international game's competitive structure has expanded to meet demand.

Real Madrid celebrate winning the FIFA Club World Cup after beating Al-Ain in Abu Dhabi.

Innovations in world competition have been introduced down to a local level, and increasingly imaginative concepts for tournament hosting have allowed more and more smaller nations to enjoy the excitement of welcoming the world. A recent example, in 2017, was the breaking of new ground with the staging of the U-17 World Cup in India – where England defeated Spain 5-2 in the final. A year earlier, in 2016, the U-17 Women's World Cup in Jordan saw the first FIFA women's tournament to be staged in a Muslim country in the Middle East. In both cases, the legacy created by upgraded stadia and training facilities has already benefited football in the countries.

In 1977, the FIFA World Youth Cup was launched. Eight years later came the FIFA Under-17 World Cup. Simultaneously, the Olympic Games men's football tournament became an Under-23 event, though three over-age players could play in the finals. In 2000, FIFA initiated the FIFA Club World Cup. These world-class events encouraged regional confederations to create their own tournaments so their teams could take to the world stage and test themselves against elite opponents.

FIFA U-20 WORLD CUP

First staged in 1977 in Tunisia and known as the FIFA Youth World Championship until 2005, the FIFA U-20 World Cup was claimed by first-time winners Ukraine in 2019, following a 3-1 win over South Korea in Poland.

TOURNAMENT TRIVIA
SUPER SUB

The Soviet Union became the first winners of the FIFA Under-20 World Cup when they beat hosts Mexico 9-8 on penalties after a 2-2 draw in the 1977 final. Their shoot-out hero was substitute goalkeeper Yuri Sivuha, who had replaced Aleksandre Novikov during extra-time. It remains the only time the Soviet Union won the event, though their striker **Oleg Salenko**, a future 1994 FIFA World Cup Golden Boot winner, took the top scorer award in 1989, with five goals.

OLEG **SALENKO**

NATIONAL LEGENDS
CAPTAIN MARVELS

Two men have lifted both the FIFA Under-20 World Cup and the FIFA World Cup as captain: Brazil's Dunga (in 1983 and 1994) and Argentina's Diego Maradona (in 1979 and 1986). Many had expected Maradona to make Argentina's full squad for the 1978 FIFA World Cup but he missed out on selection. He showed his potential by being voted best player at the 1979 youth tournament in Japan.

Only three players have won the tournament twice: Fernando Brassard (Portugal, 1989, 1991) João Vieira Pinto (Portugal, 1989, 1991) and Sergio Aguero (Argentina, 2005, 2007).

RECENT HISTORY
HISTORY BOYS

England celebrated their first world crown since 1966 when the Under-20s triumphed in South Korea in 2017. They defeated Venezuela 1-0 in the final in Suwon, thanks to a 34th-minute goal from Everton's Dominic Calvert-Lewin. Both teams hit the post during the game and Newcastle goalkeeper Freddie Woodman was England's other hero, saving a 75th-minute penalty from Adalberto Penaranda, who, ironically, was on the books of English Premier League club Watford. Woodman took the award as the tournament's top keeper while Dominic Solanke was voted best player. England manager Paul Simpson was born on 26 July 1966, four days before England's World Cup victory.

SCORING RECORD
SAVIOUR SAVIOLA

Javier Saviola has scored more goals in one FIFA Under-20 World Cup than any other player – he managed 11 in seven games at the 2001 competition, as his side Argentina went on to beat Ghana in the final, with Saviola scoring his team's three unanswered goals. Saviola, born on 11 December 1981 in Buenos Aires, was playing for River Plate at the time but joined Barcelona for £15 million not long afterwards – before later signing for the Spanish side's arch-rivals Real Madrid. When Pele picked his 125 "greatest living footballers" for FIFA in March 2004, 22-year-old Saviola was the youngest player on the list.

JAVIER
SAVIOLA

4-0

The joint-highest scoreline in a tournament final was 4-0: West Germany beat Qatar by that scoreline in 1981, and Spain beat Japan by the same margin in 1999.

18

Brazil have had the most appearances at the tournamanent – 18 – and have managed 16 of those in a row, the most consecutive appearances at the tournament.

1991
In 1991, Portugal became the first hosts to win the tournament with a team that became known as the country's "Golden Generation", featuring Luis Figo, Rui Costa, Joao Pinto, Abel Xavier and Jorge Costa.

NATIONAL LEGEND
WHAT A MESSI

Lionel Messi was the star of the show for Argentina in 2005, and not just for scoring both his country's goals in the final – both from the penalty spot. He achieved a hat-trick by not only winning the Golden Boot for top scorer and Golden Shoe for best player, but also by captaining his side to the title. This feat was emulated two years later by compatriot Sergio Aguero, who scored once in the final against the Czech Republic, before team-mate Mauro Zarate struck a late winner.

LIONEL
MESSI

TOURNAMENT TRIVIA
DOMINANT DOMINIC

Ghana became the first African country to lift the trophy when they upset Brazil in the 2009 final – despite playing 83 of the 120 minutes with just 10 men, following Daniel Addo's red card. The final finished goalless, one of only two games in which **Dominic Adiyiah** failed to score. He ended the tournament as top scorer with eight goals and also won the Golden Ball prize for best player. The Silver Ball went to Brazil's Alex Teixeira, even though it was his missed penalty, when the final shoot-out went to sudden death, which handed Ghana victory.

DOMINIC
ADIYIAH

Only one player has scored a hat-trick in the final of a FIFA Under-20 World Cup: Brazilian midfielder Oscar, who hit all his side's goals in their 3-2 triumph over Portugal to claim the latest trophy in August 2011.

FIFA U-17 WORLD CUP

First staged in China in 1985, when it was known as the FIFA Under-16 World Championship, the age limit was adjusted from 16 to 17 in 1991 and the tournament has been labelled the FIFA U-17 World Cup ever since 2007.

5-2

The highest-scoring final ever came in 2017 when England beat Spain 5-2 in India.

NATIONAL LEGEND
GOLDEN HAUL

West Germany's Marcel Witeczek is the only person to finish top scorer at both a FIFA Under-16 World Championship and the Under-20 version of the event. The Polish-born striker hit eight goals at the 1985 Under-16 tournament, followed by seven more at the Under-20 championship two years later. Brazil's Adriano – a different Adriano to the one who later played for the senior side and Serie A club Internazionale – came closest to equalling the feat: he won the Golden Shoe, for top scorer, after scoring four goals at the 1991 FIFA Under-17 World Cup, then the Golden Ball, for best player, at the Under-20 event in 1993.

TOURNAMENT TRIVIA
ENGLAND'S GLORY

England won their first world U-17 title in the most thrilling way possible by hitting back from two goals down to beat Spain 5-2 in the 2017 final in Kolkata, India. They were the second successive England age-group team, after the U-20s' victory in South Korea, to become world champions. Liverpool's **Rhian Brewster** led the recovery with a goal just before half-time, after Spain had hit England twice on the break through Sergio Gomez. Brewster ended the tournament as the Golden Boot winner with hat-tricks in the quarter- and semi-finals.

RHIAN **BREWSTER**

HOST HISTORY
SEOUL SURVIVOR

The final of the 2007 tournament was the first to be hosted by a former FIFA World Cup venue – the 68,476-capacity **Seoul FIFA World Cup Stadium** in South Korea's capital, which had been built for the 2002 FIFA World Cup. The game was watched by a crowd of 36,125, a tournament record. The 2007 event was the first to feature 24 teams instead of 16, and was won by Nigeria – after Spain missed all three of their spot-kicks in a penalty shoot-out.

HIGH-FLYING EAGLETS

In 2013, remarkably, the teams that finished first, second and third in Group F, ended the tournament in that order. Nigeria's Golden Eaglets won in fine style, whilst Mexico and Sweden finished second and third respectively.

SCORING RECORD
GOOD AND BAD BOY BOJAN

Barcelona star **Bojan Krkic** quickly went from hero to villain in the final moments of Spain's semi-final victory over Ghana in 2007 – he scored his team's winner with four minutes of extra-time remaining, but was then sent off for a second yellow-card offence just before the final whistle. His expulsion meant he was suspended for the final, which Spain lost on penalties to Nigeria.

BOJAN
KRKIC

5

Nigeria have won more U-17 titles than any other country, with 5.

HOST HISTORY
INDIAN OUTREACH

International football broke through another barrier when India played host to the world game for the first time, staging the 2017 FIFA U-17 World Cup. Despite foreign perceptions of Indian sports fans as caring about only cricket and hockey, a record 1.3 million fans attended the matches in New Delhi, Goa, Guwahati, Kochi, Mumbai and Kolkata, which staged the final where England defeated Spain 5-2. This exceeded the 1.2m fans in China in 1985 and was more than double the attendance at the 2015 finals in Chile. FIFA tournaments boss Jaime Yarza hailed it as a "fantastic tournament", while Indian officials immediately announced an intention to bid for the U-20 tournament.

9

The first player to win both the Golden Ball and the Golden Shoe at the FIFA U-17 World Cup was French striker Florent Sinama-Pongolle. His nine goals in 2001 set a tournament record for one player. His tally included two hat-tricks in the opening round.

TOURNAMENT TOP SCORERS:

1 10 – **Victor Osimhen** (Nigeria), 2015

2 9 – **Florent Sinama-Pongolle** (France), 2001

3 8 – **Marcel Witeczek** (West Germany), 1985

= 8 – **Rhian Brewster** (England), 2017

4 7 – **David** (Spain), 1997

= 7 – **Ishmael Addo** (Ghana), 1999

= 7 – **Macauley Chrisantus** (Nigeria), 2007

= 7 – **Valmir Berisha** (Sweden), 2013

5 6 – **Wilson Oruma** (Nigeria), 1993

SCORING RECORD
HOST HISTORY

Mexico became the first host country to lift the FIFA U-17 World Cup trophy on home soil, when they beat Uruguay 2-0 in the final in the Azteca Stadium in Mexico City in July 2011. The Golden Ball award for the tournament's best player went to Mexican winger **Julio Gomez**, whose brace against Germany in the semi-final including a spectacular bicycle-kick for the last-minute winner – though he played only ten minutes of the final, as a substitute, after picking up an injury in the previous game.

1991

The 1991 tournament was originally scheduled to take place in Ecuador, but a cholera outbreak in the country meant it was switched to Italy instead – though played in much smaller venues than those that had been used for the previous year's senior FIFA World Cup in the country.

JULIO
GOMEZ

J.GOMEZ
8

189

FIFA CLUB WORLD CUP

The FIFA Club World Cup has been played in several different formats since 1960, when Real Madrid defeated Penarol. In its current guise, the competition pits the champion clubs from all six continents against each other.

From 1960 until 1968, the two-team Intercontinental Cup was settled, not on aggregate scores but by using a system of two points for a win and one for a draw. This meant a third, deciding match was needed in 1961, 1963, 1964 and 1967, when Racing of Argentina beat Celtic 1-0 in a bad-tempered play-off in Montevideo. From 1980 until 2004, the annual event was a single match staged in Japan before it was swallowed up in FIFA's expanded Club World Cup.

FIFA CLUB WORLD CUP WINNERS BY COUNTRY:

1. 11 – Spain
2. 10 – Brazil
3. 9 – Argentina
   = 9 – Italy
5. 6 – Uruguay

3

Barcelona boss Pep Guardiola has won the tournament in its current guise three times. Twice with Barcelona, in 2009 and 2011, and once with Bayern Munich, in 2013.

4-0
The most one-sided FIFA Club World Cup final was 4-0, in 2011, when Barcelona thrashed Santos of Brazil.

IVAN **VACELICH**

CLUB LEGEND
VETERAN IVAN

New Zealand's Auckland City were one of the surprises of the 2014 FIFA Club World Cup, spearheaded by 38-year-old **Ivan Vacelich** who won the bronze award for third best player at the tournament. Only Real Madrid's Sergio Ramos and Cristiano Ronaldo finished ahead of him. Auckland City finished third, the highest finish for a club from Oceania. They beat Cruz Azul on penalties, after a 1-1 draw in the third- place play-off.

TOURNAMENT TRIVIA
THE REIGN OF SPAIN

Spain has dominated the FIFA Club World Cup since 2009. Between them current champions Real Madrid and Barcelona have won six of the last nine finals. Barcelona launched the era of Spanish supremacy by defeating Estudiantes de La Plata from Argentina, 2-1 after extra time, on goals from Pedro and Lionel Messi. They won again in 2015, while **Cristiano Ronaldo**'s Madrid triumphed three times in four years in 2014, 2016 and 2017 in three different host nations: Morocco, Japan and the UAE. Madrid have won the world title a record seven times.

CRISTIANO **RONALDO**

TOURNAMENT TRIVIA
CORINTHIAN SPIRIT

Corinthians of Sao Paulo are the last Brazilian club – the last South American outfit – to have won the FIFA Club World. In 2012 Peruvian striker Paulo Guerrero scored the only goal of their semi- final victory over Egypt's Al-Ahly, and repeated the feat in the final against England's Chelsea. The Corinthians line-up included goalkeeper and player-of-the-tournament **Cassio**, as well as Danilo and Fabio Santos, a pair who had both won the tournament with Sao Paulo seven years earlier.

CASSIO **RAMOS**

OVERALL FIFA CLUB WORLD CUP CHAMPIONS (1960 TO 2018):

1 7 – **Real Madrid** (Spain)

2 4 – **AC Milan** (Italy)

3 3 – **Penarol** (Uruguay)

= 3 – **Internazionale** (Italy)

= 3 – **Nacional** (Urugay)

= 3 – **Bayern Munich** (West Germany/Germany)

= 3 – **Boca Juniors** (Argentina)

= 3 – **Sao Paulo** (Brazil)

= 3 – **Barcelona** (Spain)

7 With 7 goals since 2000, Cristiano Ronaldo holds the record of being the overall top goalscorer in FIFA Club World Cup history.

5 Since 2000, Toni Kroos has won the FIFA Club World Cup five times: the record for the most by any player.

TOURNAMENT TRIVIA
LONG-DISTANCE, LONG-RUNNING RIVALRY

The precursor to the modern FIFA Club World Cup was the Intercontinental Cup, also known informally as the World Club Cup and/or the Europe–South America Cup, which pitted the champions of Europe and South America against each other. Representatives of UEFA and CONMEBOL contested the event from 1960 to 2004, but now all continental federations send at least one club to an expanded Club World Cup organized and endorsed by the world federation, FIFA. The original final, in 1960, was between Spain's Real Madrid and Uruguay's Penarol. After a goalless draw in the rain in Montevideo, Real triumphed 5-1 at their own stadium in Madrid – including three goals scored in the first eight minutes, two of them by Ferenc Puskas.

TOURNAMENT TRIVIA
AFRICAN DOUBLE

In 2010, for the first time in the overall event's history, a club not from Europe or South America contested the final. African champions TP Mazembe from the Democratic Republic of Congo defeated Internacional of Brazil 2-0 in the semi-finals before losing 3-0 to Italy's Internazionale. Mazembe achieved their surprise progress despite missing star striker and captain Tresor Mputu through suspension. In 2013, in Morocco, home favourite Raja Casablanca became the second African club to reach the final before losing 2-0 to Bayern Munich.

A third non-European club followed up in Japan in 2016 when **Kashima Antlers** took Real Madrid to extra time before losing 4-2.

6 Barcelona's triumph in 2009 made them the first club to lift six different major trophies in one calendar year: the FIFA Club World Cup, the UEFA Champions League, the UEFA European Super Cup, and a Spanish hat-trick of La Liga, Copa del Rey and Super Cup.

OLYMPIC FOOTBALL

First played at the 1900 Olympic Games in Paris, although not recognized by FIFA as an official tournament until London 1908, the men's Olympic football tournament was played in strict accordance with the Games' strong amateur tradition until 1984, when pros were allowed to play.

Sophus Nielsen is the top scorer in Olympic history with 13 goals.

23/27
Eastern European countries dominated the Olympic Games football competitions from 1948 to 1980, when professional players were officially banned from taking part. Teams comprising so-called "state amateurs" from the Eastern Bloc took 23 of the 27 medals available during those years.

TOURNAMENT TRIVIA
CZECH OUT

The climax of the 1920 Olympic Games tournament is the only time a major international football final has been abandoned. Czechoslovakia's players walked off the pitch minutes before half-time, in protest at the decisions made by 65-year-old English referee John Lewis – including the dismissal of Czech player Karel Steiner. Belgium, who were 2-0 up at the time, were awarded the victory, before Spain beat Holland 3-1 in a play-off for silver.

ORIBE
PERALTA

TOURNAMENT TRIVIA
LONDON CALLING

Mexico were the unexpected winners when Wembley Stadium became the first venue to stage two men's Olympic Games football finals as part of London 2012. The old stadium hosted the showpiece game when England's capital held the Olympics in 1948 and London is also now the only city to stage three separate summer Olympics, though the football final back in 1908 was played at White City. **Oribe Peralta** scored both goals as Mexico defeated Brazil 2-1 in the 2012 final at the renovated venue. A late reply by Hulk was little consolation for the highly-fancied South Americans, though Brazil's Leandro Damiao did end as six-goal top scorer.

LAST TEN GOLD MEDALLISTS IN OLYMPIC FOOTBALL :

2016, Rio De Janeiro:	Brazil
2012, London:	Mexico
2008, Beijing:	Argentina
2004, Athens:	Argentina
2000, Sydney:	Cameroon
1996, Atlanta:	Nigeria
1992, Barcelona:	Spain
1988, Seoul:	USSR
1984, Los Angeles:	France
1980, Moscow:	Czechoslovakia

NATIONAL LEGEND
NEYMAR'S CROWNING GLORY

Soccer is usually a sideshow at the Olympic Games but, in 2016, it took centre stage in football-mad Rio de Janeiro. Host Brazil's bid to make amends for three final failures and win gold for the first time succeeded as they defeated World Cup winners Germany in the final. Two years earlier, at Belo Horizonte, Brazil had been routed 7-1 by the Germans, so the nerves were even more acute. The 2016 gold medal game, like the 2014 World Cup final, was played at the Maracana stadium. It was left to Brazil's superstar skipper **Neymar** to make history and he duly beat Timo Horn in goal to win Brazil's first Olympic football gold medal.

NEYMAR

NATIONAL LEGEND
BARCELONA BOUND

Future Barcelona team-mates Samuel Eto'o and Xavi scored penalties for opposing sides in 2000, when Cameroon and Spain contested the first Olympic final to be settled by a shoot-out. Future FIFA World Cup or UEFA European Championship winners to have played at Summer Olympics include Italy's Cannavaro, Buffon and Alessandro Nesta, and Brazil's Roberto Carlos, Rivaldo and Ronaldo (Atlanta, 1996); Italy's Gianluca Zambrotta and Spain's Xavi, Carles Puyol and Joan Capdevila (Sydney, 2000); and Italy's Daniele De Rossi, Andrea Pirlo and Alberto Gilardino and Portugal's Cristiano Ronaldo and Bruno Alves (Athens, 2004).

Hungary are the most successful Olympic football team with three wins. Great Britain have also managed three but those three instances are their only podium places; Hungary finished second and third in 1972 and 1960 respectively.

14 SECONDS
Neymar scored the fastest goal in a men's Olympic football match in history: he netted after 14 seconds in the semi-final match against Honduras in 2016.

Two Olympic finals have been decided by penalties, including the 2016 gold medal match.

TOURNAMENT TRIVIA
AFRICAN AMBITION

Ghana became the first African country to win an Olympic football medal, picking up bronze in 1992, but Nigeria went even better four years later by claiming the continent's first Olympic football gold medal – thanks to **Emmanuel Amunike**'s stoppage-time winner against Argentina. Nigeria's triumph came as a huge surprise to many – especially as their rival teams included such future world stars as Brazil's Ronaldo and Roberto Carlos, Argentina's Hernan Crespo and Roberto Ayala, Italy's Fabio Cannavaro and Gianluigi Buffon, and France's Robert Pires and Patrick Vieira.

EMMANUEL AMUNIKE

FOOTBALL INNOVATIONS

One of great strengths of association football is its ability to move with the times. This has brought technology on board, but only after careful consideration by the International Football Association Board which commands the Laws of the Game.

The VAR Room at the 2018 FIFA World Cup was a hive of activity, with operators on hand to assist officials around the country.

HISTORICAL INNOVATIONS

It is easy nowadays to consider football as a game whose fundamentals have always been set in stone. Travel back to its formative years, however, and you'll find a sport in flux, with the laws of the game undergoing all manner of changes and revolutions.

WILLIAM 'FATTY' FOULKE

KICKING OFF IN THE ROUND

Football's adventure in technology began with the ball itself. Ancient variations of ball games were recorded during the Han Dynasty in China 2,000 years ago, at the same time as the Romans enjoyed what they called harpastum. Japan developed kemari while ritual games were being recorded among the Inca and Mayan civilisations, just as colourful calcio was being enjoyed in Renaissance Florence. Standardization began with the first formal match under the aegis of the Football Association in 1866: the ball ordered up was a 'Lillywhite's No5'. Apart from a spherical shape it bore little resemblance to today's space-age balls. An increasingly lucrative market prompted a high-tech race for perfection – and business. German company Adidas has provided the official FIFA World Cup ball ever since 1970. In Russia in 2018, its Telstar 18 was used for the group matches and its Telstar Mechta (Russian for 'dream') in the knockout stage. The ball featured an embedded information chip. This sparked controversy when Russian President Vladimir Putin presented one to United States leader Donald Trump.

SHAPES OF THE GAME TO COME

The first international match, between Scotland and England on the ground of the West of Scotland Cricket Club, Partick, Glasgow, pre-dated several of the basic tools of the game. The goalless draw was played out on 30 November 1872. Two years later, shinguards were invented by all-round sportsman Sam Widdowson of Nottingham and written into the laws of the game in 1880-81. Initially Widdowson cut down a pair of cricket pads. One year after the shinguard appeared so did the crossbar. Until 1874 a tape had been stretched across the goal from the top of two uprights, eight yards apart. In 1892, goal nets were introduced in time for the FA Cup Final. Goal posts and the bar could be either round or square until the square design was outlawed in 1987. Sheffield United's legendary **William 'Fatty' Foulke** is the first goalkeeper recorded as having snapped the crossbar by swinging from it in 1896.

HERBERT ZIMMERMANN

INNOVATORS
FOOTBALL'S FIRST RADIO STARS

Fast-progressing radio in Britain, continental Europe and South America 'discovered' football in the 1920s and 1930s. Radio technology had developed at pace for military reasons during the First World War, and the evolution of regular league football prompted an escalating interest in the game from the pioneers of broadcasting. Finding a winning style of commentary took time. The BBC, in its early days, used a background voice calling numbers to illustrate the position of play on a printed graph of the pitch: hence the phrase: "Back to square one." In time, commentators became football stars in their own right, before the 21st-century proliferation of a myriad sound-alikes across chat shows and analytical programming. The BBC's first commentator was George Allison. He 'called' horse racing's Derby and Grand National, several England v Scotland internationals and the 1927 FA Cup Final, in which Cardiff City beat Arsenal. Seven years later he became Arsenal manager, winning the league twice and the FA Cup. Perhaps the most iconic of all football radio commentaries was delivered by **Herbert Zimmermann**, describing West Germany beating odds-on favourites Hungary to win the 1954 FIFA World Cup with a resonance that reached far beyond sport. Zimmermann's commentary reached a near-hysterical climax with: "Aus, aus, aus, aus! Das Spiel ist aus! Deutschland ist Weltmeister."

TERRIFIC TECH
BLOWING FOR TIME

After the ball itself, the most arresting piece of technology in any football match is the whistle used by the referee to stop and start play. In the mid-19th century, umpires (the traditional cricket term) or referees would signal a foul by waving a handkerchief (a custom surviving in American gridiron football). In 1878, Joseph Hudson, a Birmingham toolmaker, came up with a sports whistle which was first tested at an FA Cup tie between Nottingham Forest and Sheffield. In 1884, Hudson's company developed the first Acme Thunderer, which would be refined and, for years, was the standard whistle worldwide. Hudson was not the only provider in an increasingly high-profile market. Elite referees at the 2018 World Cup used the Fox 40 Classic; their watch was the Big Bang Referee 2018 FIFA World Cup Russia from event partner Hublot.

TERRIFIC TECH
LIGHTING UP THE GLOOM

Floodlighting arrived early. The first attempt to harness the new electric light was staged at Bramall Lane, Sheffield, in 1868. But the powering mix of dynamos and batteries was not a success. Herbert Chapman, ever a visionary manager, proposed floodlighting around Arsenal's Highbury pitch in the early 1930s, but the Football League refused permission for its use in competition. In 1950, Southampton became the first league club to install floodlights though they were permitted only for friendlies. Wolves raised the pressure on the authorities with a series of high-profile clashes against foreign clubs under lights at Molyneux. A 3-2 victory over Hungary's Honved in 1954 led to a newspaper hailing Wolves as 'champions of the world'. That provoked French newspaper *L'Equipe* into creating a European Cup built around the concept of midweek floodlit competition all around the continent. The original lights on poles around the pitch were superseded by giant pylons towering over the four corners of a ground. Later, covered-stand stadia and the high-quality demands of television technology prompted new-era floodlighting units circling the pitch and providing a near-daylight radiance.

WOLVES V HONVED

MODERN INNOVATIONS

Recent years have seen plenty of changes and technological improvements in football, with each one having a profound effect on how the game is played, watched and officiated.

LAYING DOWN THE LAW

Policing the laws of the game is the role of the International Football Association Board. The four British home associations (England, Ireland, Scotland and Wales) created IFAB for precisely this purpose on June 2, 1886. In 1913, world federation FIFA, then only nine years old, was awarded a vote. In 1958 FIFA was awarded four votes on behalf of the rest of the world to balance the four British votes. Any decision to change the laws demands at least six votes.

INNOVATORS
OUT OF FOCUS ON THE SILVER SCREEN

Football is a massive worldwide TV phenomenon. But conquering the movie world has been more awkward. Directors continue to struggle with reproducing match action. The first big screen creation was a murder story, the *Arsenal Stadium Mystery*, in 1939. It featured Arsenal stars Cliff Bastin and **Eddie Hapgood** plus manager George Allison. A soon-forgotten *Goal* trilogy, directed between 2005 and 2007 by British director Danny Cannon, featured walk-on parts for stars such as David Beckham. FIFA then invested $20m in a drama depicting its own history entitled *United Passions*. The film starred Tim Roth, Gerard Depardieu and Sam Neill and proved a self-defeating flop. Its release in the United States in 2015 coincided with the FIFAGate scandal revelations, so it grossed a record low of just $918.

EDDIE
HAPGOOD

TERRIFIC TECH
FORMULA FAIR PLAY

Refereeing has never been more scientific. Each extra gadget has increased fitness demands because of the amount of equipment referees must pack as they sprint their diagonal from one corner to the other. Once a referee needed only a watch, a whistle and a notepad and pen. Not any more. Kit for today's elite referee starts with a radio receiver plus headset for communicating with assistants and the fourth official. Then come a flags signal vibration unit, a primary watch, a goal-line decision watch, red and yellow cards, the pen and notepad plus – at the referee's back – a spray can for marking the pitch at free kicks. Brazilian inventor Heine Allemagne tested his spray first at a junior tournament in 2000 in his home city of Belo Horizonte. Brazil's CBF commissioned its use in domestic competition in 2002 and, a decade later, IFAB authorised use worldwide – and added it to the referee's burden.

INNOVATORS
FIGHTING THE FUTURE

Michel Platini, nine-goal inspiration as captain of the French side who won the 1984 European Championship, led the fight against the introduction of goal-line technology. He felt vindicated in 2005 when an early test proved a disaster at the FIFA Under-17 World Cup in Peru. Belgian referee Frank de Bleekere said later: "I refereed a 1-1 draw but the technology told me the score was 5-3 because it registered a goal every time the ball went over the bar." Platini was not convinced even by events at the 2010 World Cup. By now he was a powerful president of European federation UEFA, and a vice-president of FIFA. He feared opening the door to demands for more high-tech aides and championed goal-line assistants as an alternative in UEFA competitions. Platini said: "I worry that we will soon be using technology for things that have little point. Football is the most popular sport in the world because it has simple rules that work anywhere. It is always better to use people to assess situations rather than complex and expensive technology."

RULE CHANGE
1966 AND ALL THAT

The most controversial goal in history remains Geoff Hurst's second for England, in extra time in the 1966 World Cup Final against West Germany at Wembley. Hurst's shot struck the underside of the bar, ricocheted down and bounced back out. Swiss referee Gottfried Dienst consulted his Soviet Azeri linesman, Tofik Bakhramov, before awarding the goal. England went on to win 4-2 but the veracity of the goal has been at issue ever since. Photographs from the time were inconclusive but subsequent incidents proved a spinning ball could, indeed, drop behind the line and bounce back into play. England were victims themselves at the 2010 World Cup. This time Germany were the beneficiaries. England were losing 2-0 in a second round tie in Bloemfontein, South Africa, when a shot from Frank Lampard struck the bar, bounced down behind the line and spun back into the arms of keeper Manuel Neuer. Uruguayan referee Jorge Larrionda waved play on. The next day FIFA president Sepp Blatter, until then a firm opponent of technological assistance despite evidence from other sports, announced: "I have changed my mind. We are a laughing stock around the world. We need this technology."

RULE CHANGE
ELECTRONIC EYES HAVE IT

3 March 2012, was a historic date. That was the day on which IFAB, meeting just outside London, approved the introduction of goal-line technology. IFAB was responding to extensive testing of eight rival systems by Swiss specialists. Two systems 'survived'. Hawk-Eye ran a camera-based system while GoalRef, a German/Danish company, produced a chip in the ball linked to a magnetic field beneath the goal area. Both sent an electronic signal to the referee within one second. A special meeting of IFAB in Zurich on July 5 ratified goal-line technology which made its debut five months later at the FIFA Club World Cup in Japan. The floodgates were open. FIFA commissioned goal-line technology in Brazil at the 2013 Confederations Cup and 2014 World Cup. Simultaneously, England's Premier League won a race with Europe's other top leagues – France, Germany, Italy and Spain – for domestic application.

TERRIFIC TECH
CLOCKING IN

A typical goal-line technology set-up demands 14 cameras. Six triangulate each goal and track the ball with an additional goal-line camera set up for replays. Behind the scenes, other staff members undertake data analysis. Set-up begins 24 hours before a game. Six hours ahead of kickoff on match day, dedicated staff check that camera and communications links are all active. Once the goal frames are in place, further checks ensure that the cameras are aligned with the goal line – and that it runs straight and true between the posts. Two hours before kickoff sees final field tests with the referees and his assistants.

VAR

Perhaps the most significant and controversial football innovation this century, the video assistant referee (VAR) is here to stay, following years of heated debate within the game.

GOING DUTCH – TO RUSSIA WITH LOVE

Football needed seven years to embrace goal-line technology from the first flawed experiment in 2005 to the FIFA Club World Cup in 2012. But the game needed only four years to rush on down the electronic highway to the video assistant referee (VAR). The Dutch federation was the pioneer. In 2013 it launched experiments with an off-line pilot system called Arbitrage 2.0. Results were positive so, on 5 March 2016, in Cardiff, IFAB approved two years of worldwide experimentation. Some 12 countries rushed to become initial football test beds: Australia, Belgium, Brazil, Czech Republic, France, Germany, Italy, Mexico, Netherlands, Portugal, Qatar and the United States. FIFA duly trialled VAR at its Club World Cup in December 2016. Next up was 2017 Confederations Cup in Russia. The momentum was unstoppable. IFAB, meeting in Zurich on 3 March 2018, officially endorsed VAR. Within weeks FIFA confirmed its use at the World Cup in Russia.

VAR AT THE 2018 WORLD CUP:

64 matches

455 incidents checked

20 VAR reviews (17 on field)

1 intervention every 3.2 matches

17 decisions changed

9 penalties awarded by VAR (8 by on field review, one VAR factual)

3 penalties cancelled by VAR after on field review

95.6pc of decisions correct without VAR

99.35pc of decisions correct with VAR (17 decisions changed)

81.9sec the total average time for a review

86.5sec the average time for an on-field review

55.6sec the average time for a VAR direction review

56min 55sec the actual time played (55min 14sec in Brazil in 2014)

6min 10sec the additional time average per match (5min 23sec in Brazil in 2014)

29 penalties (9 by VAR) (13 in Brazil in2014; 15 in South Africa in 2010)

223 yellow cards (3.48 per match)

2 red cards (2 second yellow cards)

NESTOR
PITANA

PITANA THE HISTORY MAN

History was made in Moscow's Luzhniki Stadium on 15 July 2018, when the video assistant referee (VAR) was used for the first time in a World Cup Final. The referee was Argentinian **Nestor Pitana**. In the 38th minute he was alerted by Massimiliano Irrati, his Italian VAR in the control room, to a possible handball. Pitana checked the pitch-side monitor and decided that Croatia's Ivan Perisic had handled the ball in trying to clear a French set-piece. Antoine Griezmann converted the spot kick to give France a 2-1 lead and they went on to win 4-2. Pitana's penalty was the 20th review in the 64 matches during which 455 incidents were reviewed by the remote VAR review teams. The vast size of Russia led FIFA to decide on a central communications base rather than use individual studios in each stadium. Former top referees Pierluigi Collina (Italy) and Massimo Busacca (Switzerland) trained the officials. They insisted that achieving 100 per cent accuracy was not the primary aim of VAR, but rather a reduction in errors. They succeeded: referees called 95 per cent of incidents correctly without VAR but the system improved that success rate to 99.35.

INNOVATORS
PRESIDENTIAL CONVERSION

Gianni Infantino saw the light on VAR as he prepared to change jobs in the spring of 2016. Swiss lawyer Infantino, in his role as general secretary of European federation UEFA, had been loyal to his president Michel Platini in opposing technological aids. However, in late 2015 Platini was suspended from football and Infantino replaced him as Europe's candidate for the leadership of FIFA. No sooner had Infantino been elected to the top job in world football than he pushed for VAR's use at the World Cup in Russia in 2018. After VAR's successful finals debut, Infantino said: "We were a little brave, maybe almost crazy, in introducing VAR. We were criticized for it before the World Cup. But, after the World Cup, everybody in the world realized it's the future."

GIANNI INFANTINO

INNOVATORS
THE REF AHEAD OF HIS TIME

Horacio Elizondo from Argentina, by his own admission, was the first referee to show the red card on the basis of video evidence. That was also 12 years before VAR. The occasion was the biggest in the game, the 2006 FIFA World Cup Final in Berlin. The player caught out was France superstar Zinedine Zidane. France and Italy were level at 1–1 in extra time when Zidane floored Italian defender Marco Materazzi. The incident was missed by Elizondo and his two linesmen. But not by the fourth official, Spain's Luis Medina Cantalejo. He re-checked the incident on a pitch-side monitor and told Elizondo: "Zidane headbutted Materazzi. If you see the video you can believe it." Elizondo trusted the advice, flourished his red card and Zidane walked. Without him France duly lost the penalty shootout.

0.89%

Percentage of errors in Serie A during its first season using VAR (down from 5.78 per cent).

HORACIO ELIZONO

22

Number of countries that use VAR in domestic competition (as of 2019).

TO BE EXACT ...

VAR can be used only for four specific types of decision: goals, penalty decisions, direct red cards and cases of mistaken identity. Hence:

1 The referee must always make a decision and that decision will stand unless it is "clearly wrong";

2 The referee can only go back to the start of the attacking phase which leads to the incident;

3 A goal scored from a throw-in which should have gone to the other team could not be disallowed under the new system; and

4 If the ball is still in play, the referee must wait until it is in a neutral zone before stopping play. If the decision is not overturned, play will restart with a drop ball.

VAR can be used only after the referee has made a decision which can include waving play on or if a serious incident has been 'missed' by match officials.

TERRIFIC TECH
CHAMPION DECISION

VAR was introduced into the UEFA Champions League for the knockout stage in the 2018-19 season. UEFA president Aleksander Ceferin accelerated its use after the World Cup success. Various European countries – including Germany, Italy, Spain and France – had struggled with the introduction of the system. Controversial incidents including a German team having to be called back from the dressing rooms at half-time and a counter-attack goal disallowed in the Netherlands because of a delayed VAR decision at the other end of the pitch. England, a leader in introducing goal-line technology, was more cautious. VAR was used only in a patchwork manner in the FA Cup in 2017-18 and 2018-19 ahead of its eventual arrival in the Premier League.

WOMEN'S FOOTBALL

More than 30 million women now play football across the globe, and the women's game has made great strides professionally in recent years, with the 2019 FIFA Women's World Cup proving a landmark event for the sport.

Such progress is long overdue considering the time wasted along the way. Although women's football was recorded in England more than a century ago, The Football Association banned it in 1921.

That led to the creation of an independent women's association with a cup competition of its own. Women's football developed simultaneously elsewhere and the surge of interest ultimately led, in the early 1980s, to the first formal European Championships and, in 1988, to a FIFA invitational tournament in Chinese Taipei.

FIFA launched an inaugural world championship in 1991, which was won by the US to establish their claim to primacy in the game. The Americans duly hosted the next FIFA Women's World Cup, which saw a record crowd of 90,185 celebrate their shoot-out victory over China in the final in Pasadena. They underlined their No.1 status by winning the first women's football gold medal at the Olympic Games in 1996, taking silver in 2000 and gold again in 2004, 2008 and 2012.

Women's football, once considered a fleeting sporting fashion, is here to stay.

United States captain Megan Rapinoe lifts the FIFA Women's World Cup trophy aloft following her side's victory over the Netherlands.

FIFA WOMEN'S WORLD CUP 2019

ELLEN WHITE

In 2019, France played host to the biggest and most high-profile edition of the FIFA Women's World Cup yet. A diverse and talented field of 24 nations battled it out for global dominance, with the United States ultimately claiming their second consecutive title, and their fourth overall.

STAR PLAYER
WHITE ON TARGET

Ellen White became the first player to share top-scoring honours in the Women's World Cup when she scored six goals as England finished fourth. However she did not collect FIFA's specific golden boot prize because Americans Megan Rapinoe and Alex Morgan had contributed more assists. Manchester City's 30-year-old striker had also been a member of the England team who reached the last four in Canada in 2015. In France she scored England's second goal in their 2-1 opening win over Scotland, both goals in the 2-0 defeat of Japan and further strikes in the knockout victories over Cameroon and Norway. White then had what would have been a late equaliser against the United States ruled out for offside by VAR in the semi-finals.

STAR PLAYER
TREBLE CHANCE CRISTIANE

Veteran Brazil striker **Cristiane** became the oldest person to score a Women's World Cup hat-trick, as her treble handed debutants Jamaica a 3-0 loss in a Group C tie in Grenoble. Aged 34 years and 25 days, Cristiane headed her first goal, scored a second from close range and rounded off her display with a free kick. Her feat even beat the overall World Cup record held by Cristiano Ronaldo, who was 33 years and 130 days old when he scored a hat-trick in Portugal's 3-3 draw with Spain at the men's finals in Russia in 2018. Brazil eventually fell in the second round where they lost 2-1 after extra time to hosts France.

TOURNAMENT TRIVIA
START TO FORGET

Thailand marked their debut at the Women's World Cup finals with the tournament's heaviest defeat – by 13-0 against the United States. The previous record had been Germany's 11-0 victory over Argentina in 2007. Alex Morgan equalled the record set by fellow American Michelle Akers by scoring five goals in one game. But the USA were not unsympathetic to their opponents' plight: Thailand's tearful goalkeeper Sukanya Chor Charoenying was comforted at the final whistle by Carli Lloyd, who had scored the last goal.

CRISTIANE

SCREENING SUCCESS

The 2019 finals in France drew one billion viewers worldwide to programming by more than 200 broadcasters. TV records were set in many countries including host nation France, champions the United States, Germany and China. Almost 59 million watched Brazil's second round defeat by the French, making it the most watched women's football match of all time. In the UK, England's semi-final defeat by the United States attracted the highest peak UK television audience of the year, with 11.7 million, a domestic record for women's football.

TOURNAMENT TRIVIA
MAKING AMERICA GREAT

The United States are the greatest power in women's international football. Their 2-0 victory over the European champions Netherlands' in the 2019 Women's World Cup final in Lyon was their record-extending fourth title after 1991, 1999 and 2015. British-born Jill Ellis thus became the first female coach to win back-to-back World Cups. In addition, the USA have won Olympic women's football gold four times in 1996, 2004, 2008 and 2012. No fewer than ten of their greatest stars have made more than 200 national team appearances, including Kristine Lilly (354), Christie Rampone (311), Carli Lloyd (281) and Mia Hamm (276). Six players boast more than 100 goals, headed by Abby Wambach (184). Wambach was voted World Women's Player of the Year by FIFA in 2012 with two similar awards apiece going to Hamm and Lloyd.

STAR PLAYER
MAGNIFICENT MEGAN

United States captain **Megan Rapinoe** was the individual who dominated the 2019 FIFA Women's World Cup. Rapinoe, a 34-year-old from Redding, California, opened the scoring in the United States' 2-0 victory over Netherlands in the final, was voted player of the match and won the golden ball as top player in the entire tournament. Rapinoe's penalty against the Dutch was her 50th goal in 158 appearances over 13 years for the US. She had also made a name for herself off the pitch. Rapinoe is an advocate for numerous LGBT organisations. She also knelt during the national anthem at an international match in support of American football star Colin Kaepernick and his anti-racism protests.

MEGAN
RAPINOE

TERRIFIC TECH
VAR TO THE RESCUE

Stephanie Frappart became the first referee to use video assistance in awarding a penalty in the Women's World Cup final. The 35-year-old French referee checked the touchline screen after Dutch defender Stefanie van der Gragt fouled American Alex Morgan early in the second half in Lyon. Megan Rapinoe converted the penalty. This was the first time VAR had been used in the Women's World Cup, and it was a constant feature throughout the finals, right from the opening match when hosts France beat South Korea 4-0. France, featuring seven players from European club champions Lyon, had a further 'goal' by Griedge Mbock Bathy ruled out after a video review.

FINAL STANDINGS:

1 USA

2 Netherlands

3 Sweden

4 England

STEPHANIE
FRAPPART

FIFA WOMEN'S WORLD CUP RECORDS

The first FIFA Women's World Cup finals were held in China in 1991, and the tournament has since grown astronomically. It expanded to 24 teams in 2015, and will be even bigger in 2023 when 32 teams will compete for glory.

ALL-TIME TOP SCORERS:

1 Marta, 17

2 Birgit Prinz, 14
= Abby Wambach, 14

4 Michelle Akers, 12

5 Cristiane, 11
= Sun Wen, 11
= Bettina Wiegmann, 11

MARTA

7

Seven of the USA's 1991 FIFA Women's World Cup-winning team were also in the squad who triumphed in 1999: Mia Hamm, Michelle Akers, Kristine Lilly, Julie Foudy, Joy Fawcett, Carla Overbeck and Brandi Chastain.

90,185
The highest-ever attendance for a FIFA Women's World Cup match remains the 90,185 fans who packed into the Rose Bowl to see the USA defeat China to win the 1999 tournament on home turf.

TOURNAMENT TRIVIA
FIRST, FAST, MORE AND LESS

The first game in the FIFA Women's World Cup finals saw hosts China defeat Norway 4-0 in front of 65,000 fans in Guangzhou on 16 November, 1991. Together, China and Norway are among eight nations to have competed in all eight tournaments – along with Brazil, Germany, Japan, Nigeria, Sweden and the United States. Following the 2019 tournament, 36 nations in all have made at least one appearance at the FIFA Women's World Cup. Chile, Jamaica, Scotland and South Africa were the most recent debutants, with each making their bow in France.

250

The lowest attendance for any match at the finals came on 8 June 1995, when only 250 spectators watched the 3-3 draw between Canada and Nigeria at Helsingborg.

TOURNAMENT TRIVIA
UNBEATEN CHINA SENT HOME

In 1999, China became the only team to go through the finals without losing a match, yet go home empty-handed. The Chinese won their group games, 2-1 against Sweden, 7-0 against Ghana and 3-1 against Australia. They beat Russia 2-0 in the quarter-finals and Norway 5-0 in the semi-finals, but they lost on penalties to the USA in the final after a 0-0 draw. In 2011, Japan became the first team to lift the trophy despite losing a match in the first-round – as had runners-up the USA.

1,353,506

The 2015 FIFA Women's World Cup still holds the total attendance for a women's tournament at 1,353,506 – even pipping the 2019 edition.

TOURNAMENT TRIVIA
A RECORD DEFENCE

In 2007, Germany became the first team to make a successful defence of the FIFA Women's World Cup. They also set another record by going through the tournament – six games and 540 minutes – without conceding a single goal. As a result, their goalkeeper Nadine Angerer overhauled Italy keeper Walter Zenga's record of 517 minutes unbeaten in the 1990 men's finals. The last player to score against the Germans had been Sweden's **Hanna Ljungberg** in the 41st minute of the 2003 final. The run ended when Christine Sinclair of Canada scored after 82 minutes of Germany's opening game in 2011.

HANNA LJUNGBERG

Brazilian midfielder Formiga set a record in 2019 by appearing at her seventh FIFA Women's World Cup – more than any other player. She had first appeared as a 17-year-old at the 1995 tournament in Sweden.

BIRGIT PRINZ

SANDRA SMISEK

TOP TEAM SCORERS:

1 **USA**, 26 (2019)
2 **USA**, 25 (1991)
= **Germany**, 25 (2003)
4 **Norway**, 23 (1995)
5 **Germany**, 21 (2007)

TOURNAMENT TRIVIA
SPANISH REBELLION

Spain's first ever FIFA Women's World Cup finals quickly turned sour. They won only one point from their three group games in Canada in 2015 and were eliminated. On returning home, the players blamed veteran coach Ignacio Quereda, citing insufficient preparation for the cooler climate, lack of warm-up friendlies and poor analysis of opponents. They concluded: "We need a change. We have conveyed this to the coach and his staff."

TOURNAMENT TRIVIA
HAVELANGE'S DREAM COMES TRUE

The FIFA Women's World Cup was the brainchild of former FIFA president **João Havelange**. The tournament began as an experimental competition in 1991 and has expanded in size and importance ever since. The success of the 1999 finals in the United States was a turning point for the tournament, which now attracts big crowds and worldwide TV coverage. The USA and Norway – countries in which football (soccer) is one of the most popular girls' sports – dominated the early competitions. The USA have dominated the competition winning four times, in 1991, 1999, 2015 and 2019. Germany, however, were first to go back-to-back, in 2003 and 2007.

JOÃO HAVELANGE

SCORING RECORD
GERMANS AT THE DOUBLE

Germany are the only team to have twice scored double figures in a game at the finals. The first time was an 11-0 thrashing of Argentina in Shanghai in the 2007 finals, when **Birgit Prinz** and **Sandra Smisek** both scored hat-tricks. Then, in Canada in 2015, the Germans crushed Ivory Coast 10-0 in the first round with trebles for strikers Celia Sasic and Anja Mittag. Norway hold the record for scoring in the most consecutive games – 15. They began their sequence with a 4-0 win over New Zealand on 19 November 1991 and ended it with a 3-1 win over Sweden in the quarter-finals on 30 June 1999.

207

UEFA WOMEN'S EUROPEAN CHAMPIONSHIP

17

The youngest player at UEFA Euro 2017 was Russia's 17-year-old midfielder Viktoriya Shkoda from the southern city of Krasnodar while the oldest was the 37-year-old Norwegian goalkeeper Ingrid Hjelmseth.

Organised women's football has taken vast steps since it was banned in England in 1921. Its modern resurgence continued in 2017, with the Dutch victorious as hosts in the UEFA Women's European Championship.

JODIE **TAYLOR**

SCORING RECORD
TAYLOR MAKES HISTORY FOR ENGLAND

England centre-forward **Jodie Taylor** enjoyed a sensational campaign at the 2017 finals of the Women's European Championship. She started with a hat-trick in a 6-0 thrashing of Scotland and followed up against Spain and in the quarter-final defeat of France to become the first England player to finish as the tournament's top scorer. Taylor's treble was the first at the finals in two decades. Her five-goal haul for the Lionesses was one short of the record set by Germany's Inka Grings in 2009. Taylor, who had played for 12 clubs in five countries before exploding at Euro 2017, was only the third player ever to score a hat-trick in the women's Euro.

TOURNAMENT TRIVIA
ORANGE FEVER LIGHTS UP EUROPE

Hosts Netherlands celebrated victory in the European women's championship for the first time in their history in 2017 by defeating Denmark 4-2 to the delight of a capacity, orange-bedecked crowd in Enschede. Some 13 members of the 23-strong Dutch squad brought to the party their experience of playing with foreign clubs – notably goalkeeper Sari van Veenendaal and centre-forward **Vivianne Miedema** (both Arsenal), midfielder Jackie Groenen (Frankfurt) and the tournament's finest player in Barcelona left winger Lieke Martens. Miedema scored once in each of Netherlands' knockout victories over Sweden and England then two in the final triumph over Denmark.

VIVIANNE **MIEDEMA**

2

Inka Grings of Germany was top scorer of two tournaments running, between 2005 and 2009.

STAR PLAYER
NADIM'S LONG ROAD TO STARDOM

Forward **Nadia Nadim** grabbed the spotlight from even experienced team-mate Pernille Harder as Denmark reached the Euro women's final for the first time after five previous semi-final exits. Nadim, her mother and sisters had fled a war-torn Afghanistan in 2000 when she was only 11. They sought refugee status in Denmark, where Nadim began playing football for Aalborg. Her talent prompted the Danish federation to obtain a special regulatory exemption from FIFA so she could play for her adopted country. Her starring role at Euro 2017, where she opened the scoring against the Netherlands in the final, prompted a transfer to Manchester City in the FA Women's Super League.

NADIA
NADIM

1-0

At the UEFA Women's European Championship in 2017, Netherlands won all three group games without conceding a goal ahead of the Danes, whom they beat 1-0 first time around.

TOURNAMENT TRIVIA
END OF AN ERA FOR THE GERMANS

Germany's 2-1 defeat by Denmark in the quarter-finals of UEFA Euro 2017 ended an astonishing run of success featuring six successive titles won since 1995. Their exit was a bad start to a new job for head coach Steffi Jones, who had succeeded title-winning specialist Silvia Neid in 2016. Neid appeared an impossible act to match. She had been a European champion three times as a player and twice as coach as well as being voted FIFA Women's Coach of the Year on three occasions.

BIGGEST ATTENDANCES:

1 **41,301 – Germany 1 Norway 0,** (Stockholm, 2013 final)

2 **29,092 – England 3 Finland 2** (Manchester, 2005 group)

3 **28,182 – Netherlands 4, Denmark 2** (Enschede, 2017 final)

4 **27,093 Netherlands 3, England 0** (Enschede, 2017 semi-final)

5 **25,694 England 0, Sweden 1** (Blackburn, 2005 group)

61

The German women's Bundesliga provided the most players (61) at UEFA Euro 2017 followed by the English club game (41). Wolfsburg were the top club in being represented by 14 players.

TOURNAMENT TRIVIA
STEP UP FOR STEINHAUS

One of the most high-profile personalities at the 2017 finals was not a player but **Bibiana Steinhaus**, the German referee. Steinhaus, a police commander from Hanover, learned shortly before the finals that she had become the first woman official promoted to referee matches in the men's Bundesliga. This was 10 years after she had become the first female referee in German professional football in the lower divisions. Highlights in the women's game included the final of the 2011 World Cup and then the gold medal match at the London 2012 Olympic Games. Six weeks before UEFA Euro 2017, she refereed the UEFA Women's Champions League Final between Lyon and Paris Saint-Germain.

BIBIANA
STEINHAUS

165M
Away from the stadia, the total television audience hit 165m for a final screened in 80 countries, for the 2017 UEFA Women's European Championship.

OTHER WOMEN'S TOURNAMENTS

Women's football continues to flourish at all levels across the globe, with more and more talented players breaking through on the big stage. Likewise, the Olympic Games also provide up-and-coming stars to shine in front of millions of fans around the world.

AZUSA IWAHIMIZU

TOURNAMENT TRIVIA
JAPAN DOUBLE JOY

Japan clinched the AFC Asian Women's Cup title for the first time in 2014, when the tournament was staged in Vietnam. Defender **Azusa Iwashimizu** not only scored the winner in extra-time stoppage-time in the semi-final against China, but also struck the only goal of the final against Australia – some solace for her red card in the 2011 FIFA Women's World Cup final. Also in 2014, Japan won the FIFA Under-17 Women's World Cup for the first time, beating Spain 2-0 in the final in Costa Rica and seeing five-goal Hina Sugita voted best player.

TOURNAMENT TRIVIA
GERMANS CHALK UP BIGGEST WIN

Germany hold the record for the biggest win in the Olympic finals. They beat China 8-0 at Patras on 11 August 2004, with Birgit Prinz scoring four times. The Germans' other goals came from Pia Wunderlich, Renate Lingor, Conny Pohlers and Martina Muller. Yet, in a major surprise, Germany failed to qualify for the women's football tournament at the 2012 Olympic Games in London. The 2011 FIFA Women's World Cup was used as UEFA's qualifiers, meaning beaten quarter-finalists Germany fell short. Semi-finalists Sweden – including their most- capped player Therese Sjogran – and France, whose stars include midfielder Louisa Necib, went through to the 2012 event instead.

2

Brazil's Cristiane is the only player to score two hat-tricks in FIFA Olympic history. She scored three in a 7-0 win over hosts Greece in 2004 and repeated the feat in a 3-1 win over Nigeria at Beijing 2008.

NATIONAL LEGEND
MAGNIFICENT MARTA

Brazil superstar **Marta** finished with an Olympic women's silver medal in both 2004 and 2008 but missed out on home turf in 2016 when the Canarinha lost the bronze medal play-off to Canada. Her consolation was in becoming, with a total of 15 goals, the all-time leading scorer in Olympic women's football, one more than Germany's Birgit Prinz. In August 2016, Marta was one of eight athletes given the honour of carrying the Olympic Flag at the Olympic Games in Rio de Janeiro.

MARTA

FIFA U-20 WOMEN'S WORLD CUP TOP SCORERS:

1 **Christine Sinclair** (Canada), **10**

2 **Brittany Timko** (Canada), **7**

3 **Ma Xiaoxu** (China), **5**

= **Kim Song Hui** (North Korea), **5**

= **Sydney Leroux** (USA), **5**

Christine Sinclair of Canada and Alexandra Popp of Germany share the record for most goals scored in a single FIFA Under-20 Women's World Cup. Each struck 10, Sinclair in 2002 and Popp eight years later.

CHRISTINE SINCLAIR

The FIFA Under-20 Women's World Cup is held every two years, in contrast to the four-yearly senior contest. Since 2010, the younger players' event has been staged by the same nation one year before they host the FIFA Women's World Cup.

🏆 TOURNAMENT TRIVIA
HOSTS WITH THE MOST

In 2014, Canada became the first country to host the FIFA Under-20 Women's World Cup twice, having previously done so in 2002 – while Germany emerged as the second three-times champions, emulating the USA. In 2016 the finals were staged in Papua Guinea, a late replacement after original host South Africa withdrew. North Korea won the tournament for a second time, defeating France 3-1 in the final. The 113 goals in the finals matched the competition's record with Chile 2008. In March 2015, the world governing body FIFA in keeping with their policy, awarded the U-20 finals in 2018 to France, hosts-in-waiting of the 2019 FIFA Women's World Cup finals.

NATIONAL LEGEND
SINCLAIR HITS FIVE

Canada's **Christine Sinclair** holds the record for the most goals in one game at the FIFA Under-20 Women's World Cup. She netted five in Canada's 6-2 quarter-final win over England at Edmonton on 25 August 2002. Germany's Alexandra Popp is the only player to score in all of her country's six games at a tournament. Only Sinclair and Popp have won both the Golden Ball for best player and Golden Shoe for top scorer. Sinclair finished the 2012 Olympics as six-goal top-scorer in the women's football tournament. Her tally included a hat-trick – in vain – in Canada's 4-3 semi-final defeat to the US.

WOMEN'S FOOTBALL MEDAL TABLE:

1 **USA** (G:4, S:1, B:0)

2 **Germany** (G:1, S:0, B:3)

3 **Norway** (G:1, S:0, B:1)

4 **Brazil** (G:0, S:2, B:0)

5 **China** (G:0, S:1, B:0)

= **Japan** (G:0, S:1, B:0)

= **Sweden** (G:0, S:1, B:0)

2012

In 2012, Olympic hosts Great Britain fielded a team for the first time and although they finished top of their first round group with a perfect three wins from three, without conceding a goal, they were beaten 2-0 by Canada in the quarter-final and missed out on a medal.

CARLI LLOYD

🏆 TOURNAMENT TRIVIA
LATE STARTS, LATE FINISHES

American **Carli Lloyd** is one of the greatest players in Olympic women's football history. In Beijing in 2008 she struck the winning goal for the USA against Brazil and, four years later in London, scored both goals in their 2-1 victory over Japan. Other memorable moments from London 2012 included Alex Morgan's winner for the USA against Canada in the semi-final – she made it 4-3 three minutes into stoppage-time at the end of extra-time, the latest goal in Olympic history.

The USA have dominated the Olympics since women's football was introduced at the 1996 Games in Atlanta. They have won four gold medals and secured silver in 2000.

FIFA AWARDS

Every year world football swaps match kit for black tie formality to hail a range of achievements and achievers from the previous year. In 2017, FIFA took the show on the road to London.

The world federation had launched its own World Player and associated awards in 1990. Between 2010 and 2015, the main award had been shared with the Ballon d'Or, launched by the Paris magazine, France Football, in the mid-1950s.

In 2016 the FIFA and France Football awards separated, the latter reclaiming sole rights to the Ballon d'Or, while FIFA stepped out with a new title. Hence the rebranding of the FIFA prize-giving as The Best awards for the outstanding team and individual achievements of the year.

The voters of both FIFA and France Football still concurred that the outstanding player of 2018 had been Luka Modric of Croatia and Real Madrid. London magazine World Soccer, which has been running its own world player poll since 1982, made it a three-way agreement. Five times FIFA's top player, Portugal and Real Madrid/Juventus's Cristiano, was again runner-up to Modric, with Mohamed Salah of Egypt and Liverpool third.

FIFA's Best Woman player was the incomparable Brazilian superstar Marta, whose performances for club and country saw her claim the award for a record sixth time.

The Men's FIFPro World 11 accept their awards onstage with host Idris Elba.

FIFA MEN'S PLAYER OF THE YEAR

The Best FIFA Men's Player has seen several name changes since its inception, but its purpose remains the same: to celebrate the players at the very pinnacle of world football.

2018 WINNER
LUKA MODRIC

Luka Modric brought down the curtain on the Ronaldo/Messi awards roadshow on being hailed FIFA's world player of the year for 2018 at The Best awards gala in London.

The 33-year-old playmaker from Croatia and Real Madrid was rewarded for a remarkable year in which he led his national team to runners-up spot at the World Cup and carried off a fourth Champions League in five years with his club. He was also among the four current Real Madrid players named in the FIFA/FIFPro World XI.

This was the first time in eight years that neither Ronaldo nor Barcelona's Argentinian Lionel Messi had been acclaimed as No1 by FIFA. It was also the first time since 2006 that Messi had not featured on the three-man FIFA shortlist. The last winning 'interloper' had been Brazil's Kaka in 2007.

Modric, who placed top in a ballot among national team managers and captains and the media, said: "It's a great honour and beautiful feeling to stand here with this amazing trophy. This trophy is not just mine but for all my Real Madrid and Croatia teammates, for all the coaches I have played for – without them this would not be possible. For this trophy I also thank my family without whom I would not be the player and person I am."

PREVIOUS WINNERS :

2017	**Cristiano Ronaldo** (Portugal)	
2016	**Cristiano Ronaldo** (Portugal)	
2015	**Lionel Messi** (Argentina)	
2014	**Cristiano Ronaldo** (Portugal)	
2013	**Cristiano Ronaldo** (Portugal)	

1991

The year the award was first issued, when it was won by Germany's Lothar Matthaus.

5

Lionel Messi and Cristiano Ronaldo are tied for most wins.

8

Brazilian players have won the award on eight occasions – more than any other nation.

Votes for the award are divided equally between media representatives, national team coaches, national team captains, and the general public.

Liberia's **George Weah** is the only African player to win the award to date.

GEORGE WEAH

FIFA WOMEN'S PLAYER OF THE YEAR

Though it's a more recent addition to the awards slate, the Women's Player of the Year award has been won by a range of players from across four continents.

2018 WINNER
MARTA

Brazil's Marta, probably the greatest woman footballer of all time, collected her record-extending sixth FIFA award in London despite the highly-rated rivalry of Norway forward Ada Hegerberg and Germany midfielder Dzsenifer Marozsan. Marta described the occasion and her latest crowning as "an amazing night" and "a moment of magic."

Marta's achievements in 2017-18 included captaining Brazil to the Copa America title and helped her club side Orlando Pride to a successful run in the National Women's Soccer League in the United States. This was the 12th time she had been named in FIFA's top three.

She summed up her passion for the game by saying: "I don't train any harder than other players but I will say this: every day that I go to training I want to shoot the best, I want to run the fastest, I want to head the best, I want to be the first to every ball, I want to be the best there."

Both Marta's closest challengers played their club football for UEFA Women's Champions League winners Lyon with whom they also won the French league title. Norway's Hegerberg scored 31 goals in 20 league appearances for Lyon and set a Women's Champions League record of 15 goals. Marozsan also captained Germany to five wins in six Women's World Cup qualifying games.

PREVIOUS WINNERS :

2017	**Lieke Martens** (Netherlands)
2016	**Carli Lloyd** (USA)
2015	**Carli Lloyd** (USA)
2014	**Nadine Kessler** (Germany)
2013	**Nadine Angerer** (Germany)

2001
The year that the inaugural Women's World Player of the Year award was given to Mia Hamm of the USA.

20
Marta's age when she became the youngest winner of the award in 2006.

Nadine Angerer is the only goalkeeper (male or female) to have won a FIFA Player of the Year award.

6
Brazilian legend Marta's six titles (including five in a row from 2006-10) are the most by any player.

3
The number of winners from both the USA and Germany: more than any other nation.

NADINE
ANGERER

OTHER FIFA AWARDS

Excellence in football is understandably measured on the pitch, but FIFA also recognizes many other outstanding achievements, from brilliance in coaching to acts of selflessness in the world of football.

Didier Deschamps's accolade as The Best coach in the game in 2018 was assured back in mid-July when his French national team won the FIFA World Cup in Russia. Victory in Moscow lifted him alongside Germany's Franz Beckenbauer and Brazil's Mario Zagallo as the only men to win the game's top prize as both player and manager. Midfielder Deschamps had captained France to World Cup glory in 1998 and his team's 4–2 victory over Croatia two decades later marked him out for the FIFA prize in London.

2018 WINNERS:

Men's Best Player: Luka Modric (Croatia, Real Madrid)

Women's Best Player: Marta (Brazil, Orlando Pride)

Goalkeeper of the Year: Thibaut Cortois (Belgium, Chelsea)

Men's Best Coach: Didier Deschamps (France)

Women's Best Coach: Reynald Pedros (Lyon)

FIFA Ferenc Puskas Award (outstanding goal): Mohamed Salah (Egypt, Liverpool)

Fair Play Award: Lennart Thy (VVV-Venlo)

Fans Award: Peru

FIFA FIFPro World 11: David De Gea (Spain, Manchester United); **Dani Alves** (Brazil, Paris Saint-Germain), **Raphael Varane** (France, Real Madrid), **Sergio Ramos** (Spain, Real Madrid), **Marcelo** (Brazil, Real Madrid); **N'Golo Kante** (France, Chelsea), **Eden Hazard** (Belgium, Chelsea), **Luka Modric** (Croatia, Real Madrid); **Cristiano Ronaldo** (Portugal, Real Madrid/Juventus), **Lionel Messi** (Argentina, Barcelona), **Kylian Mbappe** (France, Paris Saint-Germain).

FIFA's Fair Play Award went to **Lennart Thy**. The German forward missed a week's training and a match for VVV-Venlo in the Dutch Eredivisie to donate stem cells for potentially life-saving treatment for a patient battling leukaemia.

Peru's supporters scooped the Fan Award, thanks to the South American country's noisy and excited following at the World Cup finals in Russia. The travelling Peruvians made the most of their team's return to the big stage after an absence of 36 years even though they failed to progress beyond the group stage.

The women's football coaching award went to a man in **Reynald Pedros**. The one-time France and Nantes midfielder had guided Lyon to the double of UEFA European Women's Champions League and French national championship.

REYNALD **PEDROS**

Thibaut Courtois was crowned as top goalkeeper for his outstanding displays for Chelsea and Belgium while Egypt and Liverpool's Mohamed Salah won the Puskás Award for an excellent individual goal.

THIBAUT **COURTOIS**

PREVIOUS WINNERS:

2017

Men's Best Coach: Zinedine Zidane (Real Madrid)

Women's Best Coach: Sarina Niegman (Netherlands)

FIFA Ferenc Puskas Award (outstanding goal):
Olivier Giroud (France, Arsenal)

Fair Play: Francis Kone (Togo, FC Zbrojovka Brno)

Fan Award: Celtic

2016

Men's Best Coach: Claudio Ranieri (Leicester City)

Women's Best Coach: Silvia Neid (Germany)

FIFA Ferenc Puskas Award (outstanding goal): Mohd Faiz Subri (Malaysia, Penang FA)

Fair Play: Atletico Nacional (Colombia)

Fan Award: Borussia Dortmund & Liverpool supporters

Outstanding career: Falcao [Alessandro Rosa Vieira] (Brazil, futsal)

2015

Coach of the Year (men): Luis Enrique (Barcelona)

Coach of the Year (women): Jill Ellis (United States)

FIFA Ferenc Puskas Award (outstanding goal):
Wendell Lira (Goianesia, Brazil)

Fair Play: All football organizations assisting refugees

2014

Coach of the Year (men): Joachim Low (Germany)

Coach of the Year (women): Ralf Kellerman (Germany, Wolfsburg)

FIFA Ferenc Puskas Award (outstanding goal): James Rodriguez, Colombia v Uruguay

Presidential: Hiroshi Kagawa (Japanese journalist)

Fair Play Award: FIFA World Cup volunteers

2013

Coach of the Year (men): Jupp Heynckes (Bayern Munich)

Coach of the Year (women): Silvia Neid (Germany)

FIFA Ferenc Puskas Award (outstanding goal): Zlatan Ibrahimovic, Sweden v England

Presidential: Jacques Rogge (Honorary President, IOC)

Fair Play award: Afghanistan Football Federation

FIFA WORLD RANKINGS

The movement of nations throughout all levels of the FIFA World Rankings reflects the compelling and constantly shifting battle to be the world's most dominant international team.

F IFA introduced a world ranking system in December 1992 to provide a monthly statistical analysis of the rise and fall of the fortunes of all the world game's national teams in men's football. Placings are computed on results in what are termed international A games and consider match status, goals scored, strength of opposition and regional balance. The women's world rankings, introduced in 2003, are published on a quarterly basis.

The rankings are important, not least because they have previously been used as a form-guide guide by FIFA for draws of international competitions. A short break in publication accompanied the 2018 FIFA World Cup, when the system was refined to adjust anomalies concerning the assessment of friendly matches. This new iteration of FIFA's formula, named "SUM", relies on a system of addition and subtraction rather than averaging points over a given time period, as in previous versions.

Belgium's 'golden generation' have risen to the top of the FIFA rankings.

FIFA MEN'S WORLD RANKINGS 2019

Germany went into the 2018 FIFA World Cup finals in Russia holding top spot, but that single month of high-level competition saw them toppled both as world champions and as rankings leaders by France.

Didier Deschamps's 2018 FIFA World Cup-winning France did not have long to enjoy their rankings primacy, however. Their slip-ups in the new UEFA Nations League saw them overtaken by Belgium, who held their lead at the close of the 2018-19 European season.

The Nations League was only one of a clutch of national team tournaments in 2019 which prompted further changes in the power game. New South American champions Brazil ousted France from second place, while Copa America semi-finalists Argentina, and quarter-finalists Uruguay, Colombia and Venezuela, completed a quartet of South American teams in the top ten.

Elsewhere CONCACAF Gold Cup winners Mexico rose six places to 12th spot while Algeria's surprise triumph in the African Cup of Nations lifted them a remarkable 28 places to 40th. Asian champions Qatar were 62nd.

RANKINGS (as at July 2019)

Pos.	Country	Pts	(+/-)
1	Belgium	1746	0
2	Brazil	1726	+1
3	France	1718	-1
4	England	1652	0
5	Uruguay	1637	+3
6	Portugal	1631	-1
7	Croatia	1625	-1
8	Colombia	1622	+5
9	Spain	1617	-2
10	Argentina	1610	+1
11	Switzerland	1605	-2
12	Mexico	1604	+6
13	Denmark	1589	-3
14	Chile	1583	+2
15	Germany	1582	-4
16	Italy	1569	-2
16	Netherlands	1569	-2
18	Sweden	1558	-1
19	Peru	1552	+2
20	Poland	1550	-1
20	Senegal	1550	+2
22	United States	1548	+8
23	Iran	1518	-3
24	Wales	1514	-1
25	Ukraine	1513	-1
26	Venezuela	1505	+7
27	Austria	1498	-1
28	Romania	1497	-1
29	Tunisia	1496	-4
29	N Ireland	1496	-1
31	Slovakia	1491	0
32	Rep. Ireland	1489	0
33	Nigeria	1481	+12
33	Japan	1481	-5
35	Serbia	1477	-1
36	Iceland	1473	-1
37	Korea Rep.	1467	0
37	Turkey	1467	0
39	Paraguay	1464	-3
40	Algeria	1463	+28
41	Morocco	1461	+6
42	Bosnia & Herz.	1453	-3
43	Czech Republic	1448	-2
44	Costa Rica	1445	-5
45	Hungary	1442	-3
46	Australia	1436	-3
46	Russia	1436	-3
48	Scotland	1433	-3
49	Egypt	1431	+9
50	Norway	1429	-3
50	Ghana	1429	0
52	Jamaica	1425	+2

Pos.	Country	Pts	(+/-)
53	Cameroon	1409	-2
54	Greece	1403	-2
55	Montenegro	1401	-2
56	Congo DR	1395	-7
57	Ivory Coast	1394	+5
57	Finland	1394	-1
59	Mali	1389	+3
60	Bulgaria	1388	-3
61	Burkina Faso	1381	-2
62	Qatar	1375	-7
63	Slovenia	1363	+2
64	Albania	1362	+2
65	United Arab Emirates	1360	+2
66	Ecuador	1359	-6
67	Honduras	1350	-6
68	Saudi Arabia	1342	+1
68	El Salvador	1342	+1
70	South Africa	1338	+2
71	China PR	1333	+2
71	North Macedonia	1333	+2
73	Bolivia	1332	-11
74	Panama	1331	+1
75	Guinea	1325	-4
76	Cape Verde Is.	1319	0
77	Iraq	1315	0
78	Canada	1312	0
79	Curacao	1309	0
80	Uganda	1305	0
81	Zambia	1299	0
82	Benin	1295	+6
83	Haiti	1288	+18
84	Israel	1286	-2
84	Belarus	1286	-2
84	Uzbekistan	1286	-2
87	Syria	1277	-2
87	Oman	1277	-1
87	Lebanon	1277	-1
90	Gabon	1272	-1
91	Congo	1265	-1
91	Luxembourg	1265	-1
93	Cyprus	1258	0
94	Georgia	1255	0
95	Kyrgyz Republic	1252	0
96	Madagascar	1251	+12
97	Vietnam	1232	-1
98	Armenia	1230	-1
99	Jordan	1229	-1
100	Estonia	1228	-1
101	Trinidad & Tobago	1226	-9
102	Palestine	1224	-2
103	India	1214	-2
104	Niger	1209	0
105	Libya	1207	0
106	Mauritania	1205	-3
107	Kenya	1201	-2
108	Faroe Islands	1200	-1
109	Bahrain	1188	+1
109	Azerbaijan	1188	+1
111	Central African Rep.	1184	+1
112	Kazakhstan	1174	+2
112	Zimbabwe	1174	-3
114	Sierra Leone	1172	+1
115	Thailand	1165	+1
116	Mozambique	1163	+1
117	New Zealand	1157	+2
118	Korea DPR	1154	+4
119	Tajikistan	1152	+1
120	Kosovo	1149	+1
121	Namibia	1148	-8
122	Angola	1144	+1
123	Guinea-Bissau	1143	-5
124	Antigua & Barbuda	1136	0
125	Chinese Taipei	1132	0
126	Philippines	1131	0
126	Malawi	1131	0
128	Togo	1127	0
129	Sudan	1106	+1
130	Lithuania	1101	+2
131	St Kitts & Nevis	1096	+2
132	Turkmenistan	1091	+3
133	Rwanda	1088	+3
134	Latvia	1086	+3
135	Myanmar	1084	+3
136	Andorra	1082	+3
137	Tanzania	1075	-6
137	Nicaragua	1075	-8
139	Equatorial Guinea	1074	+2
139	Eswatini	1074	+2
139	Hong Kong	1074	+2
142	Solomon Islands	1073	-2
142	Yemen	1073	+2
144	Guatemala	1072	+1
144	Lesotho	1072	+1
146	Comoros	1071	+2
147	Botswana	1069	0
148	Burundi	1061	-14
149	Afghanistan	1058	0
150	Ethiopia	1049	0
151	Suriname	1045	+1
152	Maldives	1044	-1
152	Liberia	1044	+1
154	New Caledonia	1035	+1
155	Dominican Rep.	1028	-1
156	Kuwait	1022	0
157	Mauritius	1019	0
158	Tahiti	1014	0
159	Malaysia	1009	0
160	Indonesia	1008	0
161	Gambia	1006	0
162	Singapore	999	0
163	Vanuatu	996	0
163	Fiji	996	+4
163	Barbados	996	+1
166	Nepal	995	-1
167	Belize	994	-1
168	Papua New Guinea	991	+3
169	South Sudan	989	-1
170	Cambodia	988	-1
171	Moldova	985	-1
172	St Lucia	975	0
173	Grenada	973	0
174	Bermuda	972	0
175	Chad	956	+1
176	Dominica	954	+1
176	St Vincent & Grenadines	954	+1
178	Guyana	953	-1
179	Cuba	950	-4
180	Puerto Rico	940	0
181	Malta	939	0
182	Liechtenstein	922	+1
182	Bangladesh	922	+1
182	Macau	922	0
185	Sao Tome e Principe	920	0
186	Bhutan	916	0
187	Mongolia	914	0
188	Laos	912	0
189	Aruba	909	0
190	Guam	908	0
190	Cook Islands	908	0
192	Seychelles	904	+2
192	Brunei Darussalam	904	+1
194	American Samoa	900	-4
195	Djibouti	896	0
196	Montserrat	895	+1
197	Samoa	894	-2
198	Gibraltar	893	0
199	US Virgin Islands	888	0
200	Sri Lanka	886	+1
201	Timor-Leste	879	-1
202	Somalia	868	0
202	Eritrea	868	0
204	Cayman Islands	867	+1
204	Pakistan	867	+1
204	British Virgin Is	867	+1
207	Tonga	862	-5
207	Turks & Caicos Is	862	+1
209	Anguilla	857	0
210	Bahamas	855	0
211	San Marino	839	0

FIFA WOMEN'S WORLD RANKINGS 2019

Victory in France in the final of the FIFA Women's World Cup sealed the status of the United States at the top of the FIFA/Coca-Cola Women's World Rankings.

Megan Rapinoe and her all-conquering team-mates defeated four of the other top six nations in the process to extend their lead to a staggering 121 points over Germany in the largest gap in the history of the women's rankings. The world runners-up and European champions from the Netherlands moved up five places to a best-ever third. England, meanwhile, slipped two places to fifth after losing the third-place play-off to Sweden. The July rankings featured a record 158 nations, as the women's game continues to gain popularity around the world.

RANKINGS (as at July 2019)

Pos.	Country	Pts	(+/-)
1	United States	2180	0
2	Germany	2059	0
3	Netherlands	2037	+5
4	France	2029	0
5	England	2027	-2
6	Sweden	2021	+3
7	Canada	1976	-2
8	Australia	1965	-2
9	Korea DPR	1940	+2
10	Brazil	1938	0
11	Japan	1937	-4
12	Norway	1917	0
13	Spain	1899	0
14	Italy	1891	+1
15	Denmark	1839	+2
16	China PR	1838	0
17	Iceland	1822	+5
18	Switzerland	1815	0
19	Belgium	1813	+1
20	Korea Republic	1805	-6
21	Austria	1793	+2
22	Scotland	1791	-2
23	New Zealand	1766	-4
24	Ukraine	1708	0
25	Russia	1704	0
26	Colombia	1703	0
27	Mexico	1699	-1
28	Czech Republic	1679	+1
29	Poland	1675	-1
30	Portugal	1671	0
31	Finland	1668	+1
32	Wales	1667	+1
33	Rep. Ireland	1666	-2
34	Argentina	1664	+3
35	Vietnam	1659	0
36	Nigeria	1643	+2
37	Costa Rica	1630	-1
38	Chile	1621	+1
39	Thailand	1616	-5
40	Chinese Taipei	1590	0

Pos.	Country	Pts	(+/-)
41	Cameroon	1552	+5
42	Romania	1548	-1
43	Serbia	1546	0
44	Uzbekistan	1542	-2
45	Hungary	1525	0
46	Myanmar	1521	-2
47	Slovakia	1500	-1
48	Paraguay	1494	0
49	South Africa	1486	0
50	Papua New Guinea	1479	0
51	Slovenia	1453	+1
51	Jamaica	1453	+2
53	Ghana	1452	-2
54	Belarus	1446	+1
55	Croatia	1440	+1
56	Panama	1429	0
57	India	1422	+6
58	Venezuela	1421	0
59	N Ireland	1420	0
60	Jordan	1419	-6
61	Trinidad & Tobago	1414	-1
62	Turkey	1412	-1
63	Ecuador	1393	-1
64	Israel	1392	-1
65	Greece	1376	+2
65	Peru	1376	0
67	Philippines	1371	+7
67	Bosnia/Herzegovina	1371	1
69	Cote d'Ivoire	1363	0
70	IR Iran	1358	-4
71	Equatorial Guinea	1356	-1
72	Fiji	1355	-1
73	Haiti	1349	-1
73	Kazakhstan	1349	-1
75	Uruguay	1347	-1
76	Azerbaijan	1345	-
77	Hong Kong	1336	-1
78	Albania	1326	-1
79	Bulgaria	1303	-1
80	Guatemala	1288	0

Pos.	Country	Pts	(+/-)
80	Mali	1288	+5
82	Guam	1282	-1
83	Morocco	1280	-4
84	Bahrain	1274	-2
85	Faroe Islands	1272	-2
86	Algeria	1271	-2
87	Tonga	1249	0
88	Senegal	1245	0
89	Guyana	1244	0
90	Malaysia	1243	0
91	New Caledonia	1239	0
92	Bolivia	1236	0
93	Latvia	1228	0
94	Indonesia	1224	-8
94	Cuba	1224	-1
96	Moldova	1219	-1
97	Tahiti	1218	-1
98	Montenegro	1217	-1
99	Estonia	1212	0
100	United Arab Emirates	1207	-2
101	Nepal	1196	2
102	Zimbabwe	1192	0
102	Malta	1192	-1
104	El Salvador	1179	0
105	Congo	1178	-5
106	Lithuania	1172	+1
107	Puerto Rico	1171	-2
108	Dominican Republic	1169	-2
109	Vanuatu	1161	-1
110	Cook Islands	1159	-1
111	Solomon Islands	1153	-1
112	Georgia	1143	0
113	Luxembourg	1134	0
114	Palestine	1131	-3
115	Samoa	1130	-1
116	Congo DR	1128	0
117	Cyprus	1123	-2
118	Ethiopia	1122	-1
119	Zambia	1119	-3
120	Mongolia	1114	-2

Pos.	Country	Pts	(+/-)
121	Suriname	1113	-2
122	Nicaragua	1092	-1
123	Singapore	1089	-3
124	Gabon	1070	0
125	Burkina Faso	1062	-3
126	Kosovo	1059	-3
127	North Macedonia	1053	-3
128	American Samoa	1047	-3
129	Tajikistan	1031	-3
130	Bangladesh	1008	-3
131	St Lucia	992	-2
132	St Kitts and Nevis	989	-2
133	Bermuda	987	-2
134	Barbados	984	-2
135	Tanzania	978	-2
136	Sri Lanka	974	-2
137	Lebanon	967	-2
138	Namibia	966	-10
139	Maldives	957	-3
140	St Vincent & Grenadines	956	-3
141	Kenya	921	-3
142	Dominica	913	-3
143	Rwanda	899	-3
144	Grenada	892	-3
145	Afghanistan	884	-3
146	Malawi	881	+1
147	US Virgin Islands	874	-4
148	Uganda	868	-4
149	Lesotho	850	-3
150	Mozambique	823	-5
151	Eswatini	804	-3
152	Botswana	796	-1
153	Antigua and Barbuda	784	-4
154	Bhutan	769	-4
155	Curacao	752	-3
156	Andorra	749	-3
157	Aruba	742	-3
158	Madagascar	693	-3

PICTURE CREDITS

The publishers would like to thank the following sources for their kind permission to reproduce the pictures in this book. The page numbers for each of the photographs are listed below, giving the page on which they appear in the book and any location indicator (C-centre, T-top, B-bottom, L-left, R-right).

Getty Images: 137T; /2010 Qatar 2022: 149TL; /AFP: 40BR, 48B, 73BL, 101BR, 170BL, 173T, 175BR; /AMA/Corbis: 52C, 199BL; /Suhaimi Abdullah: 116BL; /Luis Acosta/AFP: 86B, 95TL; /Robin Alam/Icon Sportswire: 130B; /Allsport: 155TR, 169TR; /Vanderlei Almeida/AFP: 169BL; /Vincent Amalvy/AFP: 103BR; /Anadolu Agency: 34B; /Odd Andersen/AFP: 25BR; /Mladen Antonov/AFP: 150TR; /Raul Arboleda/AFP: 166TR, 166B; /The Asashi Shimbun: 16T; /Matthew Ashton/Corbis: 45BR, 65BR, 87T, 133BR; /Matthew Ashton – AMA: 37TR, 126-127, 140BL, 143TR; /Marc Atkins: 202-203, 205TR; /Marc Atkins/Offside: 201BL; /Naomi Baker: 204B; /Gokhan Balci/Anadolu Agency: 105TR, 107TL; /Steve Bardens: 157R; /Dennis Barnard/Fox Photos: 91L; /Lars Baron: 46T, 154-155, 190L, 210BR; /Robbie Jay Barratt – AMA: 14BR, 80, 95BL, 143C, 157BL; /Juan Barreto/AFP: 100R; /Farouk Batiche/AFP: 106B; /James Bayliss – AMA: 4BR; /Robyn Beck/AFP: 147TR; /Sandra Behne/Bongarts: 119L; /Benainous/Hounsfield/Gamma-Rapho: 17BR; /Bentley Archive/Popperfoto: 64R; /Martin Bernetti/AFP: 72TR; /Gunnar Berning/Bongarts: 197C; /Bongarts: 28BL; /Shaun Botterill: 19TR, 47B, 145L, 153BL, 161TR; /Cris Bouroncle/AFP: 127BR, 187BR; /Gabriel Bouys/AFP: 32B, 108; /Chris Brunskill: 11R, 76TR, 90TR, 142BL, 164-165; /Clive Brunskill: 94T; /Simon Bruty: 13BL, 99B; /Rodrigo Buendia/AFP: 88T; /Giuseppe Cacace/AFP: 24T, 176B, 177R, 179L; /David Cannon: 40TR, 61B, 91B; /Alex Caparros: 222; /Jean Catuffe: 17L, 35BR, 49B; /Central Press: 63BL; /Central Press/Hulton Archive: 49TR; /Graham Chadwick: 61TC; /Stanley Chou: 210T; /Matteo Ciambelli/NurPhoto: 44TR, 101T, 132TR; /Robert Cianflone: 67R, 69TL, 96T, 141TR; /Thomas Coex/AFP: 47C; /Fabrice Coffrini/AFP: 44BL, 116TR, 147C; /Chris Cole: 144R; /Phil Cole: 43BR, 104; /Yuri Cortez/AFP: 22B; /Kevin C Cox: 220; /Benjamin Cremel/AFP: 119T; /Charlie Crowhurst: 133BC; /Jonathan Daniel: 86TR; /Stephane de Sakutin/AFP: 150L; /Adrian Dennis/AFP: 56TR, 140-141, 160L; /Philippe Desmazes/AFP: 121TR; /Khaled Desouki/AFP: 176C, 180R, 181L; /Anthony Dibon/Icon Sport: 88R; /Disney/Central Press/Hulton Archive: 15BR; /Kevork Djansezian: 131TR; /Stephen Dunn: 109BR; /Johannes Eisele/AFP: 5BL, 40BL; /Paul Ellis/AFP: 20TR; /Elsa: 144BL, 206; /Alfredo Estrella/AFP: 128BL; /Jonathan Ferrey: 43TR; /Franck Fife/AFP: 18BL, 98, 162B; /Julian Finney: 11BL, 41C, 99T, 153TL, 217TL; /Stu Forster: 39BL, 41B. 78TR, 88BL; /Foto Olimpik/NurPhoto: 61TR, 136; /Stuart Franklin: 21BL, 95TR; /Sebastian Frej/MB Media: 218-219; /Romeo Gacad/AFP: 45TR; /Daniel Garcia/AFP: 96B, 142BC; /Paul Gilham: 111TR, 193T; /Otto Greule Jr: 131BC; /Laurence Griffiths: 63R, 64BL, 113TR, 194-195; /Alex Grimm: 55TR; /Jeff Gross: 133L; /Jeferson Guareze/AFP: 167BR; /Haraldur Gudjonsson/AFP: 137B; /Gianluigi Guercia/AFP: 183L; /Jack Guez/AFP: 84-85; /Matthias Hangst: 15C, 22TL, 148, 163C; /Matthias Hangst/Bongarts: 156TR; /Norman Hall/LatinContent: 173B; /Etsuo Hara: 191BR; /Ronny Hartmann/AFP: 74TR; /Alexander Hassenstein: 21R, 143BR, 215TR, 216TR, 216BR, 217L; /Richard Heathcote: 97B, 135R, 205L, 205BR; /Alexander Heimann: 31T; /Alexander Heimann/Bongarts: 132B; /Mike Hewitt: 51BL, 90BL, 127TC, 191TL, 201C; /Maja Hitij: 5TC, 209T, 209B, 209BR; /Simon Hofmann: 152; /Boris Horvat/AFP: 29BL, 161B; /Harry How: 129TR; /Arif Hudaverdi Yaman/Anadolu Agency: 74BL; /Hulton Archive: 196TR; /isifa: 69BR; /Dan Istitene: 25L; /Catherine Ivill: 16BL; /Karim Jaafar/AFP: 117L, 118B, 123BL; /Jose Jordan/AFP: 35L; /Jasper Juinen: 13TR, 33TR, 34TL; /Sia Kambou/AFP: 110BL; /Sefa Karacan/Anadolu Agency: 32T, 33TR; /Keystone: 17TC, 62R; /Keystone/Hulton Archive: 57BR, 197BR; /Mike King: 142TR; /Glyn Kirk/AFP: 192B; /Attila Kisbenedek/AFP: 48T, 162TR; /Joe Klamar/AFP: 42BL; /Christof Koepsel/Bongarts: 100TL; /Mark Kolbe: 114TR, 115C; /Ozan Kose/AFP: 66B, 106TL; /Patrick Kovarik/AFP: 82TC; /Jan Kruger: 156BL; /Nolwenn Le Gouic/Icon Sport: 75T; /David Leah/Mexsport: 128TR; /Christopher Lee: 69TR; /Eddy Lemaistre/Corbis: 26BL; /Bryn Lennon: 59BR; /Francisco Leong/AFP: 23C; /Matthew Lewis: 55L, 58T, 199T; /Christian Liewig/Corbis: 178, 181BR; /Alex Livesey: 4TR, 36BL, 45C, 50BL, 71T, 73C, 76B, 85R, 120, 146BL; /Marco Luzzani: 27B; /Juan Mabromata/AFP: 166L; /Ian MacNicol: 14TL, 41TR, 58BR; /Pierre-Philippe Marcou/AFP: 35T, 109TL; /Nigel Marple: 125TR; /Hunter Martin/LatinContent: 94BL; /Ronald Martinez: 207BL; /Clive Mason: 109TR; /Jamie McDonald: 42T, 59C, 70B; /Anatoliy Medved/Icon Sportswire: 54C; /Marty Melville/AFP: 124B; /Buda Mendes: 167BL, 188R; /Craig Mercer/CameraSport: 36R; /Merillon/Stevens/Gamma-Rapho: 18T; /Aris Messinis/AFP: 160TR; /Aurelien Meunier: 131BR; /Maddie Meyer: 198R; /Jeff Mitchell: 189BR; /Jiro Mochizuki/Icon Sport: 103TR; /Filippo Monteforte/AFP: 57L; /Alex Morton: 186BR; /Dean Mouhtaropoulos: 10, 29T, 33B, 115TL; /Peter Muhly/AFP: 59BL, 82TL; /Dan Mullan: 56BL; /Cor Mulder/AFP: 37BL; /Marwan Naamani/AFP: 123TR; /Hoang Dinh Nam/AFP: 130TR; /Cyril Ndegeya/AFP: 102-103, 201TL; /Nebe/ullstein bild: 197TL; /Francois Nel: 95BR, 112-113; /Mike Nelson/AFP: 127TR; /Alexander Nemenov/AFP: 62B, 134-135; /Fayez Nureldine/AFP: 123BR; /NurPhoto: 23TL; /Kiyoshi Ota: 117BR; /Werner Otto/ullstein bild: 159TL; /Jeff Pachoud/AFP: 158; /Minas Panagiotakis: 215BR; /Ulrik Pedersen/Action Plus: 12TR; /Ulrik Pedersen/NurPhoto: 177TL; /Valerio Pennicino: 100BL; /Frank Peters/Bongarts: 52BL; /Hannah Peters: 124TR; /Ryan Pierse: 81L; /Hrvoje Polan/AFP: 38BL; /Popperfoto: 20B, 38TR, 71BL, 85TR, 92BL, 111C, 118TR, 122TR, 141TL, 159BR, 171BR, 172R, 198BL; /Mike Powell: 149B; /Bruna Prado: 165C; /Savo Prelevic/AFP: 83C; /Craig Prentis: 129C; /Pressefoto Ulmer/ullstein bild: 83B, 163TR; /Adam Pretty: 93R; /Professional Sport/Popperfoto: 26TR; /Dean Purcell: 125L; /Ben Radford: 58L, 92T, 188BL, 214BR; /David Ramos: 146TR, 200; /Michael Regan: 77TR, 79TR, 184-185, 214TR, 217BL; /Kyle Rivas: 131TR; /Rolls Press/Popperfoto: 12B; /Quinn Rooney: 211TR; /Clive Rose: 5L, 67BL, 77BL, 151TL; /Martin Rose: 17R, 21TL; /Martin Rose/Bongarts: 75BL; /Rouxel/AFP: 181R; /Evaristo Sa/AFP: 97T, 167TL; /Karim Sahib/AFP: 190BR; /Issouf Sanogo/AFP: 107BR, 110TR, 111BL; /Genia Savilov/AFP: 55B; /Rich Schultz: 172B; /Abdelhak Senna/AFP: 182B, 183R; /Lefty Shivambu/Gallo Images: 179T, 180B; /Christophe Simon/AFP: 71BR; /Patrick Smith: 139TR; /Andreas Solaro/AFP: 25T; /Javier Soriano/AFP: 139BL, 159TR; /Cameron Spencer: 113B; /Jamie Squire: 105BR; /Ben Stansall/AFP: 212-213; /Michael Steele: 39T, 70TR, 92BR; /Srdjan Stevanovic: 67T; /Patrik Stollarz/AFP: 82B; /TF-Images: 68BL, 138T; /Mehdi Taamallah/NurPhoto: 145TR; /Trond Tandberg: 53TR; /Bob Thomas: 24BR, 27TL, 51TR, 54R, 59TL, 60TR, 79BR, 87B, 93L, 105BC, 119BR, 143TL, 151R, 153R, 155BR, 193BL, 196BL; /John Thys/AFP: 81B, 187L, 208BL; /ullstein bild: 66TR; /VCG: 79L, 121BL; /VI Images: 5TL, 22R, 31B, 63T, 65R, 208R; /Robert van den Brugge/AFP: 37C; /Geert van Erven/Soccrates: 31BR; /Manan Vatsyayana/AFP: 129BR; /Loic Venance/AFP: 204TR; /Eric Verhoeven/Soccrates: 29BR; /Pedro Vilela: 167R, 211B; /Claudio Villa: 83TR; /Visionhaus: 174-175, 177BC, 177BR, 181T; /Hector Vivas: 135BR, 150BR; /Ian Walton: 30T, 68TR, 182TR; /Lakruwan Wanniarachchi/AFP: 122B; /Koji Watanabe: 168B; /Charlotte Wilson/Offside: 6; /Dave Winter/Icon Sport: 43L

PA Images: 67BR, 170TR, 192TR; /Matthew Ashton: 30BL, 93TL, 207R; /Barry Coombs: 47TR; /DPA: 19B, 114BL, 115BR, 138BL; /Paulo Duarte/AP: 57T; /Dominic Favre/AP: 72B; /Michel Gouverneur/Reporter: 189T; /Intime Sports/AP: 46BR; /Ross Kinnaird: 171TR; /Tony Marshall: 75R, 93TR, 187T; /Peter Robinson: 28T, 50R, 64T, 89B, 186T; /S&G and Barratts: 145BR; /SMG: 65L; /Scanpix Norway: 53TL; /Ariel Schalit/AP: 107C; /Sven Simon: 91TR; /Neal Simpson: 39BR, 60B, 73BR, 171BL; /Jon Super/AP: 207T; /Topham Picturepoint: 82R; /John Walton: 81TR, 89T

Shutterstock: /360b: 175TC; /Anabela88: 165R; /BOLDG: 85BR; /Colorsport: 78B; /FMStox: 11L; /Khvost: 113TC; /Panatphong: 155TC; /RaimaD: 175L; /Namig Rustamov: 11T; /Rvector: 175TR; /Wikrom Kitsamritchai: 8-9; /Tond Van Graphcraft: 11C

Wikimedia Commons: 53BL, 168TR

Every effort has been made to acknowledge correctly and contact the source and/or copyright holder of each picture and Carlton Books Limited apologises for any unintentional errors or omissions that will be corrected in future editions of this book.

ABOUT THE AUTHOR

Keir Radnedge has been covering football for more than 50 years. He has written countless books on the subject, from tournament guides to comprehensive encyclopedias, aimed at all ages. His journalism career included the *Daily Mail* for 20 years, as well as the *Guardian* and other national newspapers and magazines in the UK and abroad. He is a former editor of *World Soccer*, generally recognized as the premier English-language magazine on global football. In addition to his writing, Keir has been a regular foreign football analyst for all UK broadcasters. He scripted official films of the early World Cups and is chairman of the football commission of AIPS, the international sports journalists' association.

ACKNOWLEDGEMENTS

Special thanks to Aidan Radnedge for support and assistance and an incomparable insight into the most intriguing corners of the world game.